EARLY CHILDHOOD DEVELOPMENT AND LATER OUTCOME

Theories of infant cognition have transformed radically over the span of less than a century. Once considered unintelligent, infants are now described as partners in their own development. Modern research analyzes the ways in which cognitive and social skills developed early in life help shape intelligence, personality, and achievement over time. In *Early Childhood Development and Later Outcome*, editor Sabina M. Pauen has compiled essays by international experts reflecting the state of infant cognition studies and developmental psychology. These essays present cutting-edge research on a broad range of topics of relevance to scientists, teachers, and policy makers alike. The volume addresses current research on skill formation as well as longitudinal studies tracing achievement beyond childhood. Collectively, this work points the way toward approaches that will deepen our understanding of infant cognition and the profound consequences of early childhood development for future achievement.

Sabina M. Pauen is professor of developmental and biological psychology at the University of Heidelberg. Her work focuses on early brain maturation and cognitive development.

THE JACOBS FOUNDATION SERIES ON ADOLESCENCE

Series Editors: Jürgen Baumert, Marta Tienda

The Jacobs Foundation Series on Adolescence addresses the question of what can be done to promote healthy development around the world. The series views this important question from different disciplines in the social sciences. Economists and sociologists may consider how we can promote human capital over time, specifically, an individual's ability to become educated and to develop earning power; demographers and sociologists may analyze development patterns over generations; psychiatrists and psychologists may tackle the problem of how much change is possible in psychological health during the life course and over generations. Drawing from these different domains of inquiry into human development, the Jacobs Foundation Series on Adolescence examines the potential for change across generations and during the life course in three areas: (1) human capital, (2) partnership behavior, and (3) psychological health and the rearing of children. The purpose of the series is to further the goals of the Jacobs Foundation – to contribute to the welfare and social productivity of the current and future generations of young people.

(*continued after index*)

EARLY CHILDHOOD DEVELOPMENT AND LATER OUTCOME

Edited by

Sabina M. Pauen

University of Heidelberg

CAMBRIDGE UNIVERSITY PRESS
Cambridge, New York, Melbourne, Madrid, Cape Town,
Singapore, São Paulo, Delhi, Mexico City

Cambridge University Press
32 Avenue of the Americas, New York, NY 10013-2473, USA

www.cambridge.org
Information on this title: www.cambridge.org/9780521765503

First published 2012

Printed in the United States of America

A catalog record for this publication is available from the British Library.

Library of Congress Cataloging in Publication data
Pauen, Sabina.
    Early childhood development and later outcome / Sabina Pauen.
        p.   cm. – (The Jacobs Foundation series on adolescence)
    Includes bibliographical references and index.
    ISBN 978-0-521-76550-3 (hbk.)
    1. Infant psychology.   2. Infants – Development.   3. Early childhood education.
    I. Title.
    BF719.P38 2012
    155.42′2–dc23   2012015693

ISBN 978-0-521-76550-3 Hardback

To everyone who makes this world a better place for children.

Contents

Notes on Contributors

Renée Baillargeon is Alumni Distinguished Professor of Psychology at the University of Illinois. Her work focuses on early conceptual development in the physical, psychological, and biological domains.

Marc H. Bornstein is Senior Investigator and Head of Child and Family Research at the National Institute of Child Health and Human Development. He investigates the dispositional, experiential, and environmental factors that contribute to early cogntive development.

Susan Carey is Professor of Psychology at Harvard University. She investigates early knowledge and conceptual change in different domains, such as the biological or the mathematical domain.

John Colombo is Professor of Psychology at the University of Kansas. His work focuses on age-related changes of attention and learning, with a special focus on early individual differences, taking a developmental neuroscience account.

Judy DeLoache is Willian R. Kenan, Jr., Professor of Psychology at the University of Virginia. She is well known for her work on the development of symbolic functioning in early childhood.

Nathan A. Fox is Professor of Human Development at the University of Maryland. He is an expert on the development of emotion and psychophysiology, infant temperament, and emotion regulation.

Usha Goswami is Professor of Cognitive Developmental Neuroscience at the University of Cambridge. Key themes of her work include reading development and dyslexia, as well as speech and language impairments.

Michael E. Lamb is Professor of Social and Developmental Psychology at the University of Cambridge and specializes in social and emotional development, including the effects of parental and non-parental care.

Jean M. Mandler is Distinguished Research Professor of Cognitive Science at the University of California and Visiting Professor at the University of London. Her research focuses on the beginnings of concept formation.

Charles A. Nelson III is Professor of Pediatrics, Neuroscience, and Psychology at Harvard Medical School and a professor in the department of Society, Health, and Human Development at the Harvard School of Public Health. He studies the development of young children, focusing especially on those who grow up under difficult conditions.

Tricia Striano is Professor of Psychology at Hunter College, City University of New York. She is an expert on social cognition in infancy, using brain and behavioral measures in her research.

Sandra R. Waxman is Professor of Cognitive Psychology at Northwestern University. Her major resarch interests are language and conceptual development in early years, including cross-linguistic and cross-cultural perspectives.

Amanda Woodward is the William S. Gray Professor of Psychology at the University of Chicago. Her work concentrates on infant social cognition, imitation, and theory of mind in early years.

Charles H. Zeanah is Professor of Psychiatry and Professor of Clinical Pediatrics at the Tulane University School of Medicine. His research focuses on child psychopathology, infant-parent relationships, and attachment and its development in high-risk environments.

1 Looking Back and Looking Forward

Milestones in Research on Early Childhood Development

Sabina M. Pauen

Looking Back at the History of Infant Research

Infant research has come a long way. Fewer than 100 years ago, psychologists began to express an interest in early childhood. During the first half of the 20th century, Sigmund Freud worked with adults suffering from a variety of psychological problems. Using the psychoanalytic interview technique, he realized that basic aspects of our personality as adults have deep roots in early experiences. Ethologists such as John Bowlby (1958) picked up Freud's ideas and related human development to evolution and biology, suggesting that experiences during the first years of life have enduring effects. Modern research supports the idea that early social experiences are of crucial and continuing importance (see Chapters 6 and 7, this volume). It quickly became evident that infants' interactions with the physical environment are equally meaningful, as Jean Piaget (1937) pointed out that even newborns interact with the physical world in active and constructive ways. These historical foci on infancy and early childhood have in turn prompted a set of important questions, such as how cognition begins, how young children come to represent the external world, and how first concepts develop. These questions continue to occupy developmental scientists, and they motivate the work presented in this book.

For a long period following Piaget, developmentalists failed to credit infants with much cognitive competence. We now acknowledge that the lack of methods suitable for assessing mental processes in preverbal infants circumscribed our early understanding of infants. Because the motor and language skills of infants are limited, it was hard to discern what happens inside a baby's head. The first attempts to develop methods for studying the infant mind were published by Darwin and Baldwin, who made close observations of their own children, and by Berlyne (1958) and Fantz (1958) who were among the first to bring babies into the psychological laboratory. For example, using a stopwatch and measuring the reflection of images in the pupil of the infant's eye, Fantz ascertained that infants look at certain stimuli (e.g., faces) for longer periods of time than at other stimuli. He took looking duration to indicate visual interest of the child, and visual interest related to cognitive processes. In this way, Fantz opened the door to studying the infant mind by focusing on infant looking. Fantz's followers have since capitalized on two variants of his methodology, the preferential looking paradigm and the habituation-dishabituation paradigm. Using these and other behavioral procedures, it has been possible to learn a great deal about the abilities of infants to discriminate, remember, and categorize entities in different domains of knowledge. Furthermore, it has been possible to ask about individual differences in infant information processing. In this way, the development of methods advanced our understanding of development.

Today, the variety of methods suitable for probing cognitive capacities of infants is rather large, and the application of these methods during the past decades has revolutionized our ideas about the infant mind. It turns out that infants possess impressive knowledge about different aspects of the world and display quite advanced skills in many domains. As authors in this volume convey, concept formation, physical and numerical reasoning, and social cognition, as well as language acquisition, have roots deep in infancy.

In recent years, too, neuropsychological methods have been added to the developmentalists' armamentarium and deepened our understanding of infant cognition. Infant brain responses provide sensitive measures for certain cognitive abilities, and it is now possible to articulate developments in behavior with those in the brain. From brain research we have also learned about early plasticity. Neural networks undergo major changes in terms of growth and connectivity throughout infancy and toddlerhood, and they can be modified by experience. As will be illustrated in some chapters of this volume, developmental neuroscience has arrived as a promising new path to study mental development in the early years.

Why Is Infant Development of Special Importance?

Views of the human infant have changed dramatically in less than a century. The once helpless little creature lacking any mental abilities is now seen as a somewhat knowledgeable partner in his or her own development. We have also learned that experiences in early childhood may be of special relevance for later development. Infancy is no longer regarded as the time before mental life starts. Rather, we have come to understand that foundations for intelligence and personality include cognitive and social skills that develop early in life. This conclusion has far-reaching practical implications: If infants come equipped with sophisticated learning abilities, if they can conceptualize experiences and acquire knowledge, and if brain development is the product of complex interactions between existing abilities and external influences, we need to think more carefully about what kinds of environments best serve children to develop their full potential.

Economic analysis of longitudinal studies supports this position. As demonstrated by the Nobelist in economics, James Heckman, the return on investment in high-quality educational programs is related to the age of the children participating (Heckman 2006). To put it in simpler words: Educational programs are most efficient in early childhood and pay by their greatest dividends, especially for children from low socioeconomic backgrounds or otherwise difficult starting situations. Children who participate in high-quality programs show improved cognitive performance and more motivation in school. They live healthier lives, are more likely to participate in social networks, and have their own families. Furthermore, they have better opportunities for better occupations in life. Infancy researchers may not be surprised by these findings. A supportive environment in early years leads to better adjustment in the children's brain and behavior alike that in turn facilitates knowledge and skill acquisition. Because the prosperity of contemporary culture and economy depend heavily on knowledge, children who receive a good education in early years are more likely to be successful in later life and contribute positively to civic responsibility.

A Book about Infant Development

Based on these general insights from infancy research, rapid scientific progress in the field, and the manifest importance of development in the early years, the Jacobs Foundation asked Sabina Pauen to organize a conference on "Early Childhood Education and Later Achievement." In 2008, world-leading experts in the field of infant development convened at a Marbach conference to exchange ideas and discuss implications of their work for caregivers, teachers, and policy makers. To share knowledge presented at this conference, Sabina Pauen agreed to edit a volume that briefly summarizes many of those presentations. The Jacobs Foundation and

Cambridge University Press have generously supported this project. We are thus able to offer the reader a summary of edge-cutting research on a broad range of topics from early childhood. Although it is not possible to cover all dimensions of development within the confines of a single volume, here we provide advanced students as well as scientifically interested practitioners and policy makers with some important insights into the state of the art of infancy research, placing special emphasis on mental development and social functioning.

Unique to this volume, most chapters are written as collaborations of outstanding international experts. This format was chosen to encourage researchers to interrelate their work. To structure the collection, we divided the contributions into two major parts: Part 1 deals with *Emerging Knowledge Structures and Their Impact on Child Development*, and Part 2 deals with *Internal and External Determinants of Childhood Development*. More detailed descriptions of the contents of each part follows.

Emerging Knowledge Structures and Their Impact on Child Development

All authors contributing to the first part of this volume share the basic assumption that knowledge development in infancy is domain specific. Chapter 1 deals with the general question about the nature of infants' first conceptual representations, and the remaining chapters address aspects of knowledge development in specific domains, such as physical and numerical knowledge (Chapter 2), social cognition (Chapter 3), and language acquisition (Chapter 4).

In Chapter 1, Jean Mandler and Judy DeLoache discuss the beginnings of conceptual representations. Mandler provides a theoretical framework that explains how core systems serve as building blocks for later conceptual development, and DeLoache studies errors that young children typically make when they apply newly acquired representations in everyday life. Together, these contributions provide the reader with good examples of how concept formation begins and can be understood by investigating infant success and infant mistakes.

Chapter 2 by Renee Baillargeon and Susan Carey covers the acquisition of physical and numerical knowledge. In the first half, Baillargeon asks how core knowledge in the domain of physics can best be described and how it differentiates during the first years of life. More specifically, she identifies key elements of an innate physical reasoning system and proposes how infants come to detect structure and its violations and how they develop explanations and extract critical variables from the environment based on their experience. Along the way, Baillargeon reports studies demonstrating how systematic training can alter infants' physical representations and so offers ideas related to early childhood education. The second half of the chapter focuses on the development of numerical knowledge. Here Carey identifies two separate core systems of numerical knowledge in human infants as well as other species. These systems are not sufficient for the infants to count, however; rather, infants need to develop a new way of representing integrals and magnitude relations that is rooted in the core system but requires additional mental skills. Corresponding knowledge develops according to a Quinian bootstrapping mechanism. Carey describes in detail how infants' increasing ability to understand the nature of symbols influences this development. Chapter 2 leaves the reader with a good impression of how infant researchers attempt to explain knowledge progression in different but related domains in early childhood.

In Chapter 3, Amanda Woodward and Tricia Striano pursue a similar general goal when discussing the development of social cognition. As pointed out by the authors, learning from social partners is a two-way street, requiring social-cognitive capacities in the learner as well as a supportive social context. First, Striano explains how infants come to interpret social signals and engage in social interactions that can either be dyadic (infant-partner) or triadic (infant and interactive partner focusing jointly on something else). She uses both behavior and neuropsychological methods in service of her goal. Next, Woodward explores how social experience helps infants to increase their understanding about other humans. More specifically, she describes her research on the development of intentional understanding, highlighting the change from conceptualizing goal-directed action to representing intentional actions as part of an enriched folk psychology that later develops into an elaborated theory of mind. The chapter concludes with an illustration of how motor experience with successful goal-directed reaching helps infants to conceptualize goal-directed actions, thus indicating how interactive experiences with the nonsocial world influence cognitive development in the social domain.

Concluding Part I of this volume, Sandra Waxman and Usha Goswami (Chapter 4) look more closely at later years of early development, asking how children come to acquire spoken and written language. As pointed out by Waxman, world learning is intimately entwined with cognitive development, because infants can only understand the meaning of a spoken word if they have previously acquired some kind of conceptual understanding. Not only do infants need to identify individual words in the stream of spoken language, they have to identify individual entities (object, events) in the stream of experience before they can map words onto meanings. As Waxman illustrates, an additional challenge consists in the fact that not all words signify objects; for example, some words correspond to features or actions rather than entities. Hence, the infant needs to learn how to discriminate between different kinds of words using knowledge about the world as well as knowledge about language. How phonological development is related to later reading acquisition is explained by Goswami in the second part of the chapter. She proposes a detailed theory that addresses developmental progress and offers information about why some children experience difficulties in learning to read and write. In sum, Waxman and Goswami's contributions complement one another by showing how young children come to master the challenges of language acquisition in different formats of hearing, understanding, reading, and writing.

Internal and External Determinants of Childhood Development

As illustrated in different chapters of Part 1 of this volume, knowledge acquisition can be profitably approached through a domain-specific orientation. Infants come equipped with elaborated information-processing abilities (e.g., to perceive, to remember, to combine, and to conceptualize) that help them to form representations of objects (Chapter 1), physical events and magnitudes (Chapter 2), social relationships (Chapter 3), and language (Chapter 4). However, early stimulation seems to have considerable effects on infant learning, a consideration that raises issues of internal and external determinants of individual differences. Do all infants come equipped with the same mental abilities?

In Chapter 5, the first contribution to Part II of this volume, Marc H. Bornstein and John Colombo provide the reader with an overview of infant studies that bear on the prediction of mental development based on assessments of infants' basic information-processing capacities. The authors focus on the most prominent paradigm to measure visual attention: habituation-dishabituation. They ask how stable individual differences in performance can be assessed with this paradigm, and how well measures of visual attention based on it predict later intelligence and achievement, thereby, highlighting the role of internal determinants of child development.

Chapter 6 adopts a complementary approach, asking about the role of early experiences on brain maturation and later functioning. Charles Nelson and Nathan Fox report results of a longitudinal study designed to test aspects of development in Romanian orphan children who either stayed in the orphanage throughout their early childhood or were put into foster care very soon. One virtue of this study is that it used a matched-control design, ensuring that the children in the two groups were comparable with respect to their physical health and family background before they were exposed to different environments. Furthermore, the study controlled for the quality of foster care and tested children on a frequent basis, gathering both behavioral and neurological data. The authors point to striking differences in brain, mental, and social development between these groups, suggesting that high-quality care, a secure environment, and adequate cognitive and emotional stimulation during the first years of life are requisite to wholesome child development.

Raising the issue of benefits and dangers related to child-care institutions in Western cultures, Michael Lamb discusses the impact of nonparental care on emotional development in Chapter 7. Lamb first gives a brief overview of the history of nonparental care, highlighting that institutionalized child-care has always been a part of normal life. Based on this general insight, he then reviews empirical studies asking how this kind of child-care influences development, and he arrives at the conclusion that both the quality of child-care and the quality of parent-child relationships predict developmental outcomes. This work suggests that investment in high-quality daycare is necessary for all children to develop their full potential.

Looking Forward into Future Infant Research

At this point, the circle closes. Child development research increases our understanding of early childhood development. This work provides the basis for advice to parents, to health-care professionals, and to policy makers for designing high-quality educational programs. Investments in early childhood pay dividends for the individual as well as for society. Thus, we have learned that infants are capable of acquiring knowledge from early on. To do so effectively and efficiently, they need an emotionally secure and cognitively stimulating environment that offers adequate support to develop those skills that help them become healthy and successful members of their culture. The present volume addresses this complete process by offering a collection of contributions that describe advances in a diversity of vital aspects of early childhood development. Reading this volume will yield an impression that developmental science has come a long way and that we now know quite a lot about infancy and early development. However, we are still far from knowing exactly how best to help people achieve their full potential. The challenges to future researchers are to advance knowledge and the science of infant development further, and to create settings that promote human development.

REFERENCES

Berlyne, D. E. (1958). The influence of the albedo and complexity of stimuli on visual fixation in the human infant. *British Journal of Psychology*, **49**, 315–318.

Bowlby. J. (1958). The nature of the child's tie to his mother. *International Journal of Psychoanalysis*, **39**, 350–373.

Fantz, R. L. (1958). Pattern vision in young infants. *Psychological Records*, **8**, 43–47.

Heckman, J. (2006). Skill formation and the economics of investing in disadvantaged children. *Science*, **312**, 5782.

Piaget, J. (1937). *La construction du réel chez l'enfant*. Delachaux et Niestle: Neuchatel.

2 The Beginnings of Conceptual Representation

Jean M. Mandler and Judy DeLoache

This chapter deals with a fundamental question that developmental psychologists have been trying to answer for more than 100 years: How do we come to represent objects and events in terms of concepts – the basic building blocks of human thinking and reasoning? Even though we are still far from knowing all the answers to this question, much progress has been made during the past several decades. One promising approach is to integrate recent findings on preverbal understanding of objects and events within a theoretical framework that describes how concept formation begins, what the core conceptual system consists of, and how it develops over time. Yet another promising approach is to study errors that young children make when they apply their newly acquired conceptual representations in everyday life. The present chapter provides the reader with one prominent example for each approach. In the first section, Jean Mandler describes how a process of *Perceptual Meaning Analysis* creates concepts from spatial information and how they become enriched in various ways. In the second section, Judy DeLoache presents her work on *scale errors* and explains how such errors inform us about the difficulty of aligning conceptual and motor representations in young children.

Creating Concepts from Spatial Information

The First Concepts

One of the things we have learned about infant development in recent years is that along with the sensorimotor skills of recognizing and acting on objects that Piaget described, infants are also learning to interpret what they observe conceptually. Even before they begin to act on objects, they show attentional biases that help create their first interpretations of events. In particular they attend to motion through space (Haith 1980; Kellman 1993). They attend to whether objects start moving by themselves (Leslie 1982), whether they interact with other objects (Frye et al. 1983), and the kinds of paths they take (Rochat, Morgan, & Carpenter 1997).

One of the results of this bias is that at least until 6 months, infants attend to and remember more about what objects do than about what they look like. For example, 5-month-olds are better at remembering where an object has been hidden than what the object looks like (Newcombe, Huttenlocher, & Learmonth 1999). They are also better at remembering the action an object took (such as brushing hair) than what the object was (for example, a brush or a bubble wand) (Bahrick, Gogate, & Ruiz 2002; see also Perone et al. 2008). Lack of attention to object detail is one of the reasons so-called basic-level concepts, such as *dog* and *cup*, are not the first kinds of concepts to be formed. Instead, early object concepts tend to be more global with less detail – that is, sketchy "superordinate" notions such as *animal, vehicle,* and *container* rather than notions such as *dog* or *cup*. Action on objects helps infants attend to the details that will eventually carve out basic-level concepts from more global ones. For example, by 11 to 12 months, infants have begun to pay attention to parts of objects that produce interesting results, and they begin to categorize objects on that basis (Träuble & Pauen 2007).

The early global concepts, which for objects are known to be formed by 7 months (Mandler & McDonough 1993) and probably as early as 3 months ground the later basic-level concepts. Young infants see a dog or a cat but think of them both as *animal*. (However, *animal* is an adult linguistic construal; as discussed later in this section, the infant concept is probably something more like *self-moving interactor*.) Similarly, a cup or a pan is understood as *a container*. For example, when 14-month-olds are asked to imitate an event in which a person drinks from a teacup, and they are provided with various objects they might use, they are as likely to choose a frying pan for their imitation as they are a mug (Mandler & McDonough 1998).

Only gradually do infants subdivide global concepts. Although as early as 3 months of age, infants are able to categorize various animals on the basis of differences in their perceptual appearance (Eimas & Quinn 1994), generalized imitation studies such as the one just mentioned show that conceptual differentiation is a slower process. For example, in Mandler and McDonough (1998, 2000) we showed that infants conceptually differentiate land animals and birds by 14 months, but do not definitively differentiate land animals such as dogs and rabbits until some time between 20 and 24 months. Infants (in our culture) are usually more advanced in their conceptual differentiation of household artifacts such as cups and pans or sinks and bathtubs, as well as vehicles, showing a good deal of correct responding by 19 months. Functional information, which begins to be added to conceptual interpretation by the end of the first year (Elsner & Pauen 2007), is presumably an important contributor to the more detailed conceptualizations of various artifacts that develop in the second year. However, without instruction, even 2-year-olds do not make many subdivisions in artifacts and familiar substances such as food – for example, airplanes versus rockets or pie versus cake (McDonough 2002).

The fact that concept formation is primarily top-down in nature (i.e., going from the more general to the particular) has far-reaching consequences for how the adult conceptual system is organized. First, because infants at first divide the world into animals and nonanimals, every time a new concept is learned within these global domains, it is necessarily learned as a subdivision of this larger division. This automatically results in a hierarchically organized conceptual system of objects, an organization that remains throughout life. Global membership is so fundamental that it is the last to be lost in semantic dementia and other degenerative diseases. Even when patients no longer know the difference between dogs and ducks, they still regard both as animals (Hodges, Graham, & Patterson 1995).

Second, some mechanism that reduces incoming perceptual information into a less detailed, more generalized form must be operating. I have proposed such a mechanism, called Perceptual Meaning Analysis (Mandler 1992, 2004, 2010, 2012) that recodes attended spatial information into a conceptual format. For example, an infant watches a small white sandwich being put into a large blue box, but Perceptual Meaning Analysis is hypothesized to output something like *THING INTO CONTAINER*. This is information that can be used implicitly to interpret what has just been seen or explicitly for thought. We know, of course, that adults engage in explicit thought. But because we associate explicit thought with verbalization, it is often assumed that preverbal babies cannot do the same thing. However, recall studies using deferred imitation have shown explicit memory for past events in infants as young as 6 months (see Bauer, DeBoer, & Lukowsky 2006 and Mandler 2006 for summaries). By 7 months, infants can recover a hidden object after a delay (McDonough 2002), and by 8 months, they begin to solve novel problems mentally (Willatts 1997). So preverbal infants are capable of explicit conceptualization, although, without verbal evidence, we usually do not know exactly what they have attended to in a particular situation or exactly what their interpretation is.

From at least 3 months of age, infants can form perceptual schemas of objects that, in contrast to *concepts* about objects, contain considerable detail. (There is some evidence that this process may also develop in a global-to-basic direction, in that 2-month-olds' perceptual categories are less detailed than those of 3-month-olds; Quinn & Johnson 2000.) This perceptual ability makes infants become familiar with and able to discriminate among many everyday objects. But responding to something as having been seen before is not the same as conceptualizing it, just as recognizing something is not the same as recalling it. This was one of Piaget's important insights. Infants live in a rich perceptual world that generates a sense of familiarity as they interact with things, but that does not tell us how they interpret what they are seeing. For example, showing that 3-month-olds can categorize pictures of cats as being different from tigers or horses as being different from giraffes (Eimas & Quinn 1994) does not tell us whether infants have any idea what a cat or a horse is.

Perception proceeds through learning of statistical regularities (e.g., Turk-Browne, Jungé, & Scholl 2005) and does not require any conceptual description, let alone an accurate one. Face perception versus our concept of a face is a good illustration. Our concept of a face is poverty-stricken compared to our exquisite ability to differentiate thousands of faces, and most people's inability to draw a face with the right proportions is an indication of how little of our perceptual knowledge is available to us conceptually. We often need explicit training to conceptualize knowledge that has not been attentively analyzed and remains implicit. This is but one example of the frequent disjunction between implicit and explicit knowledge (see Mandler 1998, 2012, for discussion), a disjunction that almost certainly begins in infancy. Although the first section of this chapter emphasizes the conceptual knowledge formed in the first year, it pales beside the enormous amount of implicit perceptual knowledge acquired in the same period.

A mechanism that reduces incoming perceptual information into an accessible format must engage in serious simplification. What kinds of information is it sensitive to, and what kind of primitives ("vocabulary") does it need to do the redescription? As adults we have words to describe perceptual analyses; young infants, who do not yet have language, must represent in some way the information being conceptualized. A good possibility are *image-schemas* (Mandler 2004, 2005, 2010, 2012), which are analog representations that schematize spatial relations and movements in space. These provide a nonverbal format for the outputs of the simplifying mechanism. In conjunction with perceptual information they can also be used to structure spatial imagery, thus making possible explicit thought in the absence of language. For instance, in the example mentioned earlier of watching someone put a sandwich into a box, the image-schematic interpretation *THING INTO CONTAINER* can be used to imagine a shape – perhaps a square one if the shape of the sandwich has been attended to, but if not, a blob will do – moving toward and into a container, realized as another amorphous shape with an opening in the top. This kind of process is known in the current literature as *simulation* (Barsalou 1999). Most discussions of simulation do not specify details, but image-schemas are a plausible format.

Consistent with this format, current evidence suggests that the first concepts are composed from spatial information, especially movements in space. Not only do very young infants pay great attention to the paths that objects take, and how they begin, but also what happens at their ends (Woodward 1999). They are also attentive to several spatial relations, as shown by learning containment and occlusion relations as early as 2.5 months (Aguiar & Baillargeon 1999; Hespos & Baillargeon 2001), support relations by 3 months (Baillargeon, Kotovsky, & Needham 1995), and caused motion by 4 months (Leslie 1982).

Spatial representations are necessarily structured. For example, containment is a notion requiring a bounded space with an inside and an outside. It is structured, because there cannot be an inside without an outside; it is the structure itself that gives the parts meaning. Although the structure can be dissected, it is primitive with respect to the conceptual system. Any concept based on spatial information will have structure, in contrast to sensory concepts such as colors, tastes, and (single) sounds. Such unstructured, nonspatial concepts are late acquisitions that may even require language – the concepts *red* or *barking*, for example, may consist primarily of a label pointing to an unanalyzed perceptual experience.

To summarize: It does not require much innate machinery to get concept formation started (although some theorists posit more, e.g., Carey 2009). There is built-in attention to paths of motion through space and a few spatial relations such as containment and contact that are perceptually salient for infants. All that is needed further is a mechanism to redescribe this information into a form that enables accessibility and some primitives to get redescription started. For example, animals can be described as things that start motion by themselves and interact with other objects even from a distance. This conceptualization of *animal* as a self-moving interactor is not a bad core definition and can be derived from information that is within the perceptual capacity of newborns.

Conceptual Primitives

This simple concept of *animal* can be represented by four primitives. (These and the following primitives are expressed in capital letters, and are described more thoroughly in Mandler 2012.) PATH represents an object's motion through space, without regard to speed, direction, or shape of either object or path. START PATH minus CONTACT specifies that an object begins movement without contact with another object. LINK represents contingent interactions, such as two objects following a common path, or back-and-forth interactions as in turn taking. This primitive specifies a linkage between objects even when they are not touching (see Mandler 1992, for detail). Infants follow object paths from birth (Haith 1980). As early as 4 months they attend to whether objects touch or not when they start motion (Leslie 1982), and they treat contingent responders as animate as early as 2 to 3 months of age (Frye et al. 1983). A related small set of primitives creates an early concept of *inanimate thing* as something that either does not move on a path at all, or if it does, START PATH + CONTACT specifies that it begins only with contact from another object; minus LINK specifies it does not respond contingently to other objects.

Both *animal* and *inanimate thing* are relatively abstract concepts. This abstract character applies to other early concepts as well, for example, *cause* in the sense of *make move*. A likely candidate for this concept is transfer of motion from one object to another. Hume thought that we cannot see causality, but we can, or at least we see what looks like motion from one object moving into another (Michotte 1963; see Mandler 1998, for discussion). In brief, we see caused motion between two objects when there is a conflict between two types of continuity cues. Spatial discontinuity says there are two objects, whereas continuous motion suggests there is only one. The conflict is resolved by perceiving the sequence as the transfer of motion from one object to the other (White 1988). So to interpret causal perception, Perceptual Meaning Analysis needs to output MOTION INTO. There is also a spatial notion of a path being blocked so that motion stops. When an object runs into something immovable, there is no motion transfer to be seen, but an abrupt cessation of motion altogether. For example, Baillargeon (1986) showed that 6-month-olds expect that a car running along a track will not pass through a block on the track but will come to a stop. To the extent that they conceptualize this situation, it needs something like BLOCKED MOTION as a primitive description.

Another important concept is *goal*. Although we have evidence that infants as young as 5 to 6 months understand something about goal-directed behavior, there is no evidence that at this young age the concept of *goal* has anything to do with people's intentions or states of mind. The information that seems to be used in early goal understanding has to do with the spatial interactions of objects. One is interaction with an object at the end of a direct PATH TO an object. Another is LINKED PATHS that persistently go around things that block a direct path. Woodward (1999) showed that 5-month-olds discriminate between a hand taking a direct path to an object and grasping it versus following a path and just resting the hand against it. Csibra (2008) showed that 6-month-olds expect that an object that has repeatedly gone to another around a barrier will take a direct path when the barrier is removed. Primitives of START PATH, PATH TO, END PATH, and LINK are sufficient to construct a spatially based concept of goal. This kind of concept of *goal* at first applies to animate beings and inanimate objects (e.g., Biro & Leslie 2007), a tendency that remains in attenuated form throughout life.

At a somewhat simpler level, event concepts involve spatial relations between objects. These can be represented by a small set of primitives (Mandler 2004, 2008), for example, CONTAINER along with the associated PATH primitives of INTO and OUT OF. There are also early concepts of tight versus loose containment (McDonough, Choi, & Mandler 2003; Spelke & Hespos 2002). Tight and loose are probably not themselves primitives; rather the default case of containment seems to be loose, and tight containment a special case of CONTAINER + BLOCKED MOTION. Infants are also sensitive to what adults call support (Baillargeon 1994). So far as we know, very young infants are not sensitive to gravity (Spelke et al. 1992); the earliest interpretation of a support relation is more like attachment (CONTACT and minus MOVE). Interestingly, there may not be an innate primitive of ON. It seems to be an aspect of everyday experience so common that it does not draw attention. There also appears to be a primitive of LOCATION. As mentioned earlier, 7-month-olds can remember where things are hidden, and the first conceptual subdivisions of animals and vehicles seem to be based on their typical LOCATION: either on the ground or in the air.

There is also intriguingly early evidence for conceptualizing occlusion relations, intriguing because it is difficult to design experiments capable of demonstrating conceptual activity in the first 2 to 3 months of life. Nevertheless, Luo and Baillargeon (2005) provide data on occlusion that suggest primitives of BEHIND, MOVE OUT OF SIGHT, and MOVE INTO SIGHT are operative as early as 2.5 months. Their research shows that as 2.5- to 4-month-olds learn about objects being occluded, they develop changing expectations of what is to be seen in such situations. Some of their expectations may be governed by the perceptual system, such as the persistence of an object that moves behind an occluder and out the other side. The perceptual system of both infants and adults briefly maintains information about occluded objects in what is called mid-level vision (Cheries et al. 2009). However, infants apparently make inferences that go beyond purely visual information. At 2.5 months they have overly simple interpretations of occlusion that lead them to find unexpected some perfectly normal sights. The first interpretation of *behind* appears to be merely that something should not be seen if it goes behind an occluding screen. So if it appears in a window or a door in the occluder, they appear surprised to see it. It is hard to think of a purely perceptual learning account of this kind of "mistake," because infants frequently see objects only partially hidden as they move behind other objects. However, Perceptual Meaning Analysis is an attentional mechanism, and many partial occlusions of objects are apt to go unnoticed, whereas people or other objects going into or out of a room are much more likely to draw attention. These primitives suggest early concepts of *seen* and *unseen*, represented by the states resulting from moving into or out of sight (see Mandler 2012).

Either singly or in combination, this small set of path, motion, and spatial relation primitives go far toward getting the conceptual system started. They provide an account of early global object concepts and crude concepts of events. There are most likely more kinds of spatial relations involved, UP and DOWN, and UNDER for example, but not many more primitives may be needed – presumably the conceptual system of a 6- to 8-month-old is quite simple. The primitives specified here are all rooted in innate saliencies in spatial attention, which set the stage for simplifying redescriptions of perceptual information to take place.

Concept Development

Although these few spatial descriptions can get the conceptual system started, we must also ask how greater complexity is achieved. One way is by subdividing existing concepts, as in differentiating animals on the ground from "up" animals. A second source of new concepts is the analogical and metaphorical extension of spatially based concepts into nonspatial realms (e.g., Goswami 1992; Lakoff 1986). This manner of learning is evident even for infants, who before they are a year old begin to show analogical transfer from one problem to another (Chen, Sanchez, & Campbell 1997). A classic example of this ability in infants was shown by Piaget (1951), who observed his infants open and close their hands as they were trying to imitate his blinking his eyes.

A third and very important development is to associate bodily feelings with the spatial conceptual base. *Force* is a good example of a non-spatial concept derived from bodily experience in conjunction with spatial primitives. As discussed earlier, perception of transfer of motion from one object to another and perception of blocked motion underlies the concept of *cause*. After infants begin to move themselves around, these representations become associated with bodily experience of forces. A spatial representation of motion being transferred into an object is used to redescribe a bodily experience of pushing or being pushed. The spatial description becomes coupled with a sensorimotor experience, with the latter adding a crude dynamic aspect. One can attend to the "umph" one feels when hitting or pushing against something immoveable. This "umph" becomes associated with the conceptual description of BLOCKED MOTION, so that one activates the other. In short, a conceptual description can be augmented by a feeling that is not itself conceptually described. It becomes a package that at some point gets labeled by language as "force."

Similarly, once infants begin to try to do things for themselves – to reach, to push, and so forth – the internal feelings of trying can gradually be associated with the spatial conceptions of goal-directed behavior that they already have. Making conceptual sense of internal states is apt to be a difficult process, especially for feelings such as desire or wanting, which may help to explain why infants do not seem to really understand intentions until near the end of the first year, or possibly later (Tomasello et al. 2005).

Finally, there is language, which has a number of vital functions. Ultimately language will provide a symbol system to express ideas not derived from event and object perception. However, in infancy, language begins to direct attention to the perceptual details that are needed to achieve basic-level concepts (e.g., Fulkerson & Waxman 2007). It also helps categorize sensory information for which there are no primitives ("Dogs say woof woof") and provides labels for already established perceptual schemas ("That's a doggie"). The fact that different-looking self-moving interactors are given different labels by the community must focus attention on their differences. An infant listening to a parent reading a picture book may understand *animal* when seeing a dog, but the parent says, "What does the doggie say? It says 'woof woof.'" A new concept (which is a subdivision of an old one) is on its way. Dog is an *animal* of a certain appearance, called "dog," and makes sounds called "woof woof."

Equally important for social and personal understanding, language enables conceptualization of bodily experiences that have no spatial basis for someone to use to conceptualize them. Feelings of trying can be associated with existing spatial conceptions of goal-directed behavior. But many other internal sensations, such as emotional arousal, are diffuse, and without language may have no way of being conceptualized. Language may be the *only* route to explicit conceptualization of unstructured sensory or bodily information such as colors or emotions that cannot be associated with spatial representations (Mandler 2010). This is presumably also why Theory of Mind concepts such as *belief* are late developing, not appearing until language learning is well underway (Mandler 2012).

Implications for Later Development
Acquiring language will arguably bring about the greatest conceptual changes, in part by allowing greater social and cultural influences on concept learning than in the preverbal period, but also by helping to make implicit information explicit. The bodily sensations that gradually enrich infant spatially based concepts often themselves remain inchoate. Even as adults we cannot describe in detail what being pushed feels like or exactly what we mean by wanting. When we try to produce such descriptions they seem incomplete and unsatisfactory. Like much sensorimotor information many bodily sensations remain implicit – recognized when they are being experienced, but difficult even to image (other than their spatial aspects) when they are not. Even adults' representation of dynamic (forceful) information is impoverished compared to kinetic (spatial) information (Proffitt & Bertenthal 1990). We speak about force without unpacking what we mean, and so the sensorimotor part of it remains vague. Perhaps this is one reason we write poetry!

The spatially based preverbal conceptual system described here enables explicit thought about spatial aspects of the world. It becomes associated with bodily information that enriches conceptual interpretation of spatially understood events, but as just discussed, the bodily information itself does not easily become explicit. Indeed, sensorimotor knowledge learned early in life typically does not become explicit on its own. For example, Spelke et al. (1992) found that 4-month-olds were surprised if an unsupported object dropped straight down but landed below an intervening surface. In contrast, Hood, Carey, and Prasada (2000) found that 2-year-olds failed a test that was similar but required them to point to where the object would land. Prediction requires activation of an explicit conceptual model of the world, which is a very different matter from the implicit procedural knowledge that makes us look longer at impossible displays. Similarly, Kyeong and Spelke (1999) found that young children recognize that when an object launched off a cliff falls straight down, this does not look right, but predict exactly that when asked.

Karmiloff-Smith and Inhelder (1974–1975) pointed out that this discrepancy between implicit and explicit knowledge can account for U-shaped developmental trends that occur when children construct explicit theories (not necessarily correct) that do not jibe with their implicit perceptual expectations. Many aspects of knowledge of the physical world remain implicit throughout life, and because of that, misconstruals of the way the world works are formed. A classic example, notably similar to those just described, is an experiment by McCloskey and Kohl (1983), asking adults to predict the direction of a ball leaving a circular tube at high speed; although when shown a circular trajectory, the adults recognized that it was incorrect, they nevertheless tended to predict that trajectory when asked.

This research suggests that one of the main functions of education, whether at home with preschoolers or at school with more formal teaching, should be to insure that basic knowledge about both bodily information and the physical world is understood in an explicit conceptual fashion. Recent studies teaching large numbers of school children the molecular properties of water found that if 9-year-olds are given explicit, spatially represented causal models, they are capable of good understanding of this non-observable subject (Stein, Hernandez, & Anggoro 2010). When not taught explicitly, children make up their own theories about the physical processes involved. Furthermore, the longer the wait before explicit knowledge is provided, the more entrenched the incorrect theories become, so that naïve 12-year-olds are worse than naive 9-year-olds. Even some elementary school teachers were found to share the same misconceptions. These problems begin in infancy. Before culture or teaching affects them, infants begin to conceptualize how the world works. Some of the mistakes they make are corrected by further experience and reflection upon it, but if they are not taught explicitly, others are not corrected for many years or ever.

In the next section of this chapter, Judy DeLoache tells us about some of the surprising things that can happen as the concepts that begin to be formed in early infancy become integrated with the motor programs that are an important part of adult understanding. Perhaps it is because the earliest concepts begin as observations of things and their spatial movements in the world, and do not involve physical action on the infants' part, that putting the two together is a bit like mixing oil and water – it takes a lot of stirring!

What Scale Errors Tell Us about the Integration of Concepts with Action Programs

Part 2 of this chapter is also concerned with the relation between early perceptual experience and category-related knowledge, with a particular focus on how both of them relate to action. More specifically, it will be demonstrated how categorization can sometimes lead very young children astray.

Typically, object-directed actions are regulated both by what one perceives when looking at an object and what one already knows about that object or that general type of object. Thus, the sight of a chair – even a rather unusual one – activates our mental representation of the category "chairs." Also activated to some extent is our motor representation for the act of sitting – the prototypical action we carry out with respect to chairs. Activation of the motor program for sitting may or may not lead to any action, depending on a variety of factors, including motivation (we may have no current desire or intention to sit) and feasibility (the chair in question may be too small, too large, or too fragile to afford comfortable sitting).

Judgments about the feasibility of a given motor act with respect to a given object are typically made automatically and accurately. We do not have to carry on an inner dialogue to decide whether we can sit in a particular chair – whether that chair is "sittable." In J. J. Gibson's (1977) terms, the *affordance* for sitting is directly perceived.

The accurate perception of affordances depends, however, on experience, as has been so elegantly demonstrated in research by Karen Adolph (2005; Adolph & Berger 2006). Only through experience with a given motor skill are children able to make accurate judgments about whether they can successfully execute a particular action in a particular situation. Thus, infants who have only recently begun walking have very poor judgment with respect to when they can and cannot do so successfully. Inexperienced walkers will, for example, heedlessly launch themselves down sloping walkways that are far too steep for them to have any chance of getting to the bottom without falling. (An experimenter is always hovering nearby so any child who misjudges what he or she is capable of doing can be prevented from falling.) However, after a few weeks of walking experience, children judiciously pause at the top of a steep slope to consider whether to proceed, and then make quite accurate assessments regarding which slopes they can and cannot get down successfully.

The perception of affordances goes on similarly with respect to young children's object-focused actions. Consider, for example, the simple act of sitting in a chair. Even a 2-year-old who sees a chair knows what it is called, understands that it is for sitting upon, and has a well-practiced motor pro-gram for sitting. The specific actions involved in a small child sitting in a child-sized chair are the same as those employed by an adult in sitting in a standard-size chair – approaching to a certain degree of proximity to the chair, turning around, bending at the knees, and lowering the body onto the surface of the chair. The desire and decision to sit can precede or follow seeing the chair: The child may seek out something to sit down on or may form an intention to sit only after encountering an inviting chair. Either way, having decided to sit on some object, young children's actions are typ-ically scaled appropriately to the size of the object.

But this is not always the case. And therein lies a remarkable phenom-enon – a type of error that young children occasionally make in which they seriously misjudge the relation between the size of their own body and the size of an object. Specifically, *scale errors* involve children mak-ing extremely large errors when interacting with replica objects, such as a dollhouse-sized chair or a small toy car (DeLoache et al. 2004). The inspi-ration for this program line of research originated with informal observa-tions that I and my colleagues had independently made. In many years of doing research with toddlers interacting with scale models of rooms, I had occasionally observed some unusual (and quite amusing) behavior on the part of the very young participants. The children sometimes tried to sit on the miniature chair in the model, and only by alertly snatching it away did we prevent its destruction. At the same time, two colleagues – David Uttal and Karl Rosengren – had observed similar types of behavior on the part of their own small children. One child had attempted, in all seriousness, to get into a small toy car, attempting to jam her foot through its tiny door. The other had tried to lie down in her doll's bed. Neither of these actions was remotely possible to carry out, given the size of the objects in question. From initially being simply amused at these peculiar actions, we became increasingly intrigued: How could typically developing young children try to perform such obviously impossible actions? How could they so seriously misperceive the affordances of miniature objects?

Documentation of the Existence and Nature of Scale Errors

To find out, we conducted a series of laboratory studies with children between 18 and 30 months of age (DeLoache et al. 2004). Each experimen-tal session began with the child interacting with a set of large playthings – a car that the child could get inside and move around the room, a child-sized armchair that the child could comfortably sit in, and an indoor slide that the child could climb up and slide down. After the child had interacted with each of the target objects at least twice, the experimenter escorted the child from the room. During the few minutes of their absence, each of the three large playthings was replaced by a miniature replica that looked just like its larger counterpart, except for size. When the child returned, nothing was said by the experimenter about the changes that had been made. She did, however, encourage the child to interact with the target objects: For example, "Wanna go down the slide?" "Come sit in your chair, and I'll read you a story."

Most of the time, most of the children's behavior with the miniature target objects was perfectly appropriate: They ignored the experimenter's encouragement to sit on the tiny chair, to go down the impossibly small slide, or to get into the little car. Instead, they simply played in ordinary ways with these toys. For example, they pushed the toy car around on the floor while producing motor sound effects or set a doll on the miniature chair. Occasionally, however, the children behaved in unusual and intriguing ways. Specifically, half of them attempted to interact with a miniature replica object as if it were its larger counterpart. The children sat down on the tiny chair, as shown in Figure 2.1, and they sometimes remained perched on top of it for a surprisingly long time before noticing its actual size.

They attempted to climb up and go down the miniature slide, sometimes falling off in the process. Most remarkably, they tried to squeeze into the much too-little car, usually by opening the tiny door and then trying to force their foot through the small opening. When executing these actions, the children gave no signs of pretense – there was no "knowing smile." Instead, their behavior appeared completely serious. (Indeed, serious intent was a criterion for judging a child's behavior to be a scale error.) Figure 2.1 shows a prototypical example of a common scale error. The remarkable nature of scale errors can be appreciated best by viewing them in action, so illustrative film clips of scale errors are available at http://www.faculty.virginia.edu/childstudycenter/clips.html.

Scale errors are not limited to actions involving a child's own body and a miniature object – children also make scale errors involving very large relative size differences between two objects. Specifically, we observed young children making scale errors when playing with a doll and miniature doll-related toys (Ware et al. 2006). The 16- to 40-month-old children in this research first played with a baby doll and a set of related toys (bathtub, bed, chair, hat, and wagon), all of which were of an appropriate size for the doll. Next, while the children were out of the room, miniature versions of the toys were substituted for the doll-sized ones. When they returned, over half of the children (46 of 74) made one or more scale errors by trying to fit

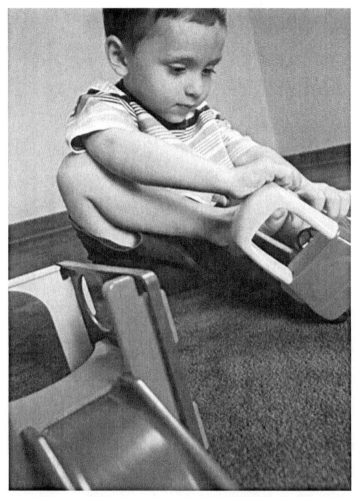

Figure 2.1. This child is committing a scale error: He is in all seriousness trying to force his foot into the small toy car.

the doll into the miniature objects. They frequently attempted, for example, to stuff the doll feet first into the tiny bathtub or to cram it into the impossibly small bed.

Although the initial research documenting the existence of scale errors involved laboratory studies, it is important to emphasize that scale errors are *not* by-products of a laboratory setting. For one thing, as mentioned earlier, the original impetus for studying this phenomenon was the fact that we had informally observed these intriguing behaviors in various settings.

Table 2.1. Examples of Participants' Descriptions of Scale Errors

Object Type	Size Description	Child's Actions	Child's Reaction
Doll's shoe	About half the size of a newborn's shoe.	Tried to put it on.	Cried out in frustration.
Toy truck	Size of a little car that you can hold inside your hand, like a Hot Wheels® car.	Tried to put leg inside the door as if he was going to drive it.	He was very mad. He asked me to help him get in the truck.
Doll bed	Fisher Price® dollhouse bed.	Tried to get into bed with foot, pulling the blanket over her toe, then lay down on top of the whole bed.	Anger and frustration, then hurt because of the uncomfortable bed under her back.
Toy horse	About the right scale for a dollhouse doll to ride.	Tried to get on the horse's back and ride it.	She tried a few times, seeming determined to ride it.

Note: Some descriptions have been edited for length or grammar.

Second, Liza Ware conducted a web-based survey examining the incidence of "everyday" scale errors (Ware, Uttal, & Deloache 2010). Parents were asked to describe in detail any scale errors that they had seen their young children commit. The instructions included a detailed description of a scale error, as well as a film clip of a child committing a prototypical scale error. The respondents provided a wide variety of accounts of scale errors, including those shown in Table 2.1. The scale errors included in the table are quite representative of scale errors in general.

Further evidence for the existence of scale errors has been provided by Celia Brownell and her colleagues (Brownell, Zerwas, & Ramani 2007). They replicated the specific scale errors reported by DeLoache et al. (2004), that is, young children trying to get into the same miniature car, to go down the miniature slide, and to sit on the tiny chair. In addition, they designed a wide array of other tasks to examine young children's ability to take their own body size into account in a variety of other situations. For example, one task involved vertical slits cut in a wall. Some of the slits were wide enough and tall enough for the children to squeeze through; others were far too narrow or too short. Similar to the classic scale errors, many of the very young children persisted in attempting to squeeze themselves through or under the impossibly small openings. Brownell et al. (2007) also documented young children attempting to put on doll's clothes (something that we had observed informally but had not recorded).

The independent documentation by three teams of investigators (Brownell et al. 2007; DeLoache et al. 2004; Ware et al. 2006, 2010) provides strong support for the existence of scale errors as a relatively common occurrence in the lives of very young children. Now the question is why: What is responsible for these common but otherwise quite remarkable behaviors early in life? Any account must interpret them within the realm of normal behavior, in recognition of the fact that they are committed so commonly by so many children.

Scale Errors: Dissociations in the Use of Visual Information for the Planning and Execution of Actions

In attempting to account for the occurrence of scale errors, we have proposed that they arise from a momentary failure to integrate visual information for planning a series of actions and for executing those actions. This account (DeLoache et al. 2004) is based on the dual processing theory of Milner and Goodale (2006), who posited that visual information is processed in different parts of the visual system with respect to action planning versus action execution. Two streams of visual information travel forward from the visual area in the occipital cortex. The ventral stream is involved with the use of visual information for the identification of objects, whereas the dorsal stream is involved in visual control of the execution of actions on objects.

The initial evidence for this theory came from patients with brain damage to different parts of the visual system who showed dissociations in the use of visual information; that is, they were able to use visual information in the service of some behaviors, but not others. For example, those with damage to the ventral stream might not be able to identify a common object sitting in front of them, but if the object were placed in their hands, they would be able to use it appropriately. Thus, if shown a pencil, they could not name it or explain how it is used. However, if they picked it up, they could use it to write or draw. Conversely, patients with damage to the dorsal stream might be able to identify a given object, but be unable to carry out appropriate actions with it. These individuals could say, "That's a pencil," but could not use it to write. These dramatic dissociations reveal that successful action requires the integration of the two streams of visual information.

Adapting this framework in the interpretation of scale errors, DeLoache et al. (2004) proposed that a scale error originates with a young child seeing a miniature replica of a familiar type of object. The child identifies it as an exemplar of a given category – for example, a chair – and decides to interact with it. The child's action plan does not, however, incorporate information about the actual size of the object; instead, it is based on a familiar large object or class of objects that it represents. Thus, the child identifies a replica object as a "chair," but the visual information about its size is not incorporated into the mental representation of the object; the representation of the object as a chair does not include the fact that it is a tiny, nonfunctional chair. A moment later, however, as the child initiates the faulty action plan, visual information about the actual size of the object is brought to bear, as shown by the fact that the child's actions are accurately scaled to the actual size of the miniature object.

In committing a scale error with the miniature car, for example, the child first approaches close to it, just as he or she would do with the larger car, and opens its tiny door, just as would be required to get into the real car. Finally, the child attempts to get inside/insert a foot through the open door. Similarly, with the chair, the child approaches it, turns around right in front of it, bends at the knees, and lowers his or her body precisely onto it. The execution of each of these actions is appropriately scaled to the actual size of the target object.

It thus appears plausible that young children's scale errors represent a dissociation in the use of visual information for the planning versus control of actions of the sort described by Milner and Goodale (2005). The young child's ventral/planning system occasionally fails to integrate size information in the process of identifying an object and forming a plan to act on it. Once the faulty action plan is initiated, however, the dorsal/control system uses visual information about the actual size of the object in the vain effort to carry the plan out.

This account of scale errors suggests that their occurrence reflects *immaturity* in the functioning of the ventral stream in very young children, either in the inferotemporal cortex itself or in the interaction of that area with other areas of the brain. The initial rise and subsequent fall that occurs in the incidence of scale errors with age (shown in Figure 2.2) suggests a complex developmental interaction. Initially, younger infants' conceptual representations of object categories are relatively impoverished. As a consequence, the level of activation that results from interacting with a given replica object may not be strong enough to override infants' visual perception of its actual size, so scale errors are initially quite rare. However, with the burgeoning conceptual development that occurs in the second year of life, children's representations of object categories become increasingly rich

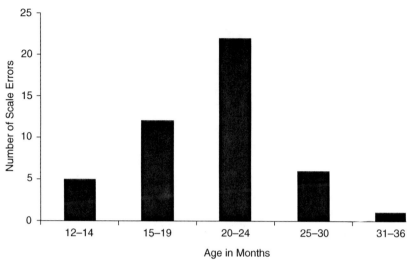

Figure 2.2. Incidence of scale errors by age.

and elaborated, and the associated motor routines become increasingly well integrated. As a result, the sight of a familiar kind of object can now override perception of its size, resulting in a scale error. Eventually, other developmental changes that occur at this age, especially increasing inhibitory control (Carlson, Davis, & Leach 2005), prevent the formation of inherently faulty action plans.

In closing, it can be noted that simple action errors are not uncommon in everyday life at any age. They are typically not so dramatic as the scale errors described here, but they involve similar miscalculations. For example, making our morning tea, we put the cup of water into the cupboard instead of the microwave. We also try to in vain to squeeze into jeans that are clearly too tight and to get more clothes in a suitcase than it can possibly hold. Nevertheless, few, if any, of the action errors that adults make are so dramatic as children's scale errors are – nor are they quite so fascinating.

Finally, it is important to emphasize the direct relation between the research discussed in the second half of this chapter and that summarized in the first half. Scale errors are essentially *categorization errors*. The young child committing a scale error has first identified a target object as an exemplar of a particular category. For example, the child sees a miniature chair, and his or her conceptual representation of chairs in general is activated. So is the motor program associated with that category. Thus, scale errors originate in the act of object categorization: A tiny chair is "a chair," and chairs are for sitting, so the child tries to sit.

Chapter Conclusions

In this chapter we have presented an account of how conceptual activity begins in infancy, along with some of the difficulties involved in aligning concepts about the world both with internal feelings and with motor activity. Our chapter differs from others in this book in that much of what we discuss is relatively impervious to social and cultural factors: What we describe are some of the universal foundations of human development. Although there are negative factors such as poor nutrition or parental neglect that have adverse effects on psychological development, given reasonably normal human conditions, the developments we describe should occur in all cultures. Details such as the age at which children develop a concept of vehicles or plants obviously depend on what the local environment offers.

The main factor that seems to predominate in determining when social and cultural practices begin to have major effects on development is language. Although parents begin social teaching before the onset of infant speech, language greatly amplifies this process. Nevertheless, language is not always used to shape development as much as it might be. One message from the research described in this chapter is that much human functioning remains implicit even when it is possible to make it at least partially explicit. Talking things out helps, not only parents talking to young children but also encouraging them to express things they are struggling with, perhaps by saying, "Use your words!" Not the whole solution, by any means, but a start. The more talk the better, not only for helping difficult experiences such as internal feelings and thoughts to become at least somewhat explicit, but also as preparation for the formal schooling to come.

REFERENCES

Adolph, K. E. (2005). Learning to learn in the development of action. In J. Lockman, J. Rieser, & C. A. Nelson (Eds.), *Action as an organizer of perception and cognition during learning and development: Minnesota Symposium on Child Development* (Vol. 33, pp. 91–133). Hillsdale, NJ: Erlbaum.

Adolph, K. E. & Berger, S. A. (2006). Motor development. In W. Damon & R. Lerner (Series Eds.) & D. Kuhn & R. S. Siegler (Vol. Eds.), *Handbook of child psychology: Vol 2: Cognition, perception, and language* (6th ed., pp. 161–213). New York: Wiley.

Aguiar, A. & Baillargeon, R. (1999). 2.5-Month-old infants' reasoning about when objects should and should not be occluded. *Cognitive Psychology, 39,* 116–157.

Bahrick, L. E., Gogate, L. J., & Ruiz, I. (2002). Attention and memory for faces and actions in infancy: The salience of actions over faces in dynamic events. *Child Development, 73,* 1629–1643.

Baillargeon, R. (1986). Representing the existence and the location of hidden objects: Object permanence in 6- and 8-month-old infants. *Cognition*, **23**, 21–41.

(1994). How do infants learn about the physical world? *Current Directions in Psychological Science*, **3**, 133–140.

(2004). Can 12 large clowns fit in a Mini Cooper? Or when are beliefs and reasoning explicit and conscious? *Developmental Science*, **7**, 422–424.

Baillargeon, R., Kotovsky, L., & Needham, A. (1995). The acquisition of physical knowledge in infancy. In D. Sperber, D. Premack, & A. J. Premack (Eds.), *Causal cognition* (pp. 79–116). New York: Oxford University Press.

Barsalou, L. W. (1999). Perceptual symbol systems. *Behavioral and Brain Sciences*, **22**, 577–660.

Bauer, P. J., DeBoer, T., & Lukowski, A. F. (2007). In the language of multiple memory systems: Defining and describing developments in long-term declarative memory. In L. M. Oakes & P. J. Bauer (Eds.), *Short- and long-term memory in infancy and early childhood: Taking the first steps towards remembering* (pp. 240–270). New York: Oxford University Press.

Biro, S. & Leslie, A. M. (2007). Infants' perception of goal-directed actions: Development through cue-based bootstrapping. *Developmental Science*, **10**, 379–398.

Bomba, P. C. & Siqueland, E. R. (1983). The nature and structure of infant form categories. *Journal of Experimental Child Psychology*, **35**, 294–328.

Brownell, C. A., Zerwas, S., & Ramani, G. B. (2007). "So big": The development of body self-awareness in toddlers. *Child Development*, **78**, 1426–1440.

Carey, S. (2009). *The origin of concepts*. New York: Oxford University Press.

Carlson, S. M., Davis, A., & Leach, J. G. (2005). Less is more: Executive function and symbolic representation in preschool children. *Psychological Science*, **16**, 609–616.

Chen, Z., Sanchez, R. P., & Campbell, T. (1997). From beyond to within their grasp: The rudiments of analogical problem-solving in 10- and 13-month olds. *Developmental Psychology*, **33**, 790–801.

Cheries, E. W., Mitroff, S. R., Wynn, K., & Scholl, B. J. (2009). Do the same principles constrain persisting object representations in infant cognition and adult perception?: The cases of continuity and cohesion. In B. Hood & L. Santos (Eds.), *The origins of object knowledge* (pp. 107–134). New York: Oxford University Press.

Csibra, G. (2008). Goal-attribution to inanimate agents by 6.5-month-old infants. *Cognition*, **107**, 705–717.

DeLoache, J. S. (2010). Everyday scale errors. *Developmental Science*, **13**, 28–36.

DeLoache, J. S., Uttal, D. H., & Rosengren, K. S. (2004). Scale errors offer evidence for a perception-action dissociation early in life. *Science*, **304**, 1047–1029.

Eimas, P. D. & Quinn, P. C. (1994). Studies on the formation of perceptually based basic-level categories in young infants. *Child Development*, **65**, 903–917.

Elsner, B. & Pauen, S. (2007). Social learning of artefact function in 12- and 15-month-olds. *European Journal of Developmental Psychology*, **4**, 80–99.

Frye, D., Rawling, P., Moore, C., & Myers, I. (1983). Object-person discrimination and communication at 3 and 10 months. *Developmental Psychology*, **19**, 303–309.

Fulkerson, A. L. & Waxman, S. R. (2007). Words (but not tones) facilitate object categorization: Evidence from 6- and 12-month-olds. *Cognition*, **105**, 218–228.

Gibson, J. J. (1977). The theory of affordances. In R. Shaw & J. Bransford (Eds.), *Perceiving, acting and knowing* (pp. 67–82). Hillsdale, NJ: Erlbaum.

Glover, S. (2004a). Separate visual representations in the planning and control of action. *Behavioral and Brain Sciences*, **27**, 3–78.

(2004b). What causes scale errors in children? *Trends in Cognitive Sciences*, **8**, 440–442.

Goswami, U. (1992). *Analogical reasoning in children*. Hove, UK: Erlbaum.

Haith, M. M. (1980). *Rules that babies look by: The organization of newborn visual activity*. Hillsdale, NJ: Erlbaum.

Hespos, S. J. & Baillargeon, R. (2001). Reasoning about containment events in very young infants. *Cognition*, **78**, 207–245.

Hood, B., Carey, S., & Prasada, S. (2000). Predicting the outcomes of physical events: Two-year-olds fail to reveal knowledge of solidity and support. *Child Development*, **71**, 1540–1554.

Hodges, J. R., Graham, N., & Patterson, K. (1995). Charting the progression of semantic dementia: Implications for the organisation of semantic memory. *Memory*, **3**, 463– 495.

Karmiloff-Smith, A. & Inhelder, B. (1974–1975). If you want to get ahead get a theory. *Cognition*, **3**, 195–212.

Kellman, P. J. (1993). Kinematic foundations of infant visual perception. In C. Granrud (Ed.), *Visual perception and cognition in infancy* (pp. 121–173). Hillsdale, NJ: Erlbaum.

Kyeong, I. K. & Spelke, E. S. (1999). Perception and understanding of effects of gravity and inertia on object motion. *Developmental Science*, **2**, 339–362.

Lakoff, G. (1986). *Women, fire, and dangerous things*. Chicago: University of Chicago Press.

Landau, B., Hoffman, J. E., & Kurz, N. (2006). Object recognition with severe spatial deficits in Williams syndrome: Sparing and breakdown. *Cognition*, 1–28.

Leslie, A. M. (1982). The perception of causality in infants. *Perception*, **11**, 173–186.

Luo, Y. & Baillargeon, R. (2005). When the ordinary seems unexpected: Evidence for incremental physical knowledge in young infants. *Cognition*, **95**, 297–328.

Mandler, J. M. (1992). How to build a baby II: Conceptual primitives. *Psychological Review*, **99**, 587–604.

(1998). Representation. In D. Kuhn & R. Siegler (Eds.), *Cognition, perception, and language: Vol. 2 of Handbook of child psychology* (pp. 255–308). New York: Wiley.

(2004). *The foundations of mind: Origins of conceptual thought*. New York: Oxford University Press.

(2005). How to build a baby III: Image-schemas and the transition to verbal thought. In Hampe, B. (Ed.), *From perception to meaning: Image-schemas in cognitive linguistics* (pp. 137–163). Berlin: Mouton de Gruyter.

(2006). How do we remember? Let me count the ways. In L. M. Oakes & P. J. Bauer (Eds.), *Short- and long-term memory in infancy and early childhood: Taking the first steps toward remembering* (pp. 271–290). New York: Oxford University Press.

(2008). On the birth and growth of concepts. *Philosophical Psychology*, **21**, 207–230.

(2010). The spatial foundations of the conceptual system. *Language & Cognition*, **2**, 21–44.

(2012). On the spatial foundations of the conceptual system and its enrichment. *Cognitive Science*, **36**, 421–451.

Mandler, J. M. & McDonough, L. (1993). Concept formation in infancy. *Cognitive Development*, **8**, 291–318.

(1998). Studies in inductive inference in infancy. *Cognitive Psychology*, **37**, 60–96.

(2000). Advancing downward to the basic level. *Journal of Cognition and Development*, **1**, 379–404.

Mareschal, D. & Johnson, M. H. (2003). The "What" and "Where" of infant object representations. *Cognition*, **88**, 259–76.

McCloskey, M. & Kohl, D. (1983). Naive physics: The curvilinear impetus principle and its role interactions with moving objects. *Journal of Experimental Psychology: Learning, Memory and Cognition*, **9**, 146–156.

McDonough, L. (1999). Early declarative memory for location. *British Journal of Developmental Psychology*, **17**, 381–402.

(2002). Basic-level nouns: First learned but misunderstood. *Journal of Child Language*, **29**, 357–377.

McDonough, L., Choi, S., & Mandler, J. M. (2003). Understanding spatial relations: flexible infants, lexical adults. *Cognitive Psychology*, **46**, 229–259.

Michotte, A. E. (1963). *The perception of causality*. London: Methuen

Milner, A. D. & Goodale, M. A. (2006). *The visual brain in action*. New York: Oxford University Press.

Newcombe, N. J., Huttenlocher, J., & Learmonth, A. (1999). Infants' encoding of location in continuous space. *Infant Behavior and Development*, **22**, 483–510.

Newman, C., Atkinson, J., & Braddick, O. (2001). The development of reaching and looking preferences in infants to objects of different sizes. *Developmental Psychology*, **37**, 561–572.

Perone, S., Madole, K. L., Ross-Sheehy, S., Carey, M., & Oakes, L. M. (2008). The relation between infants' activity with objects and attention to object appearance. *Developmental Psychology*, **44**, 1242–1248.

Piaget, J. (1951). *Play, dreams, and imitation in childhood*. London: Kegan Paul.

Proffitt, D. R. & Bertenthal, B. I. (1990). Converging operations revisited: Assessing what infants perceive using discrimination measures. *Perception & Psychophysics*, **47**, 1–11.

Quinn, P. C. & Johnson, M. H. (2000). Global-before-basic object categorization in connectionist networks and 2-month-old infants. *Infancy*, **1**, 31–46.

Rochat, P., Morgan, R., & Carpenter, M. (1997). Young infants' sensitivity to movement information specifying social causality. *Cognitive Development*, **12**, 537–561.

Spelke, E. S., Breinlinger, K., Macomber, J., & Jacobson, K. (1992). Origins of knowledge. *Psychological Review*, **99**, 605–632.

Spelke, E. S. & Hespos, S. J. (2002). Conceptual development in infancy: The case of containment. In N. L. Stein, P. Bauer, & M. Rabinowitz (Eds.), *Representation, memory, and development: Essays in honor of Jean Mandler* (pp. 223–246). Mahwah, NJ: Erlbaum.

Stein, N. L., Hernandez, M. W., & Anggoro, F. (2010). A theory of coherence and complex learning in the physical sciences: What works (and what doesn't). In N. L. Stein & S. W. Raudenbush (Eds.), *Developmental cognitive science goes to school*. New York: Taylor & Francis.

Tomasello, M., Carpenter, M., Call, J., Behne, T., & Moll, H. (2005). Understanding and sharing intentions: The origins of ocultural cognition. *Behavioral and Brain Sciences*, **28**, 675–735.

Träuble, B. & Pauen, S. (2007). The role of functional information for infant categorization. *Cognition*, **105**, 362–379.

Turk-Browne, N. B., Jungé, J. A., & Scholl, B. J. (2005). The automaticity of visual learning. *Journal of Experimental Psychology: General*, **134**, 552–564.

Ungerleider, L. G. & Mishkin, M. (1982). Two cortical visual systems. In D. J. Ingle, M. A. Goodale, & R. J. W. Mansfield (Eds.), *Analysis of visual behavior* (pp. 549–586). Cambridge, MA: MIT Press.

Vishton, P. M., Ware, E. A., & Badger, A.N. (2005). Different Gestalt processing for different actions?: Comparing object-directed reaching and looking time measures. *Journal of Experimental Child Psychology*, **90**, 89–113.

VonHofsten, C., Vishton, P. M., Spelke, E. S., Feng, Q., & Rosander, K. (1998). Predictive action in infancy: Tracking and reaching for moving objects. *Cognition*, **67**, 255–285.

Ware, E. A., Uttal, D. H., & DeLoache, J. S. (2010). Everyday scale errors. *Developmental Science*, **13**, 28–36.

Ware, E., Uttal, D. H., Wetter, E. K., & DeLoache, J. S. (2006). Young children make scale errors when playing with dolls. *Developmental Science*, **9**, 40–45.

White, P. A. (1988). Causal processing: Origins and development. *Psychological Bulletin*, **104**, 36–52.

Willatts, P. (1997). Beyond the "couch potato" infant: How infants use their knowledge to regulate action, solve problems, and achieve goals. In G. Bremner, A. Slate, & G. Butterworth (Eds.), *Infant development: Recent advances* (pp. 109–135). Hove, East Sussex, England: Psychology Press.

Woodward, A. L. (1999). Infants' ability to distinguish between purposeful and non-purposeful behaviors. *Infant Behavior and Development*, **22**, 145–160.

3   Core Cognition and Beyond

The Acquisition of Physical and Numerical Knowledge

Renée Baillargeon and Susan Carey

Only human beings create the conceptual repertoire that underlies the lexicons of natural languages and that subserves the institutions of science, mathematics, government, religion, and art. Accounting for this astonishing feat is one of the foremost challenges in the cognitive and psychological sciences. As a matter of logic, any account must have the following structure: a specification of the initial representational repertoire that serves as the input to subsequent learning, a characterization of the differences between the initial and adult repertoires, and a characterization of the learning mechanisms that make possible conceptual development.

In Part I (written by Renée Baillargeon), we first consider the question of the initial repertoire by presenting a case study of the system of representations that underlies reasoning about the physical world. We illustrate the properties of what has been called "core cognition" in the domain of physics, and also characterize how learning underlies changes in this system of representation within infancy. In Part II (written by Susan Carey), we turn to a case study of the acquisition of concepts of number. We characterize the core cognition systems with numerical content, outline the discontinuities between the initial representations and later ones, and describe the bootstrapping process that underlies the change.

The Acquisition of Physical Knowledge

Over the past two decades, substantial progress has been made in understanding how infants reason and learn about physical events. This research has led to the development of a new account of the development of infants' physical reasoning (for recent reviews, see Baillargeon et al. 2009a, 2011, 2012). In what follows, we briefly describe this account.

Like several other researchers, we assume that infants are born equipped with a *physical-reasoning (PR) system* – an abstract computational system that provides them with a skeletal causal framework for making sense of the displacements and interactions of objects and other physical entities (e.g., Gelman 1990; Leslie 1995; Premack & Premack 2003; Spelke et al. 1992). Before we describe how the PR system operates, three general comments are in order.

First, it should be understood that the PR system operates without conscious awareness. Infants are not aware of the causal framework they use when reasoning about physical events, any more than young children are aware of the grammar of their language as they begin to understand and produce sentences. Second, the PR system allows infants to reason and learn about the simple everyday physical events that were familiar to our distant evolutionary ancestors: for example, occlusion events (i.e., events in which an object moves or is placed behind another object, or occluder), containment events (i.e., events in which an object is placed inside a container), and collision events (i.e., events in which an object hits another object). In infancy, the PR system has relatively little to say about events that involve complex artifacts whose causal mechanisms are opaque to most adults – artifacts such as phones, computers, radios, and televisions. Although infants may learn to operate some of these artifacts, pedagogical processes may be necessary to support these acquisitions (e.g., Csibra & Gergely 2009; Futó et al. 2010).

Finally, although our focus here is on the PR system, it should be kept in mind that this system is only a part of the complex cognitive architecture that underlies infants' responses to objects and events. Following other researchers, we have argued that, in addition to the PR system, at least two other systems are involved in infants' responses: an *object-tracking* (OT) and an *object-representation* (OR) system (e.g., Baillargeon et al. 2011; Wang & Baillargeon 2008b; Wang & Mitroff 2009). To illustrate the distinction among the three systems, consider a simple static display involving a block and a can standing apart on an apparatus floor. As infants begin to attend to the objects, the OT system assigns an *index* to each object; each index functions as an attentional pointer that "sticks" to its object, enabling infants to keep track of it when it moves – to know where it is without having to search for it (e.g., Leslie et al. 1998; Pylyshyn 1989, 1994; Scholl & Leslie 1999). As soon as the OT system assigns indexes to the block and can, the OR system begins to build a temporary *file* for each object, listing both individual (e.g., color) and relational (e.g., relative height) features (e.g., Huttenlocher, Duffy, & Levine 2002; Kahneman, Treisman, & Gibbs 1992; Needham 2001; Rose et al. 1982). If an experimenter then places the block inside the can, the PR system also becomes involved: The objects are now engaged in a physical interaction, and the PR system's main purpose is that of interpreting and predicting the outcomes of such interactions (e.g., will the block fit through the can's opening? will the block protrude above the can, or be visible through its sidewalls? if a block is later removed from the can, is it the same block as was seen before or a different one?). In the first year of life, object representations in the PR system often contain only a small subset of the information included in the object files of the OR system; as we explain more fully in the section "Detecting structural violations," event representations in the PR system are initially very sparse (no doubt to facilitate learning) and become richer as infants gradually learn what information is useful for predicting and interpreting outcomes (for a fuller discussion of the links between the OR and PR systems, see Baillargeon et al. 2011).

Core Concepts and Core Principles

When infants watch a physical event, the PR system builds a specialized *physical representation* of the event. Any information included in this physical representation becomes subject to the PR system's causal framework, which encompasses both core concepts and core principles (e.g., Baillargeon et al. 2009a; Carey & Spelke 1984; Gelman 1990; Leslie 1995; Premack & Premack 2003; Spelke et al. 1992).

Core concepts invoke unobservable elements that help explain events' outcomes. Examples of core concepts include "force" and "internal energy" (these are listed in quote marks to emphasize that they are only primitive versions of the concepts used by scientists). When infants see an object hit another object, the PR system represents a *force* – like a directional arrow – being exerted by the first object onto the second one (e.g., Leslie 1995; Leslie & Keeble 1987). Furthermore, when infants see a novel object begin to move or change direction on its own, they categorize it as a self-propelled object and endow it with an *internal source of energy*; infants recognize that a self-propelled object can use its internal energy directly to control its own motion and indirectly – through the application of force – to control the motion of other objects (e.g., Baillargeon et al. 2009b; Gelman, Durgin, & Kaufman 1995; Leslie 1995; Luo, Kaufman, & Baillargeon 2009; Pauen & Träuble 2009; Premack 1990; Saxe, Tenenbaum, & Carey 2005; Woodward, Phillips, & Spelke 1993).

Core principles constrain infants' expectations about objects' displacements and interactions. Examples of core principles include "persistence" "inertia," and "gravity" (again, these are listed in quote marks to emphasize that they are only primitive versions of the principles used by scientists). The principle of *persistence* states that, all other things being equal, objects persist, as they are, in time and space (e.g., Baillargeon 2008; Baillargeon et al. 2009a). The persistence principle has many corollaries (e.g., Baillargeon 2008; Spelke et al. 1992; Spelke, Phillips, & Woodward 1995b), which specify that an object cannot occupy the same space as another object (solidity) and cannot spontaneously appear or disappear (continuity), break apart (cohesion), fuse with another object (boundedness), or change size, shape, pattern, or color (unchangeableness). The principle of *inertia* states that, all other things being equal, an object in motion will follow a smooth path, without abrupt changes in direction or speed (e.g., Kochukhova & Gredebäck 2007; Luo et al. 2009). Finally, the principle of *gravity* states that, all other things being equal, an object will fall when released in midair (e.g., Needham & Baillargeon 1993; Premack & Premack 2003).

Structural Information
When infants watch a physical event, the PR system begins by representing the *structural information* about the event. This structural information includes both *spatiotemporal* and *categorical* information. The spatiotemporal information describes how the objects are arranged and how this arrangement changes over time as the event unfolds (e.g., Kestenbaum, Termine, & Spelke 1987; Needham & Ormsbee 2003; Slater 1995; Yonas & Granrud 1984). The categorical information specifies what kinds of objects are involved in the event by providing categorical descriptors for each object. Early descriptors include (1) abstract *ontological* descriptors, such as whether the objects in the event are human or nonhuman, agentive or non-agentive, and inert or self-propelled (e.g., Bonatti, Frot, & Mehler 2005; Bonatti, Frot, Zangl, & Mehler 2002; Csibra 2008; Johnson, Shimizu, & Ok 2007; Luo et al. 2009; Saxe, Tzlenic, & Carey 2007; Surian & Caldi 2010; Träuble & Pauen 2011b); and (2) primitive *functional* descriptors, such as whether the objects in the event are closed, open at the top to form containers, open at the bottom to form covers, or open at both ends to form tubes (e.g., Hespos & Baillargeon 2001b; Wang & Baillargeon 2006; Wang, Baillargeon, & Paterson 2005; Wang & Kohne 2007; see also Träuble & Pauen 2007, 2011a).

Both the spatiotemporal and the categorical information about an event help specify how many objects are involved in the event. For example, if two identical objects stand apart on a table and a screen is lifted to hide them, the spatiotemporal information will specify that two objects are present behind the screen (e.g., Aguiar & Baillargeon 1999, 2002). Similarly, if a human disappears behind a large screen and what reappears is a nonhuman object, the categorical information will specify that two distinct objects are involved in the event, one human and one nonhuman (e.g., Bonatti et al. 2002, 2005).

With experience, the PR system begins to identify distinct event categories – kinds of causal interactions in which objects play specific roles. In addition to occlusion, containment, and collision events (which were described earlier), early event categories include covering events (i.e., events in which a cover is placed over an object), tube events (i.e., events in which an object is placed inside a tube), and arrested-motion events (i.e., events in which an object is brought short against an extended surface such as a wall or floor). As a rule, events that do not involve causal interactions and have no physical consequences (e.g., events in which an object is simply placed next to another object) are not identified as event categories. When infants watch an event from a known category, the PR system uses the structural information available in the physical representation to *categorize* the event (e.g., Casasola, Cohen, & Chiarello 2003; Hespos & Baillargeon 2006; McDonough, Choi, & Mandler 2003; Quinn 2007; Wang & Baillargeon 2006; Wilcox & Chapa 2002) and to assign specific *roles* to the objects in the event (e.g., Leslie & Keeble 1987; Onishi 2012). As an example, consider a simple event involving two identical blocks, block-A and block-B. If block-A is used to hit block-B, the event is categorized as a collision event, with block-A as the "hitter" and block-B as the "hittee." If block-B is lowered behind block-A, the event is categorized as an occlusion event, with block-A as the "occluder" and block-B as the "occludee." After watching one of these events repeatedly, infants look reliably longer if the two objects change roles (e.g., if block-A becomes the hittee in the collision event).

The structural information about an event thus captures its essence: It specifies how many objects are involved (e.g., two objects), what kinds of objects they are (e.g., nonhuman, non-agentive, inert, closed objects), what kind of causal interaction the objects are engaged in (e.g., a collision event), and what role each object plays in this interaction (e.g., object-A is the hitter; object-B is the hittee).

Over time, at least two changes take place in the structural information infants encode about events. One change concerns the *categorical* information: As infants begin to routinely encode objects in terms of their taxonomic categories (e.g., a spoon, a cookie), these specific categorical descriptors also come to be included at the structural level of the PR system, along with the more general (ontological and functional) categorical descriptors discussed above (e.g., Xu & Carey 1996; Xu 2002). The second change concerns the *spatiotemporal* information: Not only is this information represented more accurately over time (e.g., as depth perception improves; Yonas & Granrud 1984), but descriptions of object interactions also become more precise. For example, infants initially fail to distinguish between events in which an object is released *on top of* or *against* another object; in each case, infants simply encode "object released in contact with another object," and they hold no particular expectation about whether the released object should remain stable or fall. By 4.5 to 5.5 months of age, however, infants identify *support* as an event category: They recognize that when an object, or "supportee," is placed on top of another object, or "supporter," the supportee's fall is blocked by the supporter. As a result, infants now expect objects to remain stable when released on top of, but not against, other objects (Li, Baillargeon, & Needham 2012).

Detecting structural violations. In the first months of life, infants' physical representations typically include only structural information and are therefore rather sparse. Nevertheless, this information is still sufficient, when interpreted by the PR system's causal framework, to allow infants to hold at least some expectations about physical events. To uncover these expectations, researchers often use *violation-of-expectation* tasks. In a typical task, infants see two test events: an expected event, which is consistent with the expectation examined in the experiment, and an unexpected event, which violates this expectation. With appropriate controls, evidence that infants look reliably longer at the unexpected than at the expected event is taken to indicate that they possess the expectation under investigation and detect the violation in the unexpected event.

For example, young infants detect a *persistence violation* (see Figure 3.1) when a cover is lowered over an object, slid to the side, and then lifted to reveal no object (Leslie 1995; Wang et al. 2005); when an object is lowered inside an open container which is then slid forward and to the side to reveal the object standing in the container's initial position (Hespos & Baillargeon 2001b); when an object is placed behind a screen, which then rotates through the space occupied by the object (Baillargeon 1987; Baillargeon, Spelke, & Wasserman 1985); and when a cover is lowered over a closed object and then lifted to reveal an open object (Wu & Baillargeon 2011).

In addition, young infants detect an *inertia violation* when an inert object, after being set into motion, abruptly reverses direction to return to its starting position (Luo et al. 2009); and they detect a *gravity violation*

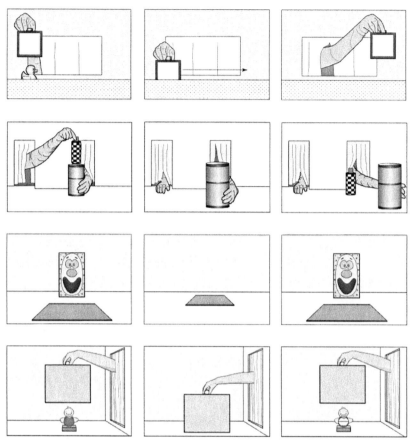

Figure 3.1. Examples of basic persistence violations young infants can detect. Infants are surprised if a cover is lowered over an object, slid to the side, and then lifted to reveal no object (Wang et al. 2005); if an object is placed inside a container which is then slid forward and to the side to reveal the object in the container's original position (Hespos & Baillargeon 2001b); if a screen rotates through the space occupied by a box in its path (Baillargeon 1987); and if a cover is lowered over a closed object (e.g., a toy duck) and then lifted to reveal an open object (e.g., a toy duck with a large hole in its midsection; Wu & Baillargeon 2011).

if an inert object remains suspended when released in midair (e.g., Luo et al. 2009; Needham & Baillargeon 1993). Interestingly, young infants do not view these last two events as violations if the object is self-propelled rather than inert (Kochukhova & Gredebäck 2007; Luo et al. 2009). This is not to say that young infants believe self-propelled objects are not subject to the same principles as inert objects. Rather, infants assume that a novel self-propelled object may be able to use its internal energy to exert some control over its horizontal and vertical displacements: In particular, it may be able to change direction at will and to "resist" falling. At the same time, young infants recognize that there are limits to what self-propelled objects can do, despite their internal energy: For example, infants appreciate that self-propelled objects cannot spontaneously disappear or pass through obstacles (e.g., Aguiar & Baillargeon 1999; Luo et al. 2009; Saxe, Tzelnic, & Carey 2006; Spelke, Kestenbaum, Simons, & Wein 1995a).

Kinds of explanations. The discussion in the preceding paragraph illustrates a key feature of physical reasoning in early infancy: Young infants' explanations for events tend to be shallow, abstract explanations almost entirely divorced of mechanistic details. Upon seeing that a novel box initiates its own motion, for example, young infants endow it with internal energy and assume it can also use this energy to "resist" falling when released in midair. As adults, we may naturally find this assumption puzzling: We possess sufficient physical knowledge to realize that (outside of the realm of science fiction) a self-propelled box would be highly unlikely to remain perfectly stationary in midair.

Infants' physical reasoning brings to mind Keil's (1995) suggestion that adults' concepts are "embedded in theory-like structures which owe their origins to a small but diverse set of fundamental modes of construal ... one key part of these early modes of construal may be more general expectations ... [that] exist before any specific explanation or detailed intuitive theory, and thus indicate *kinds of explanations* rather than any particular explanation" (pp. 260–261, italics added). In line with Keil's suggestion, we believe that the PR system's core concepts and principles provide infants with shallow kinds of explanations, rather than with specific or detailed mechanistic ones.

Variable Information

We have just seen that, in the first few months of life, the PR system includes only structural information in its physical representations of events. Although this information captures many essential elements, it is still very limited. If a spoon is placed inside a pot, for example, the structural information about the event specifies that a nonhuman, non-agentive, inert, closed object has been placed inside a nonhuman, non-agentive, inert container – but it does not specify the size, shape, pattern, and color of either object. How does this more detailed information come to be added to infants' physical representations?

For each event category, infants gradually identify a host of *variables* that help them interpret and predict outcomes within the category (e.g., Baillargeon, Needham, & DeVos 1992; Hespos & Baillargeon 2008; Kotovsky & Baillargeon 1998; Luo & Baillargeon 2005; Wang, Kaufman, Baillargeon 2003; Wilcox 1999). A variable both calls infants' information to a certain type of information in an event (e.g., features of objects or their arrangements) and provides a causal rule for interpreting this information. To illustrate, consider some of the variables infants identify for containment events (see Figure 3.2).

By about 4 months of age, most infants have identified *width* as a relevant variable, and they now detect a violation when a wide object becomes fully hidden inside a narrow container (Wang, Baillargeon, & Brueckner 2004). By about 7.5 months of age, most infants have identified *height* as a containment variable: They now detect a violation if a tall object becomes almost fully hidden inside a short container (Hespos & Baillargeon 2001a). By about 9.5 months of age, most infants have identified *container-surface* as a relevant variable: They now detect a violation if an object becomes fully hidden when placed inside a container that is made of a transparent or holey material (Luo & Baillargeon 2012). Finally, by about 14.5 months of age, infants identify color as a containment variable: They now detect a violation if a yellow toy is lowered inside a container (large enough to hide only one toy), and a purple toy is then removed from the container (Setoh & Baillargeon 2011).

With the gradual identification of variables, infants' physical representations become increasingly richer (see Figure 3.3). After representing the structural information about an event and using this information to categorize the event, the PR system accesses the list of variables that have been identified as relevant for predicting outcomes in the category selected. The PR system then gathers information about each variable and includes this information in the physical representation of the event. This variable information is then interpreted by the variable rules as well as by the PR system's causal framework.

To illustrate this process, consider what variable information 7.5-month-olds would include in their physical representation of a containment event in which a ball was lowered inside a box. By 7.5 months, as we just saw, width and height have been identified as containment variables, but container-surface and color have not. Thus, infants would include information about the relative widths and heights of the ball and box in their physical representation of the event, but *not* information about the container's

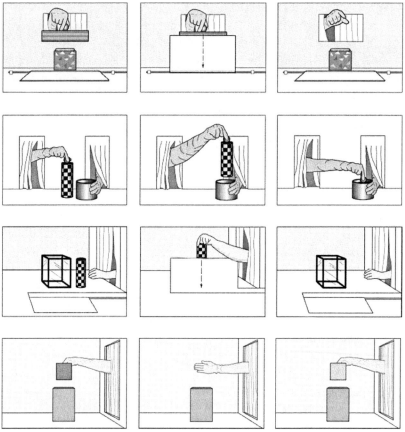

Figure 3.2. Some of the variables infants identify as they learn about containment events. By about 4 months of age, infants are surprised if a wide object becomes fully hidden inside a narrow container (Wang et al. 2004). By about 7.5 months, infants are surprised if a tall object becomes almost fully hidden inside a short container (Hespos & Baillargeon 2001a). By about 9.5 months, infants are surprised if an object becomes hidden inside a transparent container (Luo & Baillargeon 2012). Finally, by about 14.5 months, infants are surprised if an object changes color (e.g., from purple to yellow) when briefly lowered inside a container (too small to hide more than one object) (Setoh & Baillargeon 2011).

surface or about the ball's color. As a rule, the PR system does not include information about variables that have not yet been identified in its physical representation of an event (e.g., Hespos & Baillargeon 2001a; Kotovsky & Baillargeon 1998; Luo & Baillargeon 2005; Newcombe, Huttenlocher, & Learmonth 1999).

Physical-reasoning system

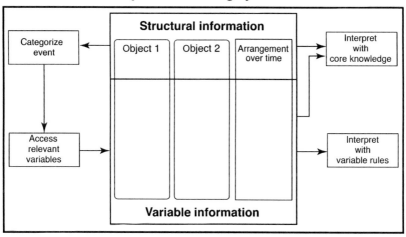

Figure 3.3. Schematic model of the physical-reasoning system: How infants represent and interpret the structural and the variable information about a physical event.

Décalages. We have just seen that, for each event category, infants gradually identify variables that enable them to better predict outcomes within the category. One might ask whether variables identified in the context of one event category are generalized to other categories, when equally relevant. For example, after infants learn to attend to height information in containment events, do they also attend to this information in covering or in tube events? Interestingly, the answer to such questions has turned out to be negative: A variable identified in the context of one category is *not* generalized to other categories, even when equally relevant (e.g., Hespos & Baillargeon 2001a, 2006; Wang et al. 2005; Wang & Baillargeon 2006; Wang & Kohne 2007). Infants thus learn separately about each event category.

In some cases, infants may identify a variable at about the same age in different event categories. For example, the variable width is identified at about the same age in occlusion and in containment events (Wang et al. 2004). In other cases, however, several months may separate the acquisition of the same variable in different event categories, resulting in marked lags or *décalages* (to use a Piagetian term) in infants' responses to similar events in different event categories. As a case in point, consider the variable height (see Figure 3.4). Although this variable is identified at about 7.5 months in containment events, as we just saw (Hespos & Baillargeon 2001a), it is identified earlier, at about 3.5 months, in occlusion events (Baillargeon & DeVos

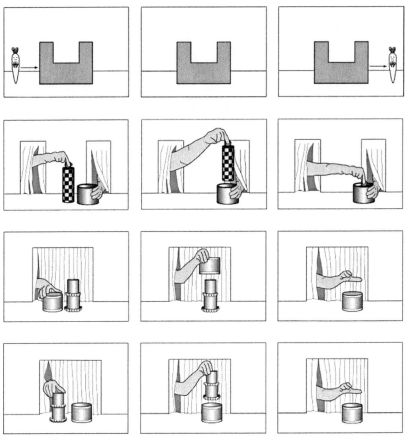

Figure 3.4. Décalages in infants' identification of the variable height across different event categories. By about 3.5 months of age, infants are surprised if a tall object remains fully hidden when passing behind an occluder with a short midsection (Baillargeon & DeVos 1991). By about 7.5 months, infants are surprised if a tall object becomes almost fully hidden inside a short container (Hespos & Baillargeon 2001a). By about 12 months, infants are surprised if a tall object becomes fully hidden under a short cover (Wang et al. 2005). Finally, by about 14.5 months, infants are surprised if a tall object becomes fully hidden inside a short tube (Wang et al. 2005). In the latter two cases, infants are first allowed to inspect the cover or tube in a brief orientation procedure.

1991); it is identified later, at about 12 months, in covering events (Wang et al. 2005); and it is identified later still, at about 14.5 months, in tube events (Wang et al. 2005).

Décalages have been observed not only in violation-of-expectation tasks, as we just saw, but also in action tasks (e.g., Hespos & Baillargeon 2006; Wang & Kohne 2007). In one experiment, for example, 6- and 7.5-month-olds first played with a tall stuffed frog (Hespos & Baillargeon 2006). Next, the frog was placed behind a large screen, which was then removed to reveal a tall and a short occluder (occlusion condition) or a tall and a short container (containment condition). The occluders were identical to the front halves of the containers; two frog feet protruded on either side of each occluder or through small holes at the bottom of each container. At both ages, infants were reliably more likely to search for the frog behind the tall as opposed to the short occluder; however, only the 7.5-months-olds (who had identified height as a containment variable) were reliably more likely to search for the frog inside the tall as opposed to the short container. Control infants who did not see the frog tended to reach about equally for the two occluders or containers.

Explanation-based learning. We suggested earlier that infants learn, with experience, what variables are helpful for interpreting and predicting outcomes in each event category. How does this learning process occur? Building on work in machine learning by DeJong (1993, 1997), we have proposed that the identification of a variable depends on an *explanation-based learning* (EBL) process that involves three main steps (e.g., Baillargeon et al. 2009a; Wang & Baillargeon 2008).

First, infants must notice *contrastive outcomes* relevant to the variable. This occurs when infants build similar physical representations for two or more events – and notice that the events have contrastive outcomes. For example, consider the variable height in covering events, which is typically identified at about 12 months of age (e.g., Wang et al. 2005). We suppose that at some point prior to 12 months of age, infants begin to notice – as they manipulate covers and objects, or as they observe others doing so – that when a cover is lowered over an object, the object sometimes remains partly visible beneath the cover and sometimes does not. Infants thus notice contrastive outcomes they cannot predict based on their current variable knowledge: Similar physical representations ("cover lowered over object") lead to contrastive outcomes ("object remains partly visible beneath cover" versus "object becomes fully hidden"), suggesting that a crucial piece of information is missing from the representations.

At this point, infants begin to search for the *conditions* that map onto these contrastive outcomes. Specifically, infants attempt to determine under what condition one outcome is observed, and under what condition the other outcome is observed. Eventually, infants uncover a regularity linking each outcome with a distinct condition (we assume that infants' statistical learning mechanisms help detect these regularities; e.g., Fiser & Aslin 2002; Saffran 2009). In the case of the variable height in covering events, infants detect that objects remain partly visible when placed under covers that are shorter than the objects, and become fully hidden when placed under covers that are as tall as or taller than the objects.

Finally, infants attempt to generate an *explanation* for the condition-outcome regularity detected, based on their prior knowledge. According to the EBL process, *only* condition-outcome regularities for which explanations can be provided are recognized as new variables. These explanations are typically very shallow (e.g., Keil 1995; Luo et al. 2009; Wilson & Keil 2000), but they still serve to integrate new variables with infants' existing causal knowledge (by the same token, these explanations also serve to prevent infants from learning incorrect or spurious variables). In the case of the variable height in covering events, infants' principle of persistence can provide a ready explanation for their observations: Because an object continues to exist and retains its height when under a cover, it can become fully hidden only if its height is equal to, or shorter than, that of the cover.

After a new variable has been identified (i.e., is added to the list of variables relevant to an event category), infants begin to routinely include information about the variable in their physical representations of events from the category.

The EBL process helps make clear why infants learn separately about each event category. Infants do not compare arbitrary groups of events and look for invariants or critical variables that might explain similarities or differences among the events. The only situation that can trigger the identification of a variable is one where events with similar physical representations yield (as yet unpredicted or unexplained) contrastive outcomes. The learning process is thus highly constrained: It is designed to compare apples with apples, and not apples with rabbits or spoons.

Teaching experiments. The EBL process predicts that infants who have not yet identified a variable in an event category should be able to identify the variable – even several months before they would normally do so – if exposed in the laboratory (or the home) to appropriate observations for the variable. And indeed, a number of "teaching" experiments have now provided evidence for this prediction (e.g., Baillargeon 2002; Wang & Baillargeon 2008a; Wang & Kohne 2007).

For example, in a series of experiments, Wang and her colleagues "taught" 9-month-old infants the variable height in covering events (recall that this variable is typically not identified until about 12 months of age; e.g., Wang et al. 2005). Infants received three pairs of teaching trials. In each pair of trials, a tall and a short cover (that differed only in height) were lowered over a tall object; infants could see that the object remained partly visible beneath the short cover, but became fully hidden under the tall cover. Different covers were used in the three pairs of teaching trials. Next, the infants received either a violation-of-expectation task or an action task involving novel covers and objects. In the violation-of-expectation task, infants looked reliably longer (even after a 24-hour delay) when a tall object became fully hidden under a short as opposed to a tall cover (Wang & Baillargeon 2008a). In the action task, infants searched correctly for a tall object under a tall as opposed to a short cover (Wang & Kohne 2007).

From an EBL perspective, these results are readily interpretable. During the teaching trials, (1) the infants noticed that events with similar physical representations led to contrastive outcomes; (2) they uncovered the specific height conditions that mapped onto these outcomes; and (3) they built an explanation for this condition-outcome regularity using their prior knowledge. Height was then added to the list of variables identified as relevant to covering events. When the infants next encountered covering events, they attended to the height information in the events, which enabled them to detect the violation in the violation-of-expectation task and to search correctly in the action task.

Two additional results supported this analysis. First, infants failed at the violation-of-expectation task if they received inappropriate teaching trials for which no explanation was possible (Wang & Baillargeon 2008a; see also Newcombe, Sluzenski, & Huttenlocher 2005). In this experiment, false bottoms were inserted into the teaching covers, rendering them all 2.5 cm deep; when the covers were rotated forward to reveal their interiors, the infants could see that they were all shallow. Thus, in each pair of teaching trials, the infants still observed that the tall object became fully hidden under the tall cover and partly hidden under the short cover – but they could no longer build an explanation for this condition-outcome regularity, because the tall and short covers were now equally shallow (i.e., it did not make sense that the tall object became fully hidden under the tall but shallow covers). Second, infants failed at the action task if they received appropriate teaching trials but were tested with tubes instead of covers (Wang & Kohne 2007). When the tops of the tall and short covers were removed to form tubes, infants searched for the tall object in either the tall or the short tube, suggesting that they had identified height as a variable relevant to covering events and did not generalize this variable to tube events.

Together, the results summarized in this section suggest that infants can be taught a new variable in an event category through brief exposure to appropriate observations for the variable. Furthermore, infants who are taught a new variable immediately attend to information about the variable in situations presenting different stimuli and calling for different responses – but only when these situations involve events from the *same* category. The EBL process ensures broad, yet circumscribed, generalization: A variable identified in an event category is attended to in *any* event from the category – but *only* in events from the category.

The Acquisition of Numerical Knowledge

A representation of a given object is a representation of a unique individual. Representations of individuals are inputs into a variety of quantificational computations, such as which of two objects is bigger, which of two sets is more numerous, exactly how many objects are in a given container, and so on. We now turn to one type of quantification – by number.

As we will see, the development of number representations provides a case study of conceptual discontinuities: Children must build representational resources qualitatively different from the initial state. In this way, number representations differ from object representations. Core cognition supports learning about objects, as Part I demonstrates, but this learning does not require forming object representations with very different properties from those available to young infants. We shall argue that core cognition contains two systems of representation with numerical content: *analog magnitude representations of number* and *parallel individuation of small sets of entities in working-memory models*. Both systems of representation continue to articulate thought throughout life and play crucial roles in later mathematical development. However, as I will show, the representations within them, alone, cannot express mathematical concepts such as integer or fraction. Thus, we need to understand how the latter concepts arise.

This question – how humans create representational resources that are discontinuous with those that are the input to the learning processes that create them – is of great scientific interest. Moreover, this case study is important for social and educational reasons also. Preschoolers vary vastly in their mastery of counting and the simple arithmetical algorithms that depend upon counting (e.g., counting up to add), and this variability predicts academic success in elementary school more than does variability in reading readiness, vocabulary, or many other predictors (Duncan et al. 2007). It is important, then, to understand what is difficult about acquiring the earliest mathematical knowledge and to understand how this learning is achieved. In what follows, we sketch answers to these questions, detailing the core cognition systems with numerical content, showing how they are

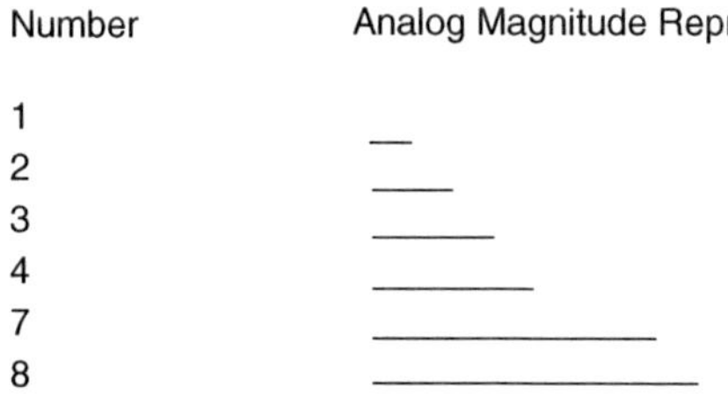

Number	Analog Magnitude Representation
1	—
2	——
3	———
4	————
7	——————
8	———————

Figure 3.5. External analog magnitude representation of number in which number is represented by line length.

discontinuous with the integers, and describe a learning process through which children navigate the conceptual achievement of creating a representational resource that is capable of expressing natural numbers.

Core Cognition System 1: Analog Magnitude Representations of Number

Human adults, human infants, and nonhuman animals deploy a system of analog magnitude representations of number. Number is represented by a physical magnitude that is roughly proportional to the number of individuals in the set being enumerated. Figure 3.5 depicts an external analog magnitude representational system in which length represents number.

A psychophysical signature of analog magnitude representations is that the discriminability of any two magnitudes depends on their ratio. That is, discriminability is in accordance with Weber's law. This is a coding scheme widely used to represent dimensions of experience, such a loudness, time, brightness, length, size, intensity of pain, and many others. Animals and humans do not confuse these different dimensions of experience, but they use similar representational systems to encode them.

Dehaene (1997) and Gallistel (1990) review the evidence for the long evolutionary history of analog magnitude number representations. Animals as disparate as pigeons, rats, and nonhuman primates all represent number, and number discriminability satisfies Weber's law. In the past years, four different laboratories have provided unequivocal evidence that preverbal infants form analog magnitude representations of number as well (Brannon 2002; Brannon, Abbot & Lutz 2004; Lipon & Spelke 2003, 2004; McCrink & Wynn 2004; Wood & Spelke 2005; Xu & Spelke 2000; Xu, Spelke & Goddard 2005). The first paper in this flurry of studies was by Fei Xu and Elizabeth Spelke, who solved the problem of how to control for other possible bases of judgment (cumulative surface area, element size, density) in a large number habituation paradigm. The authors habituated 6-month-old infants either to displays containing 8 dots, or to displays containing 16 dots. Possible confounds between number and other variables were controlled either by equating the two series of stimuli on those variables, or by making the test displays equidistant from the habituation displays on them. Infants who were habituated to 8-dot displays recovered interest when shown the novel 16-dot displays, while generalizing habituation to the novel 8-dot displays. Those habituated to 16-dot displays showed the reverse pattern. Subsequent studies duplicated this design (and the positive result) with 16-dot versus 32-dot comparisons and with 4-dot versus 8-dot comparisons.

That analog magnitude representations support these discriminations is shown by the fact that success is a function of the ratio of the set sizes. In all of the above studies, in which 6-month-old infants succeeded with a 2:1 ratio, they failed in comparisons that involved a 3:2 ratio (i.e., they failed to discriminate 8-dot from 12-dot arrays, 16-dot from 24-dot arrays, and 4-dot from 6-dot arrays). Also, these researchers have found that sensitivity improves by 9 months of age. Infants of this age succeed at 3:2 comparisons across a wide variety of absolute set sizes, but fail at 4:3 comparisons. Subsequent studies showed analog magnitude representations of number of different kinds of individuals (jumps, sounds), with the same profiles of sensitivity (Lipton & Spelke 2004; Wood & Spelke 2005).

In all the studies presented so far, we can be confident it is number infants are responding to, because every other variable has been equated either across the habituation stimuli or across the test stimuli. Of course, if the analog magnitude representations underlying performance in these habituation studies are truly numerical representations, number relevant computations other than establishing numerical equivalence should be defined over them, and indeed this is so. Elizabeth Brannon (2002) showed that 11-month-old infants represent numerical order using analog magnitude representations of sets. Koleen McCrink and Karen Wynn showed that 9-month-olds can manipulate sets of objects in the analog magnitude range to support addition, subtraction, and ratio computation (McCrink & Wynn 2004). In sum, analog magnitude representations of number are available at least by 6 months of age. Preverbal infants represent the approximate cardinal value of sets, and compute numerical equivalence, numerical order, addition, subtraction, and ratios over these representations.

Core Cognition System 2: Parallel Individuation of Small Sets

Science moves rapidly, and the infant studies reviewed above came relatively late in the history of studies designed to show that infants are sensitive to number. The first studies, some 20 years earlier, concerned *small* sets – discriminations among sets of 1, 2, and 3 objects. These include many 2 versus 3 habituation studies and Wynn's 1 + 1 = 2 or 1 violation-of-expectation study (e.g., Antell & Keating 1983; Starkey & Cooper 1980, Wynn 1992b). In the latter study, infants were shown a single object on a stage, which was then hidden by a screen. Next, another object was introduced behind the screen. Finally, the screen was lowered to reveal either one object or two objects. Infants' attention was drawn to the unexpected outcome of a single object. Although some have suggested that analog magnitude number representations underlie success in these experiments (e.g., Dehaene 1997), the evidence conclusively implicates a very different representational system (Feigenson & Carey 2003, 2005; Feigenson, Carey, & Hauser 2002; Scholl & Leslie 1999; Simon 1997; Uller, Carey, Huntley-Fenner, & Klatt 1999). In this alternative representational system, number is only implicitly encoded; there are no symbols for number at all, not even analog magnitude ones. Instead, the representations include a symbol for each individual in an attended set. Thus, a set containing one apple might be represented "O" (an iconic object file) or "apple" (a symbol for an individual of the kind apple), and a set containing two apples might be represented "O O" or "apple apple," and so forth. These representations consist of one symbol (file) for each individual, and when the content of a symbol is a spatio-temporally determined object, it is an object file (Kahneman et al. 1992). Infants also create working-memory models of small sets of other types of individuals, such as sound bursts or events, and so we shall call the system of representation "parallel individuation" and the explicit symbols within it "individual files."

There are many reasons to favor individual file representations over analog magnitude representations as underlying performance in most of the infant small number studies (see Carey 2009 for a more thorough review). First, and most important, success on many spontaneous number representation tasks involving small sets do not show the Weber-fraction signature of analog magnitude representations; rather they show the set-size signature of individual file representations. Individuals in small sets (sets of 1, 2, or 3) can be represented, and sets outside of that limit cannot, even when the sets to be contrasted have the same Weber-fraction as those small sets where the infant succeeds at that age. This is the set-size signature of individual file representations.

Here I describe just one paradigm that elicits the set-size signature of parallel individuation (see Carey 2009 for others). An infant watches as each of two opaque containers, previously shown to be empty, is baited with a different number of graham crackers. For example, the experimenter might put two crackers in one container and three in the other. After placement, the parent allows the infant to crawl toward the containers. The dependent measure is which container the baby chooses. Ten- to 12-month-olds infants succeed at 1 versus 2, 2 versus 3, and 1 versus 3, but fail at 3 versus 4, 2 versus 4, and even 1 versus 4 (Feigenson & Carey 2005; Feigenson et al. 2002). Although 1:4 is a more favorable ratio than 2:3, infants fail at 1 versus 4 comparisons and succeed at 2 versus 3. Note also that 5 crackers are involved in each choice, so the total length of time of placements is equated over these two comparisons. This is a striking result. Infants could succeed at 1 versus 4 comparisons on many different bases: putting 4 crackers into a bucket takes much longer, draws more attention to that bucket, and so on, yet infants are at chance. Although infants could solve this problem in many different ways, apparently they are attending to each cracker and creating a model of what's in the container that contains one object-file for each cracker. As soon as one of the sets exceeds the limits on parallel individuation (apparently three at this age; see also the manual-choice paradigm in Feigenson & Carey 2003, 2005), performance falls apart. This finding provides very strong evidence that parallel individuation underlies success on this task.

The purpose of parallel individuation is to create working-memory models of small sets of individuals in order to represent spatial, causal, and intentional relations among them. Unlike analog magnitude number representations, the parallel-individuation system is not a dedicated number representation system. Far from it! The symbols in the parallel-individuation system explicitly represent individuals. This ability is closely tied to knowledge development in the domain of physical reasoning (see first part of chapter): Only because the infant has core knowledge about persistence, he/she can be sure that the number of individuals perceived in a given event does not change magically. If we combine this knowledge with the individuation system, it is possible to understand occlusion or containment relations involving more than one object. Imagine, for example, an occlusion event in which two boxes are placed behind a screen. As both boxes are temporarily out of view, the infant needs to keep track of how many individuals are occluded, and to represent their relation (occlusion) to the screen. Figure 3.6 depicts several different possible individual file representations of two boxes. In none of these alternative models is there a symbol that has the content "two"; rather the symbols in working memory represent the boxes. The whole model {box box} represents two boxes, of course, but only implicitly.

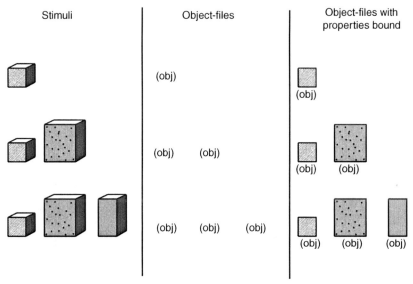

Figure 3.6. Two versions of the memory structures that might subserve parallel individuation of small sets of objects. In one, each object is represented by an object-file that abstracts away from specific features (OBJ). In the other, each object is represented by an object-file on which shape, color, texture, and spatial extent features have been bound.

If parallel individuation models do not include symbols for numbers, why are we discussing these models in the present context? The answer is that they are shot through with numerical content, even though numerical content is merely implicit in the computations that index and represent small sets, that govern the opening of new individual files, that update working-memory models of sets as individuals are added or subtracted, and that compare sets on numerical criteria. The creation of a new individual file requires principles of individuation and numerical identity (see the above section on object representations that play a role in physical reasoning; numerical identity means sameness in the sense of "same one"); models must keep track of whether this object (sound, event etc.), seen now, is the same *one* as that was perceived before. The decision the system makes dictates whether an additional individual file is established, and this guarantees that a model of a set of three boxes will contain three box symbols. Computations of numerical identity are (as their name says) numerical computations. Also, the opening of a new individual file in the presence of other active files provides an implicit representation of the process of adding one to an array of individuals. Finally, working-memory models of two sets of individuals can be simultaneously maintained, and when individual-file models are compared on the basis of 1–1 correspondence, the computations over these symbols establish numerical equivalence and numerical order (for evidence of such computations, see Feigenson 2005; Feigenson & Carey 2003).

Conceptual Discontinuity

In the adult representational system, verbal numerals represent positive integers: They are summary symbols that represent cardinal values of sets, and the system of verbal numerals satisfies Peano's axioms. The central axiom is that each integer has a unique successor; for each integer, the next integer is n + 1. Implicitly or explicitly, the adult meanings of verbal numerals must be formulated over concepts such as *exactly 1, plus, exact numerosity, set, successor*. Within this set of primitives, "four" can be defined in many different ways. Here are two: (1) four is the cardinal value of any set that can be put into 1–1 correspondence with {x, y, z, w}, where "x," "y," "z," and "w" refer to numerically distinct individuals and {} denotes a set; and (2) four is the successor of three. These two ways of defining "four" are formally equivalent, in the sense that each definition determines exactly the same concept, namely, *four*. For "four" to have the same meaning as it does in the adult representational system, its meaning must be equivalent to both of these. Of course, it is an open question just what set of primitives underlies the child's first successful representation of *four*. Whatever it is, it must provide the expressive power of the primitives listed above.

Neither of the core cognition systems discussed in the previous sections has the capacity to represent the integers. Parallel individuation includes no summary symbols for number at all, and has an upper limit of 3 or 4 on the size of sets it represents. Analog magnitude representations include summary symbols for cardinal values that are embedded within a system of arithmetical computations, but they represent only approximate cardinal values; there is no representation of exactly 1, and therefore no representation of +1. Analog magnitude representations cannot even resolve the distinction between 10 and 11 (or any two successive integers beyond its discrimination capacity), and so cannot express the successor function. Thus, neither system can represent *10*, let alone *342,689,455*. This analysis makes precise the senses in which the concepts expressed by the verbal numeral list are qualitatively different from those representations that precede it. The numeral list has more expressive power – it can represent infinitely more concepts than can either of the core cognition systems with numerical content.

Because the numeral list is qualitatively different from each of the core cognition systems with numerical content, it is indeed difficult to learn. American middle-class children learn to recite the count list and to carry out the count routine in response to the probe "how many" shortly after their second birthday. They do not learn how counting represents number for another 1½ or 2 years, however. Young two-year-olds first assign a cardinal meaning to "one," treating other numerals as equivalent plural markers that contrast in meaning with "one." Some 7 to 9 months later they assign cardinal meaning to "two," but still take all other numerals to mean essentially "some," contrasting only with "one" and "two." They then work out the cardinal meaning of "three" and then of "four." This protracted period of development is called the "subset"-knower stage, for children have worked out cardinal meanings for only a subset of the numerals in their count list. So far, we still do not know exactly what representations underlie the meanings of "one" through "four" in the subset-knower stage. It seems likely, however, that they draw on the resources of parallel individuation. LeCorre and Carey (2007) proposed a system of "enriched parallel individuation" in which the child creates long-term memory models of sets of 1 through 4 objects, mapping the verbal numerals to them using a rule that specifies that any set that can be put in 1–1 correspondence to the memory representation of a singleton set has "one" object, and similarly for sets of 2 through 4.

Many different tasks, which make totally different information-processing demands on the child, confirm that subset-knowers differ qualitatively from children who have worked out how counting represents number. Subset-knowers cannot create sets of sizes specified by their unknown numerals (Wynn 1990, 1992b), cannot estimate the cardinal values of sets outside their known numeral range (Le Corre et al. 2006), do not know what set-size is reached if 1 individual is added to a set labeled with a numeral outside their known numeral range (Sarnecka & Carey 2008), and so on. Children who succeed on one of these tasks succeed on all of them. Furthermore, a child diagnosed as a "one"-knower on one task is also a "one"-knower on all of the others, ditto for "two"-knowers, "three"-knowers and "four"-knowers.

Thus, learning how the verbal count list works is extremely difficult, with the process unfolding over a two-year period. Adults who lack a count list (because their language does not contain one) demonstrate profound limitations in nonverbal numerical reasoning (Gordon 2004; Pica et al. 2004; Spaepen et al. 2011), and preschoolers who do not fully master the numeral list representation of number are at a profound disadvantage in the elementary school curriculum. How is creating a representation of integers achieved?

Acquiring Representations of Integers

Ultimately, learning requires adjusting expectations, representations, and actions to data. Abstractly, all of these learning mechanisms are variants of hypothesis-testing algorithms. The representations most consistent with the available data are strengthened; those hypotheses are accepted. However, in cases of developmental discontinuity, the learner does not initially have the representational resources to state the hypotheses that will be tested. Carey (2009) describes one learning mechanism that underlies conceptual discontinuities – *Quinian bootstrapping*. Quinian bootstrapping can create new representational machinery, new concepts that articulate hypotheses previously unstatable.

In Quinian bootstrapping episodes, mental symbols are established that correspond to newly coined or newly learned explicit symbols. These are initially placeholders, getting whatever meaning they have from their interrelations with other explicit symbols. As is true of all word learning, newly learned symbols must be initially interpreted in terms of concepts already available. But at the onset of a bootstrapping episode, these interpretations are only partial – the learner (child or scientist) does not yet have the capacity to formulate the concepts that the symbols will come to express.

The bootstrapping process using the set of interrelated symbols in the placeholder structure to model the phenomena in the domain, where the phenomena are represented in terms of whatever concepts the child or scientist has available. Both structures (the placeholder structure and the system of available concepts) provide constraints, some only implicit and instantiated in the computations defined over the representations. These constraints are respected as much as possible in the course of the modeling activities, which include analogy construction and monitoring, limiting case analyses, thought experiments, and inductive inferences.

Bootstrapping Representations of Natural Number

In the case of the construction of the numeral list representation of the integers, the memorized count list is the placeholder structure. Its initial meaning is exhausted by the relation among the external symbols: They are stably ordered. "One, two, three, four..." initially has no more meaning for the child than "a, b, c, d..." The details of the subset-knower period suggest that the resources of parallel individuation, enriched by the machinery of linguistic set-based quantification, provide the partial meanings children assign to the placeholder structures that get the bootstrapping process off the ground. The meaning of the word "one" could be subserved by a mental model of a set of a single individual {i}, along with a procedure that determines that the word "one" can be applied to any set that can be put in 1–1 correspondence with this model. Similarly "two" is mapped onto a long-term memory model of a set of two individuals {j k}, along with a procedure that determines that the word "two" can be applied to any set that can be put in 1–1 correspondence with this model. And so on for "three" and "four." This proposal requires no mental machinery not shown to be in the repertoire of infants – parallel individuation, the capacity to compare models on the basis of 1–1 correspondence, and the set-based quantificational machinery that underlies the singular/plural distinction and makes possible the representation of dual and trial markers. The work of the subset-knower period of numeral learning, which extends in English-learners between ages 2:0 and 3:6 or so, is the creation of the long-term memory models and computations for applying them that constitute the meanings of the first numerals the child assigns numerical meaning to.

Once these meanings are in place, and the child has independently memorized the placeholder count list and the counting routine, the bootstrapping proceeds as follows. The child notices the identity between the words "one," "two," "three," and "four" that express the numerical meanings captured by the machinery of enriched parallel individuation and the first four words in the count list. The child must try to align these two independent structures. The critical analogy is between order on the list and order in a series of sets related by *one additional individual*. This analogy supports the induction that any two successive numerals will refer to sets such that the numeral farther in the list picks out a set that is 1 greater than that earlier in the list.

This proposal illustrates all of the components of bootstrapping processes: placeholder structures whose meaning is provided by relations among external symbols, partial interpretations in terms of available conceptual structures, modeling processes (in this case analogy), and an inductive leap. The greater representational power of the numeral list derives from combining distinct representational resources – a serially ordered list, the numerical content of parallel individuation (which is largely embodied in the computations carried out over sets represented in memory models with one symbol for each individual in the set). The child creates symbols that express information that previously existed only as constraints on computations. Numerical content does not come from nowhere, but the process does not consist of defining "seven" in terms of mental symbols for number available to infants.

Carey (2009) illustrates how Quinian bootstrapping underlies conceptual discontinuities of two types: (1) those that involve the construction of representational resources with more expressive power, such as is the case in mastering the verbal integer list (sketched here) or the construction of rational number, and (2) episodes of theory changes involving successive conceptual systems that are incommensurable with each other. Carey (2009) draws examples from early childhood through historical theory changes achieved by metaconceptually sophisticated scientists.

Perhaps you have noted a surprising fact about the present account of the initial construction of integer representations. The process makes no use of one of the systems of core cognition with numerical content – the analog-magnitude (AM) system. This is so, and Carey (2009) summarizes the evidence for this surprising turn of events. However, another episode of Quinian bootstrapping achieves the integration of AM number representations with verbal numerals within 6 months of the child's becoming a "cardinal principle-knower" (Le Corre & Carey 2007). This integration plays a very important role in subsequent arithmetic learning and numerical reasoning. Impairments in the AM system through brain damage lead to breakdowns of mathematical reasoning in adults, and are implicated in dyscalculia, a specific learning disability in mathematics (Butterworth 1999; Dehaene 1997). Two recent studies have shown that even within normally developing children, those with high resolution in their nonverbal AM system outperform on school arithmetic learning those with low resolution, beginning in kindergarten (Gilmore, McCarthy, & Spelke 2010; Halberda, Mazzocco, & Feigenson 2008). Thus, although Quinian bootstrapping is required to construct representations of integers, as well as fractions and other later-developing mathematical concepts, the representations within core cognition play an important role in learning and reasoning throughout all of life.

Chapter Conclusions

Systems of core cognition, such as the physical-reasoning system sketched in Part I, and the analog-magnitude and parallel-individuation systems sketched in Part II, are learning devices. They make it possible for infants to represent, and hence learn about, the objects in their world, and their spatial, causal, and quantitative relations to each other. As described in Part I, during infancy the PR system itself is enriched through explanation-based learning (EBL), as the child identifies new variables that are relevant to the predictions and explanations that constitute physical reasoning. The learning achieved in this way enriches the physical-reasoning system, but does not transcend it. It does not require creating new representational primitives; the variables identified are already available as input to the statistical processes that are part of EBL. EBL goes beyond mere statistical learning, for it is constrained by the causal/explanatory knowledge embedded in core cognition. Similarly, the quantitative machinery of the core systems of number representation makes it possible for the child to learn quantitative regularities about his or her world.

The conceptual representations that constitute systems of core cognition are part of the building blocks of later-developing conceptual representations, even those that are qualitatively different from core cognition, expressing concepts not found within it. As sketched in Part II, the resources of parallel individuation provide a large part of the meanings assigned to verbal numerals during the subset-knower stage. However, they cannot provide the full meaning of verbal numerals; parallel individuation cannot represent the meaning of "seven" or "ten," for example, because working memory has a limit of three or four items during infancy and the preschool years. Quinian bootstrapping is required for the child to work out the trick of using serial order in the count list to determine the cardinal value of any numeral in the list, that is, to come to use counting to implement the successor function. And indeed, Sarnecka and Carey (2008) showed that children who have learned how counting represents number (children called "cardinal principle-knowers," or "CP-knowers," in the literature) differ from subset-knowers precisely in this way. Only CP-knowers can derive without counting that if you add one to a set containing 5 objects, you will have 6 objects.

Our goal in this chapter was two-fold. First, we provided worked examples of the type of research that reveals rich representational resources early in infancy – representational resources that provide building blocks for later conceptual understanding of the world, illustrating that these are dynamic learning mechanisms. Second, we illustrated the point that mastery of the adult conceptual repertoire often requires creating entirely new representational resources (in this case the integer-list representation of number). Through such constructions, children become able to think thoughts unavailable to infants or to any nonhuman animal.

Acknowledgments

The preparation of this chapter was supported by a grant from the National Institute of Child Health and Human Development to Renée Baillargeon (HD-021104), and by grants from NICHHD (HD-028338) and NSF (REC-0633955) to Susan Carey. We would like to thank Amélie Bernard and Peipei Setoh for helpful comments.

REFERENCES

Aguiar, A. & Baillargeon, R. (1999). 2.5-Month-old infants' reasoning about when objects should and should not be occluded. *Cognitive Psychology*, **39**, 116–157.
  (2002). Developments in young infants' reasoning about occluded objects. *Cognitive Psychology*, **45**, 267–336.
Antell, S. & Keating, D. P. (1983). Perception of numerical invariance in neonates. *Child Development*, **54**, 695–701.
Baillargeon, R. (1987). Object permanence in 3.5- and 4.5-month-old infants. *Developmental Psychology*, **23**, 655–664.
  (2002). The acquisition of physical knowledge in infancy: A summary in eight lessons. In U. Goswami (Ed.), *Blackwell handbook of childhood cognitive development* (pp. 47–83). Oxford: Blackwell.
  (2008). Innate ideas revisited: For a principle of persistence in infants' physical reasoning. *Perspectives on Psychological Science*, **3**, 2–13.
Baillargeon, R. & DeVos, J. (1991). Object permanence in young infants: Further evidence. *Child Development*, **62**, 1227–1246.
Baillargeon, R., Li, J., Gertner, Y., & Wu, D. (2011). How do infants reason about physical events? In U. Goswami (Ed.), *The Wiley-Blackwell handbook of childhood cognitive development, second edition* (pp. 11–48). Oxford: Blackwell.
Baillargeon, R., Li, J., Ng, W., & Yuan, S. (2009a). An account of infants' physical reasoning. In A. Woodward & A. Needham (Eds.), *Learning and the infant mind* (pp. 66–116). New York: Oxford University Press.
Baillargeon, R., Needham, A., & DeVos, J. (1992). The development of young infants' intuitions about support. *Early Development and Parenting*, **1**, 69–78.
Baillargeon, R., Spelke, E. S., & Wasserman, S. (1985). Object permanence in 5-month-old infants. *Cognition*, **20**, 191–208.
Baillargeon, R., Stavans, M., Wu, D., Gertner, R., Setoh, P., Kittredge, A. K., & Bernard, A. (2012). Object individuation and physical reasoning in infancy: An integrative account. *Language Learning and Development*, **8**, 4–46.
Baillargeon, R., Wu, D., Yuan, S., Li, J., & Luo, Y. (2009b). Young infants' expectations about self-propelled objects. In B. M. Hood & L. R. Santos (Eds.), *The origins of object knowledge* (pp. 285–352). Oxford: Oxford University Press.
Bonatti, L., Frot, E., & Mehler, J. (2005). What face inversion does to infants' numerical abilities. *Psychological Science*, **16**, 506–510.
Bonatti, L., Frot, E., Zangl, R., & Mehler, J. (2002). The human first hypothesis: Identification of conspecifics and individuation of objects in the young infant. *Cognitive Psychology*, **44**, 388–426.

Brannon, E. M. (2002). The development of ordinal numerical knowledge in infancy. *Cognition*, **83**, 223–240.

Brannon, E. M., Abbott, S., & Lutz, D. J. (2004). Number bias for the discrimination of large visual sets in infancy. *Cognition*, **93**, B59–B68.

Butterworth, B. (1999). *What counts: How every brain is hardwired for math*. New York: Free Press.

Carey, S. (2009). *The origin of concepts*. New York: Oxford University Press.

Carey, S. & Spelke, E. S. (1994). Domain-specific knowledge and conceptual change. In L. A. Hirschfeld & S. A. Gelman (Eds.), *Mapping the mind: Domain specificity in cognition and culture* (pp. 169–200). New York, NY: Cambridge University Press.

Casasola, M., Cohen, L., & Chiarello, E. (2003). Six-month-old infants' categorization of containment spatial relations. *Child Development*, **74**, 679–693.

Csibra, G. (2008). Goal attribution to inanimate agents by 6.5-month-old infants. *Cognition*, **107**, 705–717.

Csibra, G. & Gergely, G. (2009). Natural pedagogy. *Trends in Cognitive Sciences*, **13**, 148–153.

Dehaene, S. (1997). *The number sense*. Oxford: Oxford University Press.

DeJong, G. F. (1993). *Investigating explanation-based learning*. Boston: Kluwer Academic Press.

(1997). Explanation-based learning. In A. Tucker (Ed.), *Encyclopedia of computer science* (pp. 499–520). Boca Raton, FL: CRC Press.

Duncan, G., Dowsett, C., Claessens, A., Magnuson, K., Huston, A., Klebanov, P., Pagani, L., Feinstein, L., Engel, M., Brooks-Gunn, J., Sexton, H., & Duckworth, K. (2007). School readiness and later achievement. *Developmental Psychology*, **43**, 128–1446.

Feigenson, L. (2005). A double-dissociation in infants' representation of object arrays. *Cognition*, **95**, B37–B48.

Feigenson, L. & Carey, S. (2003). Tracking individuals via object files: Evidence from infants' manual search. *Developmental Science*, **6**, 568–584.

Feigenson, L. & Carey, S. (2005). On the limits of infants' quantification of small object arrays. *Cognition*, **97**, 295–313.

Feigenson, L., Carey, S., & Hauser, M. D. (2002). The representations underlying infants' choice of more: Object files versus analog magnitudes. *Psychological Science*, **13**, 150–156.

Fiser, J. & Aslin, R. N. (2002) Statistical learning of new visual feature combinations by infants. *Proceedings of the National Academy of Sciences*, **99**, 15822–15826.

Futó, J., Téglás, E., Csibra, G., & Gergely, G. (2010). Communicative function demonstration induces kind-based artifact representation in preverbal infants. *Cognition*, **117**, 1–8.

Gallistel, C. R. (1990). *The organization of learning*. Cambridge, MA: MIT Press.

Gelman, R. (1990). First principles organize attention to and learning about relevant data: Number and the animate-inanimate distinction as examples. *Cognitive Science*, **14**, 79–106.

Gelman, R., Durgin, F., & Kaufman, L. (1995). Distinguishing between animates and inanimates: Not by motion alone. In D. Sperber, D. Premack, & A. J. Premack (Eds.), *Causal cognition: A multidisciplinary debate* (pp. 150–184). Oxford: Clarendon Press.

Gilmore, C. K., McCarthy, S. E., & Spelke, E. S. (2010). Non-symbolic arithmetic abilities and mathematics achievement in the first year of formal schooling. *Cognition*, **115**, 394–406.

Gordon, P. (2004). Numerical cognition without words: Evidence from Amazonia. *Science*, **306**, 496–499.

Halberda, J., Mazzocco, M. M. M., & Feigenson, L. (2008). Individual differences in non-verbal number acuity correlate with maths achievement. *Nature*, **455**, 665–668.

Hespos, S. J. & Baillargeon, R. (2001a). Infants' knowledge about occlusion and containment events: A surprising discrepancy. *Psychological Science*, **12**, 140–147.

Hespos, S. J. & Baillargeon, R. (2001b). Knowledge about containment events in very young infants. *Cognition*, **78**, 204–245.

Hespos, S. J. & Baillargeon, R. (2006). Décalage in infants' knowledge about occlusion and containment events: Converging evidence from action tasks. *Cognition*, **99**, B31–B41.

Hespos, S. J. & Baillargeon, R. (2008). Young infants' actions reveal their developing knowledge of support variables: Converging evidence for violation-of-expectation findings. *Cognition*, **107**, 304–316.

Huttenlocher, J., Duffy, S., & Levine, S.C. (2002). Infants and toddlers discriminate amount: Are they measuring? *Psychological Science*, **13**, 244–249.

Johnson, S. C., Shimizu, Y. A., & Ok, S-J. (2007). Actors and actions: The role of agent behavior in infants' attribution of goals. *Cognitive Development*, **22**, 310–322.

Kahneman, D., Treisman, A., & Gibbs, B. (1992). The reviewing of object files: Object-specific integration of information. *Cognitive Psychology*, **24**, 175–219.

Keil, F. C. (1995). The growth of causal understandings of natural kinds. In D. Sperber, D. Premack, & A. J. Premack (Eds.), *Causal cognition: A multidisciplinary debate* (pp. 234–262). Oxford: Clarendon Press.

Kestenbaum, R., Termine, N., & Spelke, E. S. (1987). Perception of objects and object boundaries by 3-month-old infants. *British Journal of Developmental Psychology*, **5**, 367–383.

Kochukhova, O., & Gredeback, G. (2007). Learning about occlusion: Initial assumptions and rapid adjustments. *Cognition*, **105**, 26–46.

Kotovsky, L., & Baillargeon, R. (1998). The development of calibration-based reasoning about collision events in young infants. *Cognition*, **67**, 311–351.

LeCorre, M., Brannon, E. M., Van deWalle, G. A., & Carey, S. (2006). Re-visiting the competence/performance debate in the acquisition of the counting principles. *Cognitive Psychology*, **52**, 130–169.

LeCorre, M. & Carey, S. (2007). One, two, three, four, nothing more: How numerals are mapped onto core knowledge of number in the acquisition of the counting principles. *Cognition*, **105**, 395–438.

Leslie, A. M. (1995). A theory of agency. In D. Sperber, D. Premack, & A. J. Premack (Eds.), *Causal cognition: A multidisciplinary debate* (pp. 121–149). Oxford: Clarendon Press.

Leslie, A. M. & Keeble, S. (1987). Do six-month-old infants perceive causality? *Cognition*, **25**, 265–288.

Leslie, A. M., Xu, F., Tremoulet, P. D., & Scholl, B. J. (1998). Indexing and the object concept: Developing 'what' and 'where' system. *Trends in Cognitive Sciences*, **2**, 10–18.

Li., J., Baillargeon, R., & Needham, A. (2012). Learning about support events in young infants. Manuscript in preparation.

Lipton, J. S. & Spelke, E. S. (2003). Origins of number sense: Large number discrimination in human infants. *Psychological Science*, **15**, 396–401.

(2004). Discrimination of large and small numerosities by human infants. *Infancy*, **5**, 271–290.

Luo, Y. & Baillargeon, R. (2005). When the ordinary seems unexpected: Evidence for rule-based physical reasoning in young infants. *Cognition*, **95**, 297–328.

(2012). Infants' reasoning about transparent occluders and containers. Manuscript in preparation.

Luo, Y., Kaufman, L., & Baillargeon, R. (2009). Young infants' reasoning about events involving inert and self-propelled objects. *Cognitive Psychology*, **58**, 441–486.

McDonough, L., Choi, S., & Mandler, J. M. (2003). Understanding spatial relations: Flexible infants, lexical adults. *Cognitive Psychology*, **46**, 229–259.

McCrink, K. & Wynn, K. (2004). Large-number addition and subtraction by 9-month old infants. *Psychological Science*, **15**, 776–781.

Needham, A. (2001). Object recognition and object segregation in 4.5-month-old infants. *Journal of Experimental Child Psychology*, **78**, 3–24.

Needham, A. & Ormsbee, S. M. (2003). The development of object segregation during the first year of life. In R. Kimchi, M. Behrmann, & C. Olson (Eds.), *Perceptual organization in vision: Behavioral and neural perspectives* (pp. 205–232). Mahwah, NJ: Erlbaum.

Needham, A. & Baillargeon, R. (1993). Intuitions about support in 4.5-month-old infants. *Cognition*, **47**, 121–148.

Newcombe, N., Huttenlocher, J., & Learmonth, A. (1999). Infants' coding of location in continuous space. *Infant Behavior and Development*, **22**, 483–510.

Newcombe, N. S., Sluzenski, J., & Huttenlocher, J. (2005). Pre-existing knowledge versus on-line learning: What do infants really know about spatial location? *Psychological Science*, **16**, 222–227.

Onishi, K. H. (2012). Perception of event roles in infancy. Manuscript in preparation.

Pauen, S. & Träuble, B. (2009). How 7-month-olds interpret ambiguous motion events: Category-specific reasoning in infancy. *Cognitive Psychology*, **59**, 275–295.

Pica, P., Lemer, C., Izard, V., & Dehaene, S. (2004). Exact and approximate arithmetic in an Amazonian Indigene group. *Science*, **306**, 499–503.

Premack, D. (1990). The infant's theory of self-propelled objects. *Cognition*, **36**, 1–16.

Premack, D. & Premack, A. (2003). *Original intelligence: Unlocking the mystery of who we are.* New York: McGraw-Hill.

Pylyshyn, Z. W. (1989). The role of location indexes in spatial perception: A sketch of the FINST spatial index model. *Cognition*, **32**, 65–97.

(1994). Some primitive mechanisms of spatial attention. *Cognition*, **50**, 363–384.

Quinn, P. (2007). On the infant's prelinguistic conception of spatial relations: Three developmental trends and their implications for spatial language learning. In J. M. Plumert & J. P. Spencer (Eds.), *The emerging spatial mind* (pp. 117–141). New York: Oxford University Press.

Rose, S. A., Gottfried, A. W., Melloy-Carminar, P., & Bridger, W. H. (1982). Familiarity and novelty preferences in infant recognition memory: Implications for information processing. *Developmental Psychology*, **18**, 704–713.

Saffran, J. R. (2009). What can statistical learning tell us about infant learning? In A. Woodward & A. Needham (Eds.), *Learning and the infant mind* (pp. 29–46). New York: Oxford University Press.

Sarnecka, B. & Carey, S. (2008). How counting represents number: What children must learn and when they learn it. *Cognition*, **108**, 662–667.

Saxe, R., Tenenbaum, J., & Carey, S. (2005). Secret agents: 10- and 12-month-old infants' inferences about hidden causes. *Psychological Science*, **16**, 995–1001.

Saxe, R., Tzelnic, T., & Carey, S. (2006). Five-month-old infants know humans are solid, like inanimate objects. *Cognition*, **101**, B1–B8.

(2007). Knowing who-dunnit: Infants identify the causal agent in an unseen causal interaction. *Developmental Psychology*, **43**, 149–158.

Scholl, B. J. & Leslie, A. M. (1999). Explaining the infant's object concept: Beyond the perception/cognition dichotomy. In E. Lepore & Z. Pylyshyn (Eds.), *What is cognitive science?* (pp. 26–73). Oxford: Blackwell.

Setoh, P. & Baillargeon, R. (2011, March). *How do infants generalize new physical expectations?* Paper presented at the biennial meeting of the Society for Research in Child Development, Montreal, Canada.

Simon, T. J. (1997). Reconceptualizing the origins of number knowledge: A "non-numerical" account. *Cognitive Development*, **12**, 349–372.

Slater, A. (1995). Visual perception and memory at birth. In C. Rovee-Collier & L. P. Lipsitt (Eds.), *Advances in infancy research* (Vol. 9, pp. 107–162). Norwood: Ablex.

Spaepen, E., Coppola, M., Spelke. E, Carey, S., & Goldin-Meadow, S. (2011). Number without a language model. *Proceedings of the National Academy of Sciences*, **108**, 3163–3168.

Spelke, E. S., Breinlinger, K., Macomber, J., & Jacobson, K. (1992). Origins of knowledge. *Psychological Review*, **99**, 605–632.

Spelke, E. S., Kestenbaum, R., Simons, D. J., & Wein, D. (1995a). Spatiotemporal continuity, smoothness of motion, and object identity in infancy. *British Journal of Developmental Psychology*, **13**, 1–30.

Spelke, E. S., Phillips, A., & Woodward, A. L. (1995b). Infants' knowledge of object motion and human action. In D. Sperber, D. Premack, & A. J. Premack (Eds.), *Causal cognition: A multidisciplinary debate* (pp. 44–78). Oxford: Clarendon Press.

Starkey, P. & Cooper, R. (1980). Perception of numbers by human infants. *Science*, **210**, 1033–1035.

Surian, L. & Caldi, S. (2010). Infants' individuation of agents and inert objects. *Developmental Science*, **13**, 143–150.

Träuble, B. & Pauen, S. (2007). The role of functional information for infant categorization. *Cognition*, **105**, 362–379.

(2011a). Cause of effect – what matters? How 12-month-old infants learn to categorize artifacts. *British Journal of Developmental Psychology*. DOI: 10.1348/026151009X479547.

(2011b). Infants' reasoning about ambiguous motion events: The role of spatiotemporal and dispositional status information. *Cognitive Development*, **26**, 1–15.

Uller, C., Carey, S., Huntley-Fenner, G., & Klatt, L. (1999). What representations might underlie infant numerical knowledge. *Cognitive Development*, **14**, 1–36.

Wang, S. & Baillargeon, R. (2006). Infants' physical knowledge affects their change detection. *Developmental Science*, **9**, 173–181.

(2008a). Can infants be "taught" to attend to a new physical variable in an event category? The case of height in covering events. *Cognitive Psychology*, **56**, 284–326.

(2008b). Detecting impossible changes in infancy: A three-system account. *Trends in Cognitive Sciences*, **12**, 17–23.

Wang, S., Baillargeon, R., & Brueckner, L. (2004). Young infants' reasoning about hidden objects: Evidence from violation-of-expectation tasks with test trials only. *Cognition*, **93**, 167–198.

Wang, S., Baillargeon, R., & Paterson, S. (2005). Detecting continuity and solidity violations in infancy: A new account and new evidence from covering events. *Cognition*, **95**, 129–173.

Wang, S., Kaufman, L., & Baillargeon, R. (2003). Should all stationary objects move when hit? Developments in infants' causal and statistical expectations about collision events. *Infant Behavior and Development*, **26**, 529–568.

Wang, S. & Kohne, L. (2007). Visual experience enhances infants' use of task-relevant information in an action task. *Developmental Psychology*, **43**, 1513–1522.

Wang, S. & Mitroff, S. R. (2009). Preserved visual representations despite change blindness in 11-month-old infants. *Developmental Science*, **12**, 681–687.

Wilcox, T. (1999). Object individuation: Infants' use of shape, size, pattern, and color. *Cognition*, **72**, 125–166.

Wilcox, T. & Chapa, C. (2002). Infants' reasoning about opaque and transparent occluders in an object individuation task. *Cognition*, **85**, B1–B10.

Wilson, R. A. & Keil, F. C. (2000). The shadows and shallows of explanation. In F. C. Keil & R. A. Wilson (Eds.), *Explanation and cognition* (pp. 87–114). Cambridge, MA: MIT Press.

Wood, J. & Spelke, E. (2005). Infants' enumeration of actions: Numerical discrimination and its signature limits. *Developmental Science*, **8**, 173–181.

Woodward, A. L., Phillips, A., & Spelke, E. S. (1993). Infants' expectations about the motion of animate versus inanimate objects. *Proceedings of the Fifteenth Annual Meeting of the Cognitive Science Society* (pp. 1087–1091). Hillsdale, NJ: Erlbaum.

Wu, D. & Baillargeon, R. (2011, March). *Young infants detect open-close but not variable changes to objects in covering events.* Paper presented at the biennial meeting of the Society for Research in Child Development, Montreal, Canada.

Wynn, K. (1990). Children's understanding of counting. *Cognition*, **36**, 155–193.

(1992a). Children's acquisition of the number words and the counting system. *Cognitive Psychology*, **24**, 220–251.

(1992b). Addition and subtraction by human infants. *Nature*, **358**, 749–750.

Xu, F. (2002). The role of language in the acquiring object kind concepts in infancy. *Cognition*, **85**, 223–250.

Xu, F. & Carey, S. (1996). Infants' metaphysics: The case of numerical identity. *Cognitive Psychology*, **30**, 111–153.

Xu, F. & Spelke, E. S. (2000). Large number discrimination in 6-month old infants. *Cognition*, **74**, B1–B11.

Xu, F., Spelke, E., & Goddard, S. (2005). Number sense in human infants. *Developmental Science*, **8**, 88–101.

Yonas, A. & Granrud, C. E. (1984). The development of sensitivity to kinetic, binocular, and pictorial depth information in human infants. In D. Engle, D. Lee, & M. Jeannerod (Eds.), *Brain mechanisms and spatial vision* (pp. 113–145). Dordrecht: Martinus Nijhoff.

4   Learning from and about the Social World

Tricia Striano and Amanda Woodward

In no other period of ontogeny is achievement more critical than in infancy. In the first months, infants must overcome limited coordination, not to mention immature social and cognitive abilities. Infants must achieve feats such as communicating their needs without spoken language; sucking, reaching, and grabbing to explore the world; distinguishing between threatening and safe situations; deciding upon which people to attend to or avoid, whom and what to focus on; and determining how to use the information that people give them. Not only do infants have to master many skills in a few short months, but the way that they achieve these skills and the context in which they achieve them in the early months will set the stage for later development and success.

Human infants engage these developmental tasks in a social context that provides both support and challenge. On one hand, the actions of social partners support infants' attention to and learning about the world. Indeed, much of what children learn in the first years of life depends critically on interactions with social partners. On the other hand, making full use of this rich social support requires that the infant mounts organized and selective responses to others' actions. That is, learning from social partners is a two-way street, requiring social-cognitive capacities in the learner as well as a supportive social context. In this chapter, we consider young infants' ability to meet these challenges in order to learn from and learn about the social world.

Our focus on these issues highlights the role of the environment and experience in supporting developmental achievements. As the chapters in this volume document, the social environment and the experiences it supports have profound and wide-ranging effects on development in childhood. An initial question is whether it is plausible that these kinds of effects in the social cognitive domain exist early in infancy. If social and cognitive capacities are limited in early infancy, why not focus our attention instead on older children, children of school age who need to learn to write and read and to communicate to become effective adults. The answer is simple and straightforward: The social and cognitive capacities of young infants are not always apparent to the naked eye, and not always apparent without age-appropriate sensitive measures, but the social and cognitive capacities of infants in the first year are robust and critical, and set the stage for later development and achievements.

In this chapter, we describe research from our two laboratories that elucidates the processes by which infants learn from and about the social world. In the first section, Tricia Striano considers the way that an infant's developing sensitivity to social cues helps him or her to successfully learn during social interactions. Her research has revealed infants' sensitivities to relevant social cues around them, and sheds light on how and when in development these sensitivities give rise to learning opportunities. Having considered how infants learn *from* their social partners, we will turn to the issue of how they learn *about* them. In the second section, Amanda Woodward reviews recent work showing that in the first year, infants come to not only respond to others' actions, but also to understand others' actions as intentional. Her research has begun to reveal the processes by which infants acquire this understanding.

Learning from Social Partners

Infants' Sensitivity to Dyadic Social Cues

Early in development infants often engage in dyadic, face-to-face interactions with other people. Dyadic interactions are characterized by a sharing and coordination of affect and attention. What might infants learn as they interact with people in face-to-face or general dyadic (person-person) interaction? One possibility is that they learn something about the relevance of social cues, or when social cues are intended for them. Detecting the relevance of social signals is an important skill to acquire early on given that it is necessary for effective learning to take place. Being able to determine when someone is directing communication to you helps guide your attention to the information the other one tries to convey or share. When do infants become sensitive to relevant social signals as being directed at them?

To answer this question, we developed an interpersonal contingency paradigm. In this paradigm, we had a mother and her infant sit in different rooms and interact over a television monitor. Eye-to-eye contact was achieved by filming through one-way mirrors (see Striano, Henning, & Stahl 2006). This setup allowed us to carefully manipulate key elements on the ongoing interaction. We asked the mothers to interact with their infants as they normally would, albeit via a television monitor. What the mothers did not know was that the infants would observe their behavior delayed by one second for part of the social interaction. We chose a one-second delay based on prior research on adult conversation suggesting that matching of speech rhythms is related to perceived quality of interaction and interpersonal attunement. We also know that adult conversational partners tend to match pause duration both within and between turns (Jaffe & Feldstein 1970), and that pauses during speech that exceed a duration of one second are perceived as disruptive (Clark 1996). This "vocal congruence" is thought to reflect interpersonal attunement, as evidenced by more positive ratings of relationships by adults whose speech rhythms are more tightly matched (Feldstein & Welkowitz 1978). In these early face-to-face interactions, parents often mirror the infant's behavior in affective quality and properties such as intensity and rhythm (Stern 1985; Gergely & Watson 1999). Moreover, parental responses generally occur within one to two seconds after an infant's behavior (van Egeren, Barratt, & Roach 2001; Keller et al. 1999; Nicely, Tamis-LeMonda, & Bornstein 1999; Papousek & Papousek 1987). Therefore, in addition to form and content, the timing of parental behavior provides infants with cues for detecting socially relevant behavior.

For the current study we tested approximately 40 3-month-old infants (Striano, Henning, & Stahl 2006). Infants interacted for a total of four minutes with their mother, two minutes which were presented live and two minutes in which the mother's behavior was presented with a delay of one second. In the delay condition, all of the mother's behavior was contingent and all aspects were delayed by one second (the effect being something akin to a long-distance video chat with a slow computer modem). Based on research on early temporal coordination in caregiver–infant interaction (e.g., Beebe et al. 1988; Crown et al. 2002), and given infants' early abilities in temporal perception (e.g., Lewkowicz 2000), we expected that by 3 months of age infants would detect a change in timing of maternal responses. Mothers tend to respond to infants within a one-second range (see Keller et al. 1999; Papousek & Papousek 1987). Also, when talking to 3-month-olds, adults' vocal utterances are less than one second in duration, and their vocal pauses are close to one second (Stern et al. 1977). Based on this promptness of response latency, the duration of adult vocal phrases and pauses, and the successful use of a one-second time interval in analyses of contingency in mother–infant interaction (e.g., Bigelow 1998; Symons & Moran 1994), we expected that a one-second delay would be within the range detectable by infants.

We measured the amount of time that infants gazed at their mother as a function of condition. We found that at 3 months of age infants gazed reliably more at their mother when she was live compared to when she was delayed by one second. These results show that by 3 months, infants are sensitive to temporal aspects of communicative signals directed at them. Such sensitivity ultimately helps them to achieve new goals, as they are able to attend to more relevant social information and use this to guide their attention outside of the dyad, or into triadic interactions. Sensitivity to interpersonal timing may also come to play a role in triadic contexts in which two partners' interaction is about a third entity, as timing may provide cues about the referential aspects of communicative signals. Understanding referentiality requires understanding that signals are about something and are perceived as being relevant. Relevance of communicative signals is determined not only by the quality of information, but also by the timing of such signals. In studies assessing older infants' understanding of the intentions underlying others' actions (e.g., Carpenter, Akhtar, & Tomasello 1998; Tomasello & Barton 1994), adults utter expressions such as "There!" or "Whoops!" to mark a performed action as a success or failure of achieving the intended goal. The timing of these cues is likely essential for infants to perceive the performed action as intentional or accidental, once they understand intentionality. When 12-month-old infants encounter a new situation and are given the choice between checking someone who has previously engaged with them in a contingent interaction compared to a noncontingent interaction, they selectively look toward the contingent partner. In sum, there is a close link between what infants detect in dyadic interaction and the people they choose to consult when learning about the world. A key to learning achievement in infancy is attending to relevant people.

From Dyadic to Triadic Interaction. By the middle of the first year of postnatal development, interactions become increasingly triadic in nature. Now rather than exchanging and sharing affect, infants increasingly use others to guide their attention to the outside world. These interactions are known as triadic interactions, and they are essential for skills such as language learning and object learning (Tomasello 1995).

This shift from dyadic to triadic interactions is demonstrated in one study in which we had had infants of 3, 6, and 9 months interacting with an adult stranger. Infants sat across from the adult. We measured social interaction between infant and adult in several ways. In one condition, the joint-attention condition, the adult coordinated attention between the infant and a toy on the infant's side. She did this by shifting her gaze between the infant and the toy while talking about the toy in a positive tone of voice. In another condition, the look-away condition, the adult looked away at the toy while vocalizing in a positive way, but without shifting her attention back and forth. We compared these conditions to a normal dyadic (face-to-face) interaction in which the adult talked to the infant and did not look at the object.

We found that at all ages infants discriminated among these three inter-active conditions. However, the way that infants discriminated among these types of interactions varied according to age. At 3 months of age, infants preferred the dyadic interaction, whereas, at the older ages, infants preferred (or at least looked more at the adult during) joint-attention interactions (Striano 2004; Striano & Stahl 2005). The likely reason for this is that the demands placed on the 6- and 9-month-olds are very differ-ent from the demands placed on a 3-month-old. At older ages, infants are capable of manipulating objects and moving around, whereas at younger ages this is much harder without assistance (Campos & Sternberg 1981). Social interactions between infants and adults start out primarily dyadic (Stern 1985; van Wulfften Palthe & Hopkins 1993). This changes when the need for triadic interactions becomes more important – as infants begin to interact with unfamiliar objects and situations, and as they must become sensitive to cues directed at them. In terms of helping infants to achieve goals, it is important that social contexts are adjusted to the infant's goals and abilities.

Using Social Cues to Learn.   A sensitivity to joint attention is essential for learning. For example, by 18 months of age, infants use others' gaze toward objects to learn labels (see, e.g., Baldwin 1993). In order to benefit from tri-adic attention or joint attention, an infant must have developed an ability to integrate a number of social and cognitive skills. When do infants use triadic social cues to gain information about new things? The function of joint attention for the infant in terms of gaining knowledge remains poorly understood. Few studies have addressed the issue of how triadic interac-tion involving adult, infant, and object facilitates learning about objects in the surrounding world. Although many studies indicate that infants modify their own behavior according to the social signals they receive, little is known about the influence of the behavior of the social partner on infants' processing of the surrounding world. Some research has shown that maternal behavior during mother–infant play sessions is related to 4-month-old infants' ability to recognize and discern a familiar from a novel stimulus. Specifically, infants whose mothers were less involved during toy play (e.g., vocalization, visual encouragement of attention) exhibited higher novelty preference – the type of visual preference that is associated with superior information processing (Miceli et al. 1998).

Itakura (2001) tested older infants (9- to 13-month-olds) to assess whether social and nonsocial events led to differential behavior on subsequent visual preference tasks. In this study, infants observed either the mother point to one of two line drawings (social event) or saw one of the line drawings blink (nonsocial event). In both conditions, infants looked longer at the stimulus-enhanced drawing (i.e., the one that was pointed at or the one that blinked). However, when the line drawings were presented again alone (without pointing or blinking), only the infants who were in the social condition showed a significant difference in their preference for the drawing that had been pointed at versus the one at which the mother had not pointed. Thus, looking behavior was influenced by the preceding social and nonsocial events.

In our research we have started to address the issue of how cues provided by adult social partners are beneficial to infants in these contexts. We examined the effects of differing social cues on object processing in 9- and 12-month-old infants (Striano et al. 2006). In a within-subject design, an adult experimenter spoke to the infants about a novel object in one of two conditions. In the joint-attention condition, the experimenter spoke to the infant about the toy while alternating gaze between the toy and the infant. The object-only condition was identical, except that the experimenter looked to the toy and to a spot on the ceiling, but never to the infant. In the test trials, infants viewed the toy used in the social interaction along with a novel toy. The 12-month-old infants looked to the novel toy equally following both conditions. In contrast, 9-month-olds looked to the novel toy significantly longer following the joint-attention condition relative to the object-only condition. These results suggest that joint-attention interactions aided object processing in the 9-month-old infants, but not in the 12-month-old infants. This indicates that, by 12 months of age, infants learned about the object as long as some social cue was provided, whether it was directed only at the object (i.e., object only) or both to the infant and the object (i.e., joint attention).

In subsequent studies, using similar paradigms (see Cleveland & Striano 2007; Cleveland, Schug, & Striano 2007), we were able to show that by 7 months of age infants profited from joint-attention interactions. Learning about objects was enhanced when infants viewed novel toys in the context of a joint-attention social cue. In a series of studies, we tested infants as young as 4 months of age. We found that 4- and 5-month-old infants did not benefit from joint-attention interactions (Cleveland & Striano 2007; Cleveland et al. 2007). This is interesting, given that, by 3 months of age, infants are already sensitive to joint-attention or triadic cues (Striano & Stahl 2005; Striano et al. 2007). However, when we observed their behavior in the types of paradigms described above, we found that they do not show a preference for one object over another. One reason for this result may be the sensitivity of our measure. That is, young infants have a limited behavioral repertoire. May it be possible that their brain is processing information based on social cues that we do not observe in behavior? This is one question that we put to the test.

Infants' Use of Social Cues as Measured by ERP.   To assess the way that the infant brain may be detecting social cues and using these cues to process the world, we measure event-related potentials, or ERPs (a more detailed description of our methods can be found in Striano & Reid 2008). Event-related potentials are derived from electrical brain activity related to a stimulus that we present to the infant. This measure can tell us something about the way that infants are processing information over the course of milliseconds and well before the onset of a behavioral response. In the past 10 years, knowledge of how the functional brain develops has increased dramatically (Johnson 2005). One component of the infant ERP that is well mapped in terms of cognitive properties is the mid-latency *negative component*, or Nc. The Nc occurs approximately 300–700 milliseconds after stimulus onset, is most prominent at fronto-central electrodes, and is thought to relate to the development of memory processes during the first 12 postnatal months (Webb et al. 2005). In our study, infants interacted with an adult in one of two conditions. In the joint attention condition, the adult looked at the infant and then at the computer screen, which displayed a new object. In the non–joint attention condition the adult looked at the computer screen only while talking and vocalizing. We measured ERPs as infants looked at the object presented on the screen. For a trial to be included, infants needed to look at the adult and then to the object presented on the computer screen. We predicted an enhanced Nc for objects that infants viewed in the context of joint attention compared to non–joint attention contexts. Our results confirmed these predictions. We found that at 9 months of age, the infant brain responded differently toward objects that have been cued by joint attention versus non–joint attention contexts. We found an enhanced negativity, which is an index of attention, already at 300 milliseconds after stimulus onset. These results were helpful as they demonstrated the usefulness of this new paradigm to understand how the infant brain processes information as a function of social cues.

Because ERPs provide a more sensitive measure of the way that infants process information, could we also find signs that much younger infants were gaining something from joint attention interactions? Recall that behavioral findings showed that at 4 and 5 months of age, infants did show evidence of differential attention to objects when these were presented in a joint attention context. In a recent study, we asked whether 5-month-old infants would process objects better as a function of joint attention contexts. The setup differed from the prior study in a couple of ways. Infants interacted with an adult in two different ways. In one condition, the joint attention condition, the adult looked at the infant's face and then to the object on the computer monitor and back to the infant. In the non–joint attention condition, the adult looked at the infant's chest and then to the object on the computer monitor and back to the infant's chest. This way we were able to control for movement cues and facial information. What differed across conditions was that there was direct eye contact in the joint attention condition and not in the non–joint attention condition. Following an interaction phase in which infants saw objects in these two conditions, they were then presented again with the objects. Like in the prior study, we measured how 5-month-old infant brains processed information as a function of social interaction. We found an enhanced Nc after stimulus onset when objects were presented in the context of joint attention interaction (Parise et al. 2008). These results were parallel to what we found with the 9-month-olds. What is important to recall is that at 5 months of age, in the behavioral studies (Cleveland et al. 2007) we did not see evidence that infants used joint attention cues. When we used a more sensitive measure, however, and in particular when we assessed how the brain was processing information in joint attention contexts, the picture was different. The sensitivity to joint attention cues was more than a sensitivity; it was functional – at the level of brain activity. We have obtained similar results with infants as young as 3 months of age (Hoehl, Wiese, & Striano 2008; Hoehl & Striano 2008) and extended these findings to language learning (Hirotani et al. 2009).

These results are important because they suggest that brain measures can give us information about development that behavior alone cannot. It also shows that although young infants primarily engage in dyadic interactions, they are using social cues to learn about the world in very specific ways. Social cues not only guide infants' attention to the external world, but infants are picking up on the precise referents of these social cues (Hoehl et al. 2008; Hoehl & Striano 2008). This is important not only for understanding the relation between brain and behavioral development across typical ontogeny, but especially for the early identification of infants who may be at risk for later social cognitive impairments such as autism. That is, we predict that an infant whose brain is not manifesting enhanced processing of relevant social information might be at risk for a range of impairments. We expect that many infants would have difficulty in parsing social information, in detecting the relevance of information, and in using these cues to interact and learn most effectively.

Implications.   In order to achieve learning, infants must attend to relevant social cues. Caregivers, in turn, must be sensitive to the rapidly developing cognitive, motor, and perceptual skills that influence which cues are advantageous. These findings show that the mechanisms that give way to language and object learning start in very early infancy. For this reason, it is important to engage infants in person and object play in the early months, whether this is at home or in school settings. These findings also suggest that using sensitive measures such as event-related potentials may be one way to predict some infants who may show later social or cognitive impairments.

Learning about Social Partners

The research just described makes clear the critical role of social partners in guiding infants' engagement with and learning from the external environment. This process is a two-way street, with adult behaviors and infant sensitivities working hand in hand from the start. As this process plays out, infants are also learning about the social partners with whom they are interacting. Specifically, during the first years of life, children come to view other people as intentional agents, understanding that human movements are structured by goals and states of attention rather than simply being physical movements through space. We turn now to focus on this aspect of social cognition – the ability not only to attend and respond to others' actions, but also to conceptualize others' actions as intentional.

This ability to analyze others' actions as intentional is of fundamental importance. By adulthood, it pervades social cognition from the initial encoding of event structure to long-term memory for, reasoning about, and communication about events (see Shipley & Zacks 2008). In development, intention understanding undergirds the conceptual distinction between animate agents and inanimate objects, provides a critical foundation for language learning (Baldwin & Moses 2001; Tomasello 1999), and provides the foundation for children's emerging theory of mind (Barresi & Moore 1996; Wellman 1992). How early can this cornerstone of social cognition be traced in development?

Observers of infant social behavior have long hypothesized that infants understand other people as intentional agents. Indeed the rich and adaptive social sensitivities described in the first half of this chapter can be construed as being driven by infants' understanding of others as intentional agents. However, on their own, infants' spontaneous responses to others' actions often leave open the question of whether, and when, infants represent others' actions as intentional. On one hand, infants' social responses may lead to overestimation of their intention understanding. To illustrate, debates have persisted as to whether infants' spontaneous tendency to follow others' gaze direction reflects an understanding of the person's state of attention (e.g., Bretherton 1991; Tomasello 1995) or instead is driven by behavioral conditioning or other low level factors (Moore & Corkum 1994). On the other hand, reliance on infants' overt social responses can also lead to underestimation of infants' understanding of others' intentions because infants may understand something about others' intentions before they can control complex social responses. To illustrate, it has been argued that the lack of robust triadic and communicative behaviors early in the first year of life reflects a lack of insight into others' intentions (e.g., Behne et al. 2005; Tomasello 1999). However, as we describe next, there is now strong evidence against this conclusion.

To gain clearer insights into the nature of infants' understanding of intentional action, researchers have recruited visual habituation methods, which are appropriate for even very young infants and can provide insight into how infants represent the structure of events. Infants, like adults, tend to look longer at novel stimuli following habituation to a repeated stimulus. Thus, infants' visual responses can shed light on their conceptualization of observed events because they provide evidence concerning the kinds of changes infants detect and attend to. A common approach is to compare infants' responses to post-habituation test events that alter either the perceptually obvious surface properties or the conceptually central aspects of the original event. In the social domain, this approach has been recruited to ask whether infants represent others' actions as structured by intentions rather than as simply physical movements through space. This approach has yielded several critical insights concerning infants' knowledge about their social partners. We turn to these now.

Early in the First Year of Life, Infants Discern the Intentional Structure of Others' Actions

Adults view even the simplest, most concrete actions as driven by intentions. Imagine a woman who reaches across a table to grasp a coffee cup. Although the movement of the woman's arm could be described in purely physical terms, that is not how we see it. Rather, we understand the action as goal-directed (she is reaching for the coffee cup) and thus we view the relation between the woman and the cup as more central to the event than the details of her movements. By 5 months of age, infants see it the same way. Having been habituated to an event in which a person reaches for and grasps an object, infants respond selectively to changes in the goal of the action compared to changes in the physical movements involved (Woodward 1998; see Woodward 2005, and Woodward et al. 2009 for reviews). That is, infants show a strong novelty response (sustained looking) when the actor moves through the same path to grasp a new object and no such response when the actor moves through a new path to grasp her prior goal object. These findings indicate that infants represent human actions in terms of the relation between agent and goal, that is, as goal-directed. Recently, we found that young infants' understanding of action goals is evident not only in their visual responses to others' actions, but also in their overt social responses. Seven-month-old infants selectively imitate the goals of actions they have observed (Hamlin, Hallinan & Woodward 2008; Mahajan & Woodward in press).

Critically, infants' response to action goals is selective for events involving animate agents and goal-directed actions. Infants do not respond to "goal" changes when the moving entity is not readily identified as an agent (Guajardo & Woodward 2004; Hofer, Hauf, & Aschersleben 2005; Mahajan & Woodward in press; Woodward 1998), or when the action is ambiguous (Hamlin et al. 2008; Luo & Johnson 2009; Woodward 1999). Across several experiments, infants have been presented with control events in which an inanimate object or a hand in an ambiguous posture that moves toward and contacts an object (e.g., Biro & Leslie 2007; Hamlin et al. 2008; Hofer et al. 2005; Mahajan & Woodward in press; Woodward 1998, 1999). These events entrain infants' attention in much the same way that intentional actions do – infants look at the contacted object in all cases. However, infants do not respond selectively to changes in the relation between "agent" and "goal" for these events. Taken together, the findings from these experiments indicated that by 5 months, and in some cases 3 months (Gerson & Woodward under review; Sommerville, Woodward, & Needham 2005), of age infants do more than simply follow others' actions – they represent others' actions as goal-directed.

Infants' Understanding of Goal-Directed Action Is Enriched over the First Year of Life. Often findings of systematic abilities in young infants are taken as evidence that the abilities are innate, arising independent of experience. However, recent findings in the social domain highlight the plasticity of infants' knowledge. Infants' understanding of intentional action undergoes developmental change during the first year, and these changes suggest a strong role for experience.

Infants' sensitivity to action goals is first evident for simple, concrete actions, such as grasping or moving objects, by 5–6 months of age (Biro & Leslie 2007, Luo & Johnson 2009; Woodward 1998, 1999). Under supportive conditions, described in the next section, this sensitivity is evident at 3 months of age (Gerson & Woodward under review; Sommerville et al. 2005). However, a number of aspects of intentional action that are obvious to adults do not seem to be obvious to infants until later in the first year of life. To start, adults readily understand not only the goals that structure individual actions, but also the higher-level plans that structure strings of actions. For example, on seeing someone use a tool to obtain an object that is too far away to reach directly, adults readily understand the actions on the tool as being directed at the object, rather than only at the tool itself. That is, adults understand the actions on the tool as the means to the end of obtaining the object. By 10–12 months, infants engage in similar means–end reasoning, showing selective attention to changes in the ultimate goal as compared to changes in the tool used (Sommerville, Hildebrandt, & Crane 2008; Sommerville & Woodward 2005; Woodward & Sommerville 2000). Before 10–12 moths, infants seem unable to detect action plans, and, in some cases, misinterpret actions as only directed at the means, not the end (Sommerville & Woodward 2005).

Adults readily detect intentional actions that do not involve concrete contact with the object, for example, the intentional connections inherent in acts of attention. When a person turns to look at something, adults automatically infer a mental connection between the person and the object at which her gaze is directed. As detailed earlier, young infants are extremely sensitive to others' eyes and spontaneously follow their gaze shifts. However, these responses do not guarantee that infants understand the intentional relation between a person and the object of her attention. Indeed, using the visual habituation paradigm, we found that 7-month-old infants follow an adult's gaze to an object under conditions in which they fail to compute that the adult is looking at the object (Woodward 2003a). Infants viewed a person who turned to look at one of two toys repeatedly during habituation. Then the locations of the toys were reversed and infants saw test events which disrupted either the relation between the person and the object of her attention (she turned to the prior side to fixate the other toy) or the person's physical movements (she turned to the other side to fixate the same object). Seven-month-old infants systematically followed the person's gaze to the objects, but they did not respond (with longer looking) to the change in relation between the person and the object of her attention. Twelve-month-old infants, tested in the same procedure, not only followed the adult's gaze, but also encoded the relation between the adult and the object of her attention, that is, they represented the adult's gaze as being object-directed (Woodward 2003a). Under more supportive conditions, 9-month-old infants have also shown sensitivity to the object-directed nature of gaze (Johnson, Ok, & Luo 2007). Further, by early in the second year of life, infants can use information about a person's focus of attention to predict and interpret her subsequent actions, integrating information about a person's focus attention with other aspects of her intentional action (Onishi & Baillargeon 2005; Phillips, Wellman, & Spelke 2002; Sodian & Thoermer 2004; Southgate, Senju, & Csibra 2007; Vaish & Woodward under review).

Central to mature folk psychology is the understanding that intentions reside within the person. By 3 years of age, children's explicit folk psychology represents intentions as "in the head" of the agent, that is, as private states (Wellman 1992). In addition to its conceptual significance, understanding the personal nature of intentions is critical for on-line social reasoning, allowing for the effective tracking and integration of a person's actions over time. Recent findings indicate that the seeds of this aspect of intentional understanding are evident by late in the first year of life, when infants begin to track action goals as specific to the individual agent. By 9 months of age, infants' propensity to track action goals in the habituation experiments described earlier is modulated by changes in the agent's identity. When the identity of the actor changes between habituation and test trials, infants no longer respond to changes in the action goal. That is, infants seem not to view the first actor's goals as relevant to the second actor's actions (Buresh & Woodward 2007). In contrast, when the actions involved information that should generalize across different individuals, in this case, the use of a linguistic label, infants used the first actor's actions to interpret the second actor's actions (Buresh & Woodward 2007). Therefore, by 9 months infants are able to integrate information across different agents, but, like adults, they seem to understand that an individual's goals are person specific. Although these findings cannot tell us whether infants view goals as mental states per se, they do suggest that infants have begun to understand goals as residing in the individual.

To summarize, over the first year of life, infants' initial sensitivity to action goals grows into richer, more abstract conceptualizations of intentional action that reflect key aspects of mature folk psychology. Early in the first year of life, infants view a person's concrete actions as organized by goals. By the end of the first year, they can discern the higher-order plans that organize actions, they understand that people are connected to the objects of their visual attention, and they understand that intentions reside in individuals. These achievements provide the conceptual foundation for theory of mind. Indeed, recent findings demonstrate longitudinal continuity between these infant abilities and later explicit theory of mind. Infants' responses in visual habituation experiments that tap early intention understanding predict their subsequent responses, as preschoolers, on verbal theory-of-mind tasks (Wellman et al. 2004, 2008).

Infants' Sensitivity to Goal-Directed Action Is Related to, and Informed by Experience. Findings that infants' intentional action knowledge develops during the first year raise questions about the processes that drive these changes and suggest a strong role for learning and experience. Pursuing these issues requires departure from both typical ways of thinking about infant conceptual development and typical ways of studying it. When visual habituation techniques first revealed conceptual structure in infants, it was assumed that these abilities arose independent of experience, the product of evolved systems for ensuring the presence of basic conceptual abilities that are critical for survival (e.g., Spelke et al. 1992). However, basic, universal, and early-emerging abilities may also reflect the contributions of early and universal aspects of experience. Indeed, developmental systems often recruit reliable aspects of the environment to ensure the development of species-typical abilities. For example, bird song, navigation, and social imprinting in various species all depend on information from the environment to develop typically (Gallistel et al. 1991; Gottlieb 1991; Marler 1991). Certainly the ability to view others' actions as intentional is both a universal (in all typically developing humans) and critical for survival and, as just described, this ability is evident during infancy. But these facts do not license the conclusion that this ability emerges independent of experience.

To establish how experience contributes to infants' social cognitive development, new kinds of empirical approaches are needed. Typically, infant cognition studies take a "snapshot" approach, testing what infants know at different ages, but not investigating the ways in which this knowledge varies among individuals or relates to variations in experience. In our work, we have begun to work against this trend, taking two strategies. First, we have undertaken correlational studies testing whether and how infants' emerging understanding of intentions relates to variations in the experiences that may contribute to this knowledge. Although correlational studies cannot support strong conclusions about causation, they do provide ecologically rich evidence about how infants' cognitive abilities relate to their broader experiences. Second, informed by correlational findings, we have begun to conduct intervention experiments, in which we alter infants' experience and assess the effects of this on their sensitivity to others' intentions.

Two general hypotheses guided our investigation of the factors that may contribute to infants' intentional action knowledge. First, it has been hypothesized that infants' own experience as intentional agents provides them with insights into others' intentions, helping them to understand others as "like me" (e.g., Meltzoff 2007; Tomasello 1999). Second, it has also been hypothesized that infants' engagement with social partners provides insights into others' intentions (e.g., Barresi & Moore 1996). Testing these general hypotheses requires methods that index infants' intention understanding independent of the factors that are hypothesized to affect it, and therefore we have recruited visual habituation methods as measures of infants' intention understanding in these studies (see Brune & Woodward 2007 for a discussion).

We began by focusing on periods during which infants' intention understanding is beginning to emerge and thus is variable across individuals. During these periods of emergence, we investigated the factors that correlate with infants' intention understanding by testing infants in both visual habituation methods and measures of their own actions and interactions with others. Our findings indicate that both kinds of factors correlate with infants' emerging intention understanding. To start, developments in infants' own actions correlate with developments in their sensitivity to others' intentions. At 10 months, infants are variable in their understanding of others' means–end actions, and this variability correlates with their own actions. Infants who are relatively skilled at means–end actions understand others' actions on tools as directed at the ultimate goal, whereas infants who are less skilled interpret the actions as directed at the tool itself (Sommerville & Woodward 2005).

Further, we found that variation in infants' experiences also correlates with their understanding of the object-directed nature of attention. As noted earlier, by 12 months, infants are sensitive to the relation between a person and the object of her attention, but younger infants are more variable in their sensitivity to this relation. Brune and Woodward (2007) tested a group of 10-month-old infants, assessing their understanding of attentional relations using habituation paradigms like those described earlier, for events involving gaze and events involving pointing. We also assessed infants' social responsiveness and social experiences, measuring their propensity to follow an adult's direction of gaze, their production of object-directed points, and their engagement with their caretakers in "supported" joint attention (i.e., times when the parent's actions draws infants into triadic attention).

Our findings revealed a pattern of specific relations among the factors we assessed. To start, although infants followed others' gaze robustly, gaze-following did not relate to infants' understanding of others' attention, thus pointing out that social responses may not always reflect underlying knowledge about others' actions. But other factors did correlate with infants' attention understanding. Infants who produced object-directed points understood others' points as implying a relation between the person and the object at which she pointed. Thus, in this case, infants' own actions correlated with their understanding of others' actions (see also Woodward & Guajardo 2002). We also found that infants' social experience correlated with their understanding of others' actions: Infants whose parents engaged them in more supported joint attention showed a stronger understanding of the object-directed nature of others' gaze shifts.

Taken together, these correlational findings raise the question of whether these aspects of infants' experience render changes in their intention understanding. We have begun to address this question by investigating the effects of infants' own actions on their understanding of others' actions. The strategy in these experiments is to intervene to support infants' engagement in a new form of goal-directed activity, and then assess the effects of this intervention on their understanding of others' actions. We began by testing infants at 3 months, an age at which infants do not typically show sensitivity to the goal-structure of others' actions and at which their own goal-directed actions are quite limited. Infants at this age are not yet skilled at reaching for objects, but they can learn to use Velcro-covered "sticky" mittens to apprehend objects by swiping at them (Needham, Peterman, & Barrett 2002). We tested whether engaging in sticky mittens actions would lead infants to view others' actions as goal-directed, and found that it did: After sticky mittens practice, infants responded selectively to the goal-structure of reaching events that they observed in the habituation paradigm (Sommerville, Woodward, & Needham 2005). In recent work, we have found that infants' own engagement in the actions is critical. Infants who simply observe others using the mittens do not show the same benefit (Gerson & Woodward under review). Similar effects have been found in older infants as well: Infants who are trained to use a tool to retrieve a toy subsequently show sensitivity to the means–end goal structure of others' actions, and, as is the case for younger infants, this effect seems to depend on infants' own production of the action (Sommerville et al. 2008).

These findings demonstrate that infants' experiences, in this case their experience producing goal-directed actions, influence their understanding of others' actions. Self-produced experiences have long been assumed to be critical for development broadly construed (e.g., Piaget 1929). The current findings elucidate one way in which this broad assumption is true: Infants' engagement in actions that are structured with respect to a goal informs their analysis of others' actions as structured by goals. These results are consistent with recent hypotheses that developing social knowledge is structured, in part, by systems that govern the child's own actions (Decety & Sommerville 2003; Gerson & Woodward in press; Meltzoff 2007). Indeed, recent findings indicate that that these effects in infants may be mediated by neurocognitive representations in motor cortex that subserve both action production and action perception (Southgate et al. 2009).

These findings raise the question of whether and how other kinds of experiences, in particular interactions with social partners, shape infants' understanding of others' actions. Consistent with a number of proposals, our correlational findings (Brune & Woodward 2007) suggest that infants' engagement in triadic interactions with caretakers may support their understanding of attention in others. More generally, as hypothesized by Barresi and Moore (1996), we expect that situations in which infants are able to align their own intentional states with those of social partners may be particularly powerful contexts for helping them to understand others' intentions. Such contexts could include not only triadic attention, but also engagement in collaborative instrumental actions and emotion sharing. These issues are ripe for further investigation.

Chapter Conclusions

Human infants develop immersed in the social world, surrounded by the complex and potentially informative actions of other people. As we have reviewed here, recent findings show that infants are prepared to thrive in this sea of action in two critical ways. To start, infants are highly responsive to others' actions, including the timing of others' contingent responses and their patterns of visual attention. Infants respond selectively to others' actions – differentiating between contexts in which attention is or is not directed at them, distinguishing between well-timed and ill-timed social responses, and using others' attention to guide their own attention to objects. Second, infants not only respond in adaptive ways to their social partners, they also understand social partners as intentional agents. Infants understand others' actions not as purely physical movements through space, but rather as actions structured by goals and objects of attention. Early in the first year, infants' show initial understanding of the intentional nature of others' actions, and this understanding broadens over the first year of life. Recent findings highlight the plasticity of this early-emerging social knowledge, indicating a strong role for experience in its development.

Thus, in the first year of life, infants are actively engaged in both *learning from* and *learning about* their social partners. The relation between these two aspects of early social learning seems obvious, but, surprisingly, has rarely been directly studied. Investigators tend to focus either on measures of social responsiveness or on measures of intention understanding, with few attempting to put the two together. The study by Brune and Woodward (2007) is an exception to this rule, and its findings suggest that there is a much to be learned by integrating these two approaches.

We suspect that the interactions between learning-from and learning-about are bidirectional. Infants' early sensitivity to critical aspects of human behavior seems likely to set the stage for discoveries about the intentions that structure others actions. For example, infants' close attention to others' eyes and gaze shifts not only leads infants to engage in triadic attention, it may also create conditions under which infants can align their own states of attention with those of others, and this may help infants to understand attention in others (see Barresi & Moore 1996). In turn, as infants attain new levels of intention understanding, these new insights seem likely to inform their future learning from social partners. Indeed, social learning in the second year of life recruits the aspects of intention understanding that emerge in the first year of life. As examples, by 18 months, infants use others' states of attention to inform their word learning (Baldwin & Moses 2001), and they use an analysis of others' action goals to inform their imitative learning (Meltzoff 1995).

Both vantage points on early social learning, considering how infants learn from and learn about others, highlight the role of experience in shaping foundational developmental abilities. Infants are attentive to and cognitively engaged with the actions of others. This engagement sets the foundation for later social learning, including the acquisition of language, culture, and systems of human knowledge they support.

Acknowledgments

The research reviewed in this chapter was supported by the Sofja Kovalevskaja Award of the Alexander von Humboldt Foundation to T. Striano and by grants from NICHD (R01–HD35707) and NSF (0446706) to A. Woodward.

REFERENCES

Baldwin, D. A. (1993). Infants' ability to consult the speaker for clues to word reference. *Journal of Child Language*, **20**(2), 395–418.

Baldwin, D. A. & Moses, J. A. (2001). Links between social understanding and early word learning: Challenges to current accounts. *Social Development*, **10**, 311–329.

Barresi, J. & Moore, C. (1996). Intentional relations and social understanding. *Behavioral and Brain Sciences*, **19**, 107–154.

Beebe, B., Alson, D., Jaffe, J., Feldstein, S. et al. (1988). Vocal congruence in mother-infant play. *Journal of Psycholinguistic Research*, **17**(3), 245–259.

Behne, T., Carpenter, M., Call, J., & Tomasello, M. (2005). Unwilling versus unable? Infants' understanding of intentional action. *Developmental Psychology*, **41**(2), 328–337.

Bigelow, A. E. (1998). Infants' sensitivity to familiar imperfect contingencies in social interaction. *Infant Behavior and Development*, **21**(1), 149–162.

Biro, S. & Leslie, A. M. (2007). Infants' perception of goal-directed actions: Development through cue-based bootstrapping. *Developmental Science*, **10**(3), 379–398.

Bretherton, I. (1991). Intentional communication and the development of an understanding of mind. In D. Frye & C. Moore (Eds.), *Children's theories of mind: Mental states and social understanding* (pp. 49–75). Hillsdale, NJ: Lawrence Erlbaum Associates.

Brune, C. W. & Woodward, A. L. (2007). Social cognition and social responsiveness in 10-month-old infants. *Journal of Cognition and Development*, **8**(2), 133–158.

Buresh, J. S. & Woodward, A. L. (2007). Infants track action goals within and across agents. *Cognition*, **104**(2), 287–314.

Campos, J. J. & Stenberg, C. (1981). Perception, appraisal, and emotion: The onset of social referencing. In M. E. Lamb & L. R. Sherrod (Eds.), *Infant social cognition: Empirical and theoretical considerations* (pp. 273–314). Hillsdale, NJ: Erlbaum.

Carpenter, M., Akhtar, N., & Tomasello, M. (1998). Fourteen- through 18-month-old infants differentially imitate intentional and accidental actions. *Infant Behavior and Development*, **21**(2), 315–330.

Clark, H. (1996). *Using language.* Cambridge: Cambridge University Press.

Cleveland, A., Schug, M., & Striano, T. (2007). Joint attention and object learning in 5- and 7-month old infants. *Infant and Child Development*, **16**(3), 295–306.

Cleveland, A. & Striano, T. (2007). The effects of joint attention on object processing in 4- and 9-month-old infants. *Infant Behavior and Development*, **30**(3), 529–534.

Crown, C. L., Feldstein, S., Jasnow, M. D., Beebe, B., & Jaffe, J. (2002). The cross-modal coordination of interpersonal timing: Six-week-olds infants' gaze with adults' vocal behavior. *Journal of Psycholinguistic Research*, **31**, 1–23.

Decety, J. & Sommerville, J. A. (2003). Shared representations between self and other: A social cognitive neuroscience view. *Trends in Cognitive Sciences*, **7**(12), 527–533.

Feldstein, S. & Welkowitz, J. (1978). A chronography of conversation: In defense of an objective approach. In A. W. Siegman & S. Feldstein (Eds.), *Nonverbal behavior and communication*. Hillsdale, NJ: Lawrence Erlbaum Associates.

Gallistel, C. R., Brown, A. L., Carey, S., Gelman, R., & Keil, F. C. (1991). Lessons from animal learning for the study of cognitive development. In S. Carey & R. Gelman (Eds.), *The epigenesis of mind: Essays on biology and cognition* (pp. 3–36). Hillsdale, NJ: Erlbaum.

Gergely, G. & Watson, J. (1999). Early social-emotional development: Contingency perception and the social biofeedback model. In P. Rochat (Ed). *Early social cognition*. Hillsdale, NJ: Lawrence Erlbaum Associates.

Gerson, S. & Woodward, A. L. (2010). Building intentional action knowledge with one's hands. In S. P. Johnson (Ed.), *Neo-constructivism*. Oxford: Oxford University Press.

(under review). What's in a mitten? The effects of active versus passive experience on infants' attribution of goals.

Gottlieb, G. (1991). Experiential canalization of behavioral development: Results. *Developmental Psychology*, **27**, 35–39.

Guajardo, J. J. & Woodward, A. L. (2004). Is agency skin-deep? Surface features influence infants' sensitivity to goal-directed action. *Infancy*, **6**, 361–384.

Hamlin, J. K., Hallinan, E. V., & Woodward, A. L. (2008). Do as I do: 7-month-old infants selectively reproduce others' goals. *Developmental Science*, **11**(4), 487–494.

Hirotani, M., Stets, M., Striano, T., & Friederici, A. (2009). Joint attention helps infants learn new words: Event-related potential evidence. *NeuroReport*, **20**(6), 600–605.

Hoehl, S., Reid, V. M., Mooney, J., & Striano, T. (2008). What are you looking at? Infants' neural processing of an adult's object-directed eye gaze. *Developmental Science*, **11**(1), 10–16.

Hoehl, S., Wiese, L., & Striano, T. (2008). Young infants' neural processing of objects is affected by eye gaze direction and emotional expression. *PLOS One*, **3**(6), 1–6.

Hoehl, S. & Striano, T. (2008). Neural processing of eye gaze and threat-related emotional facial expressions in infancy. *Child Development*, **79**(9), 1752–1760.

Hofer, T., Hauf, P., & Aschersleben, G. (2005). Infant's perception of goal-directed actions performed by a mechanical device. *Infant Behavior & Development*, **28**(4), 466–480.

Itakura, S. (2001). Attention to repeated events in human infants (Homo sapiens): Effects of joint visual attention versus stimulus change. *Animal Cognition*, **4**(3–4), 281–284.

Jaffe, J. & Feldstein, S. (1970). *Rhythms of dialogue*. New York: Academic Press.

Johnson, M. H. (2005). *Developmental cognitive neuroscience*, 2nd ed. Oxford: Blackwell.

Johnson, S. C., Ok, S.-J., & Luo, Y. (2007). The attribution of attention: Nine-month-olds' interpretation of gaze as goal-directed action. *Developmental Science*, **10**, 530–537.

Keller, H., Lohaus, A., Völker, S., Cappenberg, M., & Chasiotis, A. (1999). Temporal contingency as an independent component of parenting behavior. *Child Development*, **70**(2), 474–485.

Lewkowicz, D. J. (2000). The development of intersensory temporal perception: An epigenetic systems/limitations view. *Psychological Bulletin*, **126**(2), 281–308.

Luo, Y. & Johnson, S. C. (2009). Recognizing the role of perception in action at 6 months. *Developmental Science*, **12**, 142–149.

Mahajan, N. & Woodward, A. L. (2009). Infants imitate human agents but not inanimate objects. *Infancy*, **14**(6), 667–679.

Marler, P. (1991). The instinct to learn. In S. Carey & R. Gelman (Eds.), *The epigenesis of mind: Essays on biology and cognition* (pp. 37–66). Hillsdale, NJ: Erlbaum.

Meltzoff, A. N. (1995). Understanding the intentions of others: Re-enactments of intended acts by 18-month-old children. *Developmental Psychology*, **31**, 838–850.

    (2007). The "like me" framework for recognizing and becoming an intentional agent. *Acta Psychologica*, **124**, 26–43.

Miceli, P. J., Whitman, T. L., Borkowski, J. G., Braungart-Rieker, J. M., & Mitchell, D. W. (1998). Individual differences in infant information processing: The role of temperamental and maternal factors. *Infant Behavior and Development*, **21**, 119–136.

Moore, C. & Corkum, V. (1994). Social understanding at the end of the first year of life. *Developmental Review*, **14**, 349–372.

Needham, A., Barrett, T., & Peterman, K. (2002). A pick-me-up for infants' exploratory skills. *Infant Behavior and Development*, **25**, 279–295.

Nicely, P., Tamis-LeMonda, C. S., & Bornstein, M. H. (1999). Mothers' attuned responses to infant affect expressivity promote earlier achievement of language milestones. *Infant Behavior and Development*, **22**(4), 557–568.

Onishi, K. H. & Baillargeon, R. (2005). Do 15-month-old infants understand false belief? *Science*, **308**, 255–258.

Papousek, H. & Papousek, M. (1987). *Handbook of infant development*. New York: Wiley.

Parise, E., Reid, V., Stets, M., & Striano, T. (2008). Direct eye contact influences the neural processing of objects in 5-month-old infants. *Social Neuroscience*, **3**(2), 141–150.

Parise, E., Cleveland, A., Costabile, A., & Striano, T. (2007). Influence of vocal cues on learning about objects in joint attention contexts. *Infant Behavior and Development*, **30**(2), 380–384.

Phillips, A. T., Wellman, H. M., & Spelke, E. S. (2002). Infants' ability to connect gaze and emotional expression to intentional action. *Cognition*, **85**, 53–78.

Piaget, J. (1929). *The child's conception of the world* (J. Tomlinson & A. Tomlinson, Trans.). London: Routledge and Kegan Paul, Ltd.

Shipley, T. F. & Zacks, J. M. (Eds.). (2008). *Understanding events: From perception to action*. New York: Oxford University Press.

Sodian, B. & Thoermer, C. (2004). Infants' understanding of looking, pointing and reaching as cues to goal-directed action. *Journal of Cognition and Development*, **53**, 289–316.

Sommerville, J. A., Hildebrand, E. A., & Crane, C. C. (2008). Experience matters: The impact of doing versus watching on infants' subsequent perception of tool use events. *Developmental Psychology*, **44**, 1249–1256.

Sommerville, J. A. & Woodward, A. L. (2005). Pulling out the intentional structure of human action: The relation between action production and processing in infancy. *Cognition*, **95**, 1–30.

Sommerville, J. A., Woodward, A. L., & Needham, A. (2005). Action experience alters 3-month-old infants' perception of others' actions. *Cognition*, **96**, B1–B11.

Southgate, V., Johnson, M. H., Osborne, T., & Csibra, G. (2009). Predictive motor activation during action observation in human infants. *Biology Letters*, **5**, 769–772.

Southgate, V., Senju, A., & Csibra, G. (2007). Action anticipation through attribution of false belief by 2-year-olds. *Psychological Science*, **18**(7), 587–592.

Spelke, E. S., Breinlinger, K., Macomber, J., & Jacobson, K. (1992). Origins of knowledge. *Psychological Review*, **99**, 605–632.

Stern, D. N. (1985). *The interpersonal world of the infant – A view from psychoanalysis and developmental psychology.* New York: Basic Books.

Stern, D., Beebe, B., Jaffe, J., & Bennett, S. (1977). The infant's stimulus world during social interaction: A study of caregiver behaviors with particular reference to repetition and timing. In H.R. Shaffer (Ed.), *Studies on mother-infant interaction* (pp. 177–203). New York: Academic Press.

Striano, T. (2004). Direction of regard and the still-face effect in the first year: Does intention matter? *Child Development*, **75**(2), 468–479.

Striano, T., Reid, V. M., & Hoehl, S. (2006). Neural mechanisms of joint attention in infancy. *European Journal of Neuroscience*, **23**(10), 2819–2823.

Striano, T., Stahl, D., Cleveland, A., & Hoehl, S. (2007). Sensitivity to triadic attention between 6 weeks and 3 months of age. *Infant Behavior and Development*, **30**(3), 529–534.

Striano, T. & Stahl, D. (2005) Sensitivity to triadic attention in early infancy. *Developmental Science*, (**8**)4, 333–343.

Striano, T., Chen, X., Cleveland, A., & Bradshaw, S. (2006). Joint attention social cues influence infant learning. *European Journal of Developmental Psychology*, **3**(3), 289–299.

Striano, T. & Reid, V. M. (Eds.) (2008). *Social cognition: Development, neuroscience and autism.* London: Wiley-Blackwell Publishing.

Symons, D. & Moran, G. (1994). Responsiveness and dependency are different aspects of social contingencies: An example from mother and infant smiles. *Infant Behavior and Development*, **17**(2), 209–214.

Tomasello, M. (1995). Joint attention as social cognition. In C. Moore, & P. J. Dunham (Eds), *Joint attention: Its origins and role in development* (pp. 103–130). Hillsdale, NJ, England: Lawrence Erlbaum Associates.

(1999). *The cultural origins of human cognition.* Cambridge, MA: Harvard University Press.

Tomasello, M., Carpenter, M., Call, J., Behne, T., & Moll, H. (2005). Understanding and sharing intentions: The origins of cultural cognition. *Behavioral and Brain Sciences*, **28**, 675–735.

Tomasello, M. & Barton, M. (1994). Learning words in nonostensive contexts. *Developmental Psychology*, **30**(5), 639–650.

Vaish, A. & Woodward, A. (2010). Infants use attention but not emotions to predict others' actions. *Infant Behavior and Development*, **33**(1), 79–87.

vanEgeren, L.A., Barratt, M. S., & Roach, M. A. (2001). Mother-infant responsiveness: Timing, mutual regulation, and interactional context. *Developmental Psychology*, **37**, 684–697.

vanWulfften Palthe, T. & Hopkins, B. (1993). A longitudinal study of neural maturation and early mother-infant interaction: A research note. *Journal of Child Psychology and Psychiatry*, **34**(6), 1031–1041.

Webb, S. J., Long, J. D., & Nelson, C. A. (2005). A longitudinal investigation of visual event-related potentials in the first year. *Developmental Science*, **8**, 605–616.

Wellman, H. M. (1992). *The child's theory of mind*. Cambridge, MA: MIT Press.

Wellman, H. M., Phillips, A. T., Dunphy-Lelii, S., & LaLonde, N. (2004). Infant social attention predicts preschool social cognition. *Developmental Science*, **7**, 283–288.

Wellman, H. M., Lopez-Duran, S., LaBounty, J., & Hamilton, B. (2008). Infant attention to intentional action predicts preschool theory of mind. *Developmental Psychology*, **44**, 618–623.

Woodward, A. L. (1998). Infants selectively encode the goal object of an actor's reach. *Cognition*, **69**, 1–34.

(1999). Infants' ability to distinguish between purposeful and non-purposeful behaviors. *Infant Behavior and Development*, **22**, 145–160.

(2003a). Infants' developing understanding of the link between looker and object. *Developmental Science*, **6**(3), 297–311.

(2003b). Infants' use of action knowledge to get a grasp on words. In D. G. Hall & S. R. Waxman (Eds.), *Weaving a lexicon* (pp. 149–172). Cambridge, MA: MIT Press.

(2005). The infant origins of intentional understanding. In R. V. Kail (Ed.), *Advances in child development and behavior* (Vol. 33, pp. 229–262). Oxford: Elsevier.

Woodward, A. L. & Guajardo, J. J. (2002). Infants' understanding of the point gesture as an object-directed action. *Cognitive Development*, **17**, 1061–1084.

Woodward, A. L. & Sommerville, J. A. (2000). Twelve-month-old infants interpret action in context, *Psychological Science*, **11**, 73–76.

Woodward, A. L., Sommerville, J. A., Gerson, S., Henderson, A. M. E., & Buresh, J. S. (2009). The emergence of intention attribution in infancy. In B. Ross (Ed.), *The psychology of learning and motivation, Volume 51*. New York: Academic Press.

5 Learning about Language: Acquiring the Spoken and Written Word

Sandra R. Waxman and Usha Goswami

Language acquisition is critical not only in infancy, but also for later achievement. Language supports cognitive and social development, enhances memory and reasoning abilities, and underpins the development of executive function – the capacity to organize and manage one's own behavior. For example, because language permits children to construct extended, temporally organized, narratively coherent representations of their own experiences that can be accessed efficiently, language acquisition can promote capacities as fundamental as memory. Language acquisition is tuned by the language input children receive. By the time they enter school, there is considerable variability in the language experiences and language capacities of young children. Hart and Risley (1995) estimated that by four years of age, children from high-SES families in the United States had been exposed to around 44 million utterances, compared to 12 million utterances for lower SES children (see also, Huttenlocher et al. 2002). Because these enormous differences in young children's language exposure affect their subsequent learning and development, language interventions aimed at providing young children with richer and more complex linguistic experiences (and going beyond "empty language" such as "Don't do that," "bring it here") have well-documented positive effects on how well children flourish in school (Landry 2005).

Because a primary function of language is, of course, communication, infants need to learn what words *mean*. To succeed, infants must identify not only the relevant linguistic units and conceptual units, but must establish a mapping between them. But how do infants accomplish this task? And how do they learn that for any given scene (e.g., a cardinal flying behind a stone fence), we can use not only different words (e.g., "bird," "cardinal") but also different *kinds* of words (e.g., nouns, adjectives, verbs) to focus in on different aspects of the scene (e.g., "bird," "red," "flying," respectively).

Because words are perhaps the primary unit of language, in this chapter, we focus on the acquisition of words in spoken and written language. We adopt a cross-linguistic developmental approach, focusing on evidence from infants and young children. With regard to spoken language, Waxman (Waxman & Gelman 2009; Waxman & Markow 1995) has proposed that infants cross the threshold into word-learning equipped with a broad initial expectation linking words to concepts, and that this initial expectation becomes increasingly fine-tuned on the basis of infants' experience with the objects and events they encounter and the native language they hear. In addition to linking words and concepts, infants and young children must also learn the sound structure of spoken words, and how to reproduce these sound structures exactly. With regard to written language, this awareness of sound structure, or phonology, is critical for learning to read, a key educational achievement. Goswami has developed a cross-language theory of phonological development and reading acquisition, which we also illustrate in the second part of this chapter.

Learning What Words Mean

Even before they begin to speak, infants have already begun to establish a repertoire of concepts and to focus on the sound patterns of their native language. Consider first the infants' conceptual capacities. In the first year of life, infants begin to form categories that capture important relations among the objects and events that they encounter, and use these early concepts as a foundation for learning about new objects and events (Waxman & Gelman 2009). Infants' early object and event categories provide strong starting points for the more elaborated concepts and theories that emerge later in development. In other words, there is conceptual continuity from infancy through adulthood.

Consider next, infants' burgeoning language capacities. Infants begin to recognize a few words (notably, their own names) at about 7 months of age, and typically produce their first words by their first birthdays. Infants' first words tend to be those that refer to important individuals (e.g., "Mama"), objects (e.g., "cup," "doggie"), social routines (e.g., "night-night"), and actions (e.g., "up"). Across languages, infants tend to show a "noun advantage," with nouns referring to basic-level object categories being the predominant form (Bornstein et al. 2004, provide a cross-linguistic review). By their second birthdays, infants typically have command of hundreds of words; they also typically begin to combine words to form short phrases that respect the grammatical properties of their native language.

The Puzzle of Word-Learning

To learn the meaning of a word, infants must solve a difficult three-part puzzle: they must (1) parse the relevant *word* from the ongoing stream of speech, (2) identify the relevant entity or relation in the ongoing stream of activity in the *world*, and (3) establish a word-to-world mapping. Put differently, successful word-learning rests on an ability to discover the relevant linguistic units, the relevant conceptual units, and the mappings between them.

Solving each piece of this puzzle depends on infants' ability to recruit other perceptual and psychological capacities. For example, consider what it takes for an infant to parse a word from fluent speech. We know that newborns prefer human speech – and particularly infant-directed speech – over other kinds of auditory stimulation. We also know that the function of infant-directed speech changes with development. Within the first six months, infant-directed speech serves primarily to engage and modulate infants' attention. But in the latter six months, infants begin to cull words from the speech stream, and to pay attention to the morphologic, phonetic, and prosodic cues that mark word and phrase boundaries in their language (Jusczyk & Aslin 1995; Kemler Nelson et al. 1989). At this point, infants begin to distinguish two very broad classes of words: *open class* words (or, *content* words, including nouns, adjectives, verbs) and *closed class* words (or, *function* words, including determiners and prepositions). Infants as young as six months of age prefer listening to open class words (Gomez 2002; Shi & Werker 2003). This early listening preference provides an important step on the way to establishing meaning, for it insures that infants will pay particular attention to just those words (the open class, content words) that will serve to anchor their first word-to-world mappings. (Morgan & Demuth 1996; Werker et al. 1996).

Early word-learning also calls on infants' ability to identify objects and events in their environment, and to notice commonalities among them. Even in the first six months of life, infants have a great deal of core knowledge, including abstract notions of animacy, intentionality, and physical causation (Baillargeon 2000; Pauen & Träuble 2009; Spelke 2000). They also have a repertoire of prelinguistic concepts, including category-based (e.g., cup, dog) and property-based (e.g., red, soft) commonalities. Because these concepts emerge before infants begin to learn words, it is reasonable to assume that these concepts are independent of language and are universally available. Each concept that the infant is capable of representing is, in essence, a candidate for word-meaning. What infants must do, then, is to home in on *which* words refer to *which* of a range of available concepts.

This brings us to the third piece of the word-learning puzzle, known as the mapping problem. In solving this piece of the puzzle, infants reveal an ability to grasp the symbolic and referential power of words. Moreover, they draw on fundamental notions related to human behavior: inferring the goals and intentions of others (Waxman & Gelman 2009). For example, the ability to map a word to its referent is predicated on an ability to infer that the speaker *intended to name* the designated object (Fennell & Waxman 2010; Jaswal 2004). By their first birthdays, infants have begun to make such connections.

Finally, if infants are to extend words appropriately beyond the particular individual(s) with which they were introduced, infants must go beyond word-to-*object* mappings to establish word-to-*concept* mappings (Gelman 2006; Waxman & Leddon 2009; Waxman & Lidz 2006). In essence, then, to apply a word (e.g., *bird*) to a new and (as yet) unlabeled object, infants must make an inference regarding the novel word's extension.

Different Kinds of Words Highlight Different Aspects of a Scene

To make matters more complicated, many different *types* of words can be appropriately offered in a single naming episode, with each type of word highlighting a different aspect of the very same scene and each supporting a unique pattern of extension. For example, across languages, nouns (count nouns, if there is a mass-count distinction in the language) ("Look, it's a *bird*") typically refer to the named object itself and are extended spontaneously to other members of the same object kind (other birds); proper nouns ("Look, it's *Clara*") also refer to the named individual, but these are not extended further. Adjectives can also be applied correctly to that individual ("Look, it's *red*"); they refer to a property of the individual, and are extended to other objects sharing that property, whether or not they are birds. Verbs, in contrast, are used to describe the event, or the relation in which the individual(s) are participating ("Look, it's *pecking*, or *flying*"), and are extended to other relations of the same type.

For over a decade, we have known that by two-and-a-half years of age, children are sensitive to many of these links between kinds of words and kinds of relations among objects, and recruit them in the process of word-learning (for a review, see Waxman & Lidz 2006). Thus, they have the *linguistic* capacity to distinguish among the relevant syntactic forms (e.g., count noun vs. adjective) and the *conceptual* or *perceptual* ability to appreciate many different kinds of relations, and a tacit expectation that these linguistic and conceptual abilities are linked.

But how do these links emerge? Which, if any, are available as infants begin the process of word-learning, and how are these links shaped over the course of development? As we have pointed out, even before they reach their first birthdays or produce their first words, infants have a rich repertoire of concepts and perceptual categories. But in addition, they harbor a broad tacit expectation that novel (open class) words, independent of their grammatical form, highlight commonalities among named objects. This broad initial link serves (at least) three essential functions. First, words direct attention to commonalities, and in this way facilitate the formation of an expanding repertoire of concepts, including those that infants may not have detected as readily in the absence of a novel word. Second, this broad initial expectation (that words refer to commonalities) supports the establishment of a rudimentary lexicon. Third, and perhaps most radically, this broad initial expectation sets the stage for the discovery of more specific expectations linking *particular* types of words (nouns, adjectives, verbs) to *particular* types of meaning (object categories, object properties, event categories) in the particular language being acquired by the infant. In other words, infants' initial broad expectation (linking words (in general) to commonalities (in general)) will direct their attention in such a way as to promote their discovery of the distinct grammatical forms present in their native language, and the ways these link to meaning.

Naming and Categorization

In a series of experiments, Waxman and her colleagues examined the influence of novel words in infants ranging from 12 months of age (see Waxman & Markow 1995 for a complete description). We used a novelty-preference task (see Figure 5.1 for a sample set of stimuli and introductory phrases). During a familiarization phase, an experimenter offered an infant four different toys from a given category (e.g., four animals) one at a time, in random order. This was immediately followed by a test phase, in which the experimenter simultaneously presented both (1) a new member of the now-familiar category (e.g., another animal) and (2) an object from a novel category (e.g., a fruit). To identify the influence of novel words, infants were randomly assigned to different conditions, each varying in the experimenter's comments during familiarization. Each infant completed this task with four different sets of objects.

	Familiarization Phase				Test Phase	
	Trail 1	Trail 2	Trail 3	Trail 4		
Animal Set:						
	yellow duck	green raccoon	blue dog	orange lion	red cat	red apple
Noun	This one is. a(n) X	This one is. a(n) X	See what I have?	This one is. a(n) X	see what I have?	
Adjective	This one is. X-ish	This one is. X-ish	See what I have?	This one is. a(n) X	see what I have?	
No Word	Look at this.	Look at this.	See what I have?	This one is. a(n) X	see what I have?	

Figure 5.1. Sample set of stimuli and introductory phrases used by Waxman and Markow (1995).

We reasoned as follows: If infants detect the novel word, and if novel words direct infants' attention to commonalities among objects, then infants who hear novel words during familiarization should be more likely than those in the No Word condition to form object categories. Including both a Novel Noun and Novel Adjective condition permitted us to test the specificity of infants' initial expectation. If the expectation is initially general, as we have proposed, then infants hearing either novel nouns or adjectives should be more likely than those hearing no novel words to form object categories.

The data were consistent with this prediction: Infants on the threshold of producing language reliably detected the novel words, and these novel words (both adjectives and nouns) directed infants' attention to commonalities among the objects. In essence, then, words serve as "invitations to form categories." This invitation has several consequences. First, novel words invite infants to discover similarities among objects that might otherwise have gone unnoticed (Gelman 2006; Gentner & Namy 1999; Keates & Graham 2008; Welder & Graham 2006). Second, naming has dramatic consequences in situations in which infants have already formed object categories. After all, infants' knowledge about these categories is not as detailed as that of an older child or adult. Novel words are instrumental in motivating infants and young children to discover the deeper commonalities that underlie our richly structured object categories (Ahn & Luhmann 2004; Barsalou et al. 2008; Gelman & Kalish 2006; Landau 1994; Macnamara 1994; Markman 1989; Murphy 2004). Most importantly, the results of this series document that a link between words and concepts is in place early enough to guide infants in their very first efforts to establish word-to-world mappings.

When Do Infants Tease Apart Different Kinds of Words and Map Them to Different Kinds of Meaning?

Another closely related experimental series reveals even more precise and nuanced effects. By 14 months of age, different *kinds* of words highlight different *kinds* of commonalities. Infants were familiarized to objects sharing *both* category- and property-based commonalities (e.g., four purple animals). See Figure 5.2.

As predicted, at 11 months, infants' link was broad: They mapped novel words (either nouns or adjectives) broadly to either category- or property-based relations (Waxman & Booth 2003). But by 14 months, their expectations were more nuanced: Infants mapped nouns specifically to category-based (and not to property-based) commonalities, but they continued to map adjectives broadly to either category- or property-based relations (Waxman & Booth 2001). Later, by 18 to 21 months, infants' mappings are more precise: Infants hearing these objects described with novel nouns focused on object categories (e.g., animal); those hearing the same objects described with novel adjectives focused on object properties (e.g., purple things) (Booth & Waxman 2009; Waxman & Markow 1998).

Another series of experiments illustrated infants' acquisition of verbs. For most infants, and across most languages, verbs do not appear in appreciable number in infants' lexicons until roughly 20- to 24-months of age, several months after the appearance of nouns (for reviews, see Gleitman et al. 2005; Waxman & Lidz 2006). What accounts for this developmental phenomenon, favoring the acquisition of nouns over verbs? The conceptual underpinnings of verb meaning appear to be in place, at least in rudimentary ways, by the time infants reach their first birthdays. By 7 to 12 months, infants are sensitive to fundamental components of events, including notions of animacy, agency, and cause (Buresh, Wilson-Brune, & Woodward 2006; Casasola & Cohen 2000; Gergely et al. 1995; Gertner, Fisher, & Eisengart 2006; Leslie & Keeble 1987; Pauen & Träuble 2009; Sommerville, Woodward, & Needham 2005; Wagner & Carey 2005). Between 12 and 24 months, infants demonstrate sensitivity to other key elements of verb-meaning, including changes of state, result, manner, and path of motion (Bunger & Lidz 2004; Pruden et al. 2004; Pulverman et al. 2006).

Based on findings such as these, it seems clear that infants' delay in acquiring verbs cannot be attributed to an inability on their part to represent the kinds of concepts that underlie verb-meaning. What, then, might be holding them back? This relative delay appears to reflect a fundamental feature of verbs: The meaning of a verb depends on the linguistic arguments that it takes (and the relation among them). That is, to identify the

Figure 5.2. Sample set of stimuli and introductory phrases used by Waxman and Booth (2003).

	Familiarization		Contrast	Test	
	Trial 1	Trial 2		Category	Property
Purple Animal Set:	bear lion	---- dog	red apple	purple horse vs. purple chair	purple horse vs. blue horse
Noun	These are blickets. This one is blicket & This one is blicket	These are blickets. This one is blicket & This one is blicket	Uh-oh, this one is not a blicket!	Can you give me the blicket?	Can you give me the blicket?
Adjective	These are blickish. This one is blickish & This one is blickish	These are blickish. This one is blickish & This one is blickish	Uh-oh, this one is not a blickish!	Can you give me the blickish one?	Can you give me the blickish one?
No Word	Look at these. Look at this one & Look at this one	Look at these. Look at this one & Look at this one	Uh-oh, look at this one!	Can you give one?	Can you give me one?

event labeled by a verb, we depend on the noun phrases that represent the event participants and the linguistic relations among these phrases (Fisher et al. 1994; Gleitman et al. 2005; Landau & Gleitman 1985; Piccin & Waxman 2007; Waxman & Lidz 2006). Apparently, then, infants must first acquire at least some nouns before they can establish the meaning of verbs.

This fits well with the "noun advantage" in infants' earliest lexicons. By roughly 24 months, when infants begin to produce an appreciable number of verbs, they are also sensitive to a great deal of syntactic information (e.g., the number and types of frames in which novel verbs appear; the relations among the noun phrases in these frames) to establish a novel verb's meaning (Arunachalam & Waxman 2010; Akhtar & Tomasello 1996; Bunger & Lidz 2004; Fernandes et al. 2006; Fisher 2002; Gertner, Fisher, & Eisengart 2006; Gleitman 1990; Gleitman et al. 2005; Hirsch-Pasek, Golinkoff, & Naigles 1996; Landau & Gleitman 1985; Naigles 1990, 1996; Naigles & Kako 1993). At the same time, however, infants' efforts at verb-learning in the laboratory also reveal some striking failures, many of which persist beyond infancy into the preschool years (Imai et al. 2008; see also Kersten & Smith 2002; Meyer et al. 2003). For example, in lab tasks, 3- and 5-year-olds often map novel verbs to categories of objects, rather than events.

How can we reconcile what, until now, has been a large and largely unexplained gap between 24-month-old infants' well-documented ability to acquire verbs in the natural course of their lives and 3- and 5-year-olds' rather surprising failures in many laboratory-based tasks? Waxman and her colleagues designed a task to unravel this mystery (Waxman et al. 2009). They presented 24-month-old infants with dynamic scenes (e.g., a man waving a balloon), and asked (1) whether infants could construe these scenes flexibly, noticing the consistent action (e.g., waving) as well as the consistent object (e.g., the balloon) and (2) whether their construals were influenced by the grammatical form of a novel word used to describe them (verb or noun). See Figure 5.3. In this task, 24-month-olds successfully mapped novel verbs to event categories (e.g., waving events) and novel nouns to object categories (e.g., balloons). Considered in conjunction with other recent work, this outcome beckons the field to move beyond asking *whether* infants can learn verbs (they can), and to consider instead which conditions best support successful verb-learning in infants and young children.

Summarizing to this point, as they learn words, infants attend not only to the novel word itself: They depend crucially on its surrounding linguistic elements (e.g., determiners, arguments). They distinguish among distinct

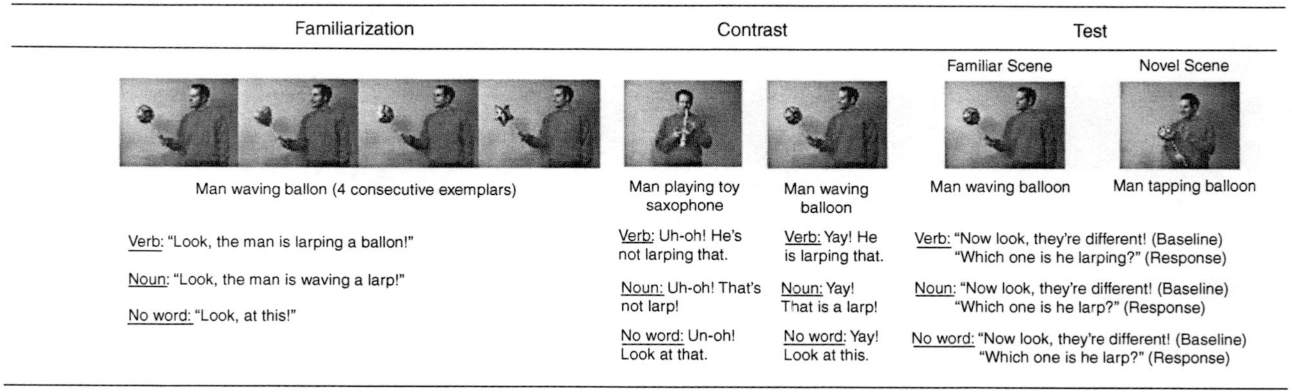

Familiarization | Contrast | Test

Familiarization

Man waving balloon (4 consecutive exemplars)

Verb: "Look, the man is larping a balloon!"

Noun: "Look, the man is waving a larp!"

No word: "Look, at this!"

Contrast

Man playing toy saxophone | Man waving balloon

Verb: Uh-oh! He's not larping that.

Noun: Uh-oh! That's not larp!

No word: Un-oh! Look at that.

Verb: Yay! He is larping that.

Noun: Yay! That is a larp!

No word: Yay! Look at this.

Test

Familiar Scene | Novel Scene

Man waving balloon | Man tapping balloon

Verb: "Now look, they're different! (Baseline) "Which one is he larping?" (Response)

Noun: "Now look, they're different! (Baseline) "Which one is he larp?" (Response)

No word: "Now look, they're different! (Baseline) "Which one is he larp?" (Response)

Figure 5.3. Sample set of stimuli and introductory phrases used by Waxman et al. (2009).

98

kinds of words, and recruit these distinctions precisely in establishing distinct kinds of meaning (e.g., categories of objects, properties, events).

Prelinguistic infants: Effects of naming. In the previous section, we traced the increasingly precise expectations regarding word-to-world mappings of infants as they crossed the important developmental thresholds of producing words on their own, and later combining them. Here, we ask whether words have cognitive consequences for infants who have not yet begun to speak. Surprisingly, the answer is yes. For example, 10-month-old infants look longer at objects that have been named than to objects presented in silence (Baldwin & Markman 1989). But does this increased attention stem from a general attention-engaging function of auditory stimuli, or does it reflect something special about words? And does naming direct infants' attention to the named exemplar only, or does it support categorization, as we have seen in infants at 11 months and older?

To address these questions, researchers have compared the effect of novel words to other kinds of auditory stimuli on infants' categorization behavior. Even for prelinguistic infants, words are indeed special (Balaban & Waxman 1997; Ferry, Hespos, & Waxman 2010). In one task, researchers have assessed 3-, 6-, and 12-month-old infants' categorization when presented with words versus tones in a novelty-preference task. During the familiarization phase, infants saw a sequence of colorful slides, each depicting a different member of a category (e.g., dinosaurs). To examine the influence of words, infants were randomly assigned to either a Word or a Tone condition. For infants in the Word condition, a naming phrase (e.g., "Oh look, it's a *toma*! Do you see the *toma*?") accompanied the familiarization trials. For infants in the Tone condition, a sine-wave tone (matched to the naming phrase in amplitude, duration, and pause length) accompanied the familiarization trials. Infants then viewed a test trial, including (1) a new member of the now-familiar category (e.g., another dinosaur) and (2) an object from a novel category (e.g., a fish). Test trials were presented in silence. If words focus attention on commonalities among objects, then infants in the Word condition should notice the commonalities among the familiarization objects. In that case, the infants should reveal a preference for the novel test object (e.g., the fish). If this effect is specific to words, and not to auditory stimulation more generally, then infants in the Tone condition should be less likely to notice these commonalities and less likely to reveal a novelty preference at test. The results supported this prediction entirely: For infants as young as 3 months of age, there is indeed something special about words. Providing a shared name for distinct individuals highlights commonalities among them.

Naming also helps infants trace the identity of distinct objects over time (Waxman & Braun 2005; Xu & Carey 1996). For example, 10-month-olds can find it taxing to keep track of the unique identities of two distinct objects (e.g., a ball and a duck), especially if these objects are presented in constant motion, with one appearing and disappearing from one side of an opaque screen, and the other appearing and disappearing from the other side (Xu & Carey 1996). However, infants' difficulty in tracking the identity of these distinct objects diminishes dramatically if each is labeled with a distinct name as it emerges from behind the screen.

Together, these results reveal that even before the advent of productive language, naming has powerful cognitive consequences. Naming supports the establishment of a repertoire of object categories and provides infants with a means of tracing the identity of individuals within these categories throughout development (Waxman & Braun 2005).

The evidence from early word-learning provides considerable support for Waxman's proposal that even before infants begin to speak, they are sensitive to a broad initial link between words (independent of their grammatical form) and a wide range of commonalities among named objects and events. By roughly 14 months, this general expectation had become more fine-tuned. Infants distinguish nouns from adjectives, and treat this distinction as relevant to establishing the meaning of novel words; they map nouns specifically to category-based (and not property-based) commonalities. Yet discovering the specific links between adjectives and properties of objects emerges later, toward the end of the second year of life. At this point, infants also successfully link verbs to event categories. In essence, then, there is a developmental cascade: Some word-world links emerge first, and others follow. At the same time, there is substantial developmental continuity. From infancy, words are powerful engines, promoting conceptual development, advancing us beyond our initial groupings, and fueling the acquisition of the rich relations that characterize our most powerful concepts.

Implications for Education

From infancy through adulthood, language and conceptual organization are intricately and powerfully linked. Language is a prime conduit for communicating our own knowledge and intentions, and conveying this information to others. As a result, language is essential not only to conceptual development in infants and preschool-aged children, but also to education. The results of the work described in this section will advance our efforts to promote positive development outcomes for the ever-increasing number of infants and young children who enter classrooms having acquired languages other than the language of the classroom. This work will also set the stage for examining infants growing up bilingual, and identifying the consequences of processing two languages in the first years of life. Finally, this basic research can also serve as a springboard for developing targeted interventions for young children diagnosed with language delay and impairments.

Learning How Words Sound

As they learn the meaning of novel words, infants also learn about the sounds of words in their language. Earlier in this chapter, we saw also that newborns prefer to listen to human speech, particularly infant-directed speech, rather than to other sources of auditory stimulation. The rhythmical and melodic contours of infant-directed speech appear to have a specific language-learning function, for example in word boundary segmentation. Infant-directed speech (IDS) emphasizes prosodic cues: Pitch is typically heightened, duration is increased, and rhythm and intonation are exaggerated. These features are found in IDS across the world's languages (Fernald et al. 1989). So the acoustic features that are important for phonological acquisition seem to be similar across languages.

Child phonologists propose that infants learn language-specific "phonotactic templates" (Vihman & Croft 2007). A phonotactic template is basically a phonological pattern. Each template contains variations in sound intensity, pitch, duration, and rhythm which together constitute a unit, usually of meaning. For spoken English, a common template is a bi-syllabic pattern with stronger first syllable stress (a strong – weak stress template). In the English template, the "strong" first syllable is typically louder, longer, and higher in pitch than the second syllable. Early acquired words that follow this pattern are "Mummy," "Daddy," and "baby." This rhythmic pattern is so strong in English that caregivers frequently change the words that they use with babies and young children to fit the pattern ("milkie," "doggie"). Developmental phonologists such as Vihman and Croft (2007) have shown that babies' own babbling also conforms to these rhythmic patterns. Babies do not babble single-syllable words. So, both auditory perception and spoken language production appear to converge onto these rhythmic templates.

These first acquisitions have been termed "prosodic structures" by the linguist Pierrehumbert (2003). Of course, typical prosodic structures or phonotactic templates vary across languages. In French, the dominant prosodic pattern depends on lengthening the final syllable, whereas Hungarian utilizes first-syllable stress. Prosody is a term used in linguistic theory to cover all aspects of grouping, rhythm, and prominence, from subparts of the syllable up through the organization of words in the phrase (Lehiste 1977; Pierrehumbert 2003). Prosody and speech rhythm are intimately linked, and languages conform to different rhythm "types." English is a stress-timed language. It has a rhythm determined by the stressing of syllables that occur at roughly equal intervals in speech. French and Hungarian are syllable-timed languages. They have rhythms determined by stressing particular syllables in particular words. The phonotactic templates that organize a preliterate child's phonological development will therefore differ across languages. This will naturally have implications for learning to be literate.

Cross-Language Similarities
Despite these differences in prosodic organization, there is widespread agreement among linguists that the syllable is the primary perceptual phonological unit across languages. Young children can be asked to reflect on their knowledge of spoken language by asking them to perform "phonological awareness" tasks. Phonological awareness tasks are performed most easily at the syllable level. For example, young children can be asked to tap once with a wooden dowel for each syllable in a word (e.g., butterfly = 3 taps), to put out a counter for each syllable in a word (e.g., president = 3 counters), or to make "same–different" judgments about words (e.g., whether "repeat" and "compete" share a syllable). High levels of performance are found across languages in tasks measuring children's awareness of syllabic structure, from age 3 to 4 years (e.g., Liberman et al. 1974; Treiman & Zukowski 1991). When Treiman and Zukowski used a same–different judgment task to measure syllable awareness, 100% of 5-year-olds, 90% of 6-year-olds, and 100% of 7-year-olds made accurate same–different judgments about syllables. Similar performance levels have been reported for Turkish kindergartners (age 6) (Durgunoglu & Oney 1999), who tapped out 94% of syllable structures correctly, Norwegian kindergartners (age 6), who counted out 83% of syllable structures correctly (Hoien et al. 1995), and German kindergarten children (age 6), who performed at 81% correct in a syllable counting task (Wimmer et al. 1991). Clearly, when pre-reading children are asked to reflect on the phonological structure of spoken language at the syllable level, they perform extremely well regardless of language.

Cross-Language Differences

Despite the ubiquity of the syllable as a perceptual linguistic unit across languages, structural elements of the syllable appear to vary across languages. Different factors that vary systematically across languages include the number of sound elements within syllables (syllable complexity – a consonant-vowel or CV syllable is "simple," a CCVCC syllable is "complex"), the types of sound elements within syllables ("sonority profile"), and phonological "neighborhood density" (the number of similar-sounding syllables to a particular target syllable in a given language). All of these factors affect the development of well-specified phonological representations of words and the development of phonological awareness skills by young children.

Syllable complexity. A simple syllable is a CV syllable, comprising a consonant sound and a vowel sound. Strikingly, most world languages have syllables with a simple CV structure. Logically, it should be easier to become "phonologically aware" of the individual sound elements in syllables that have this simple CV structure. Developing an awareness of these individual sound elements is an integral part of learning to read. However, despite its prominence as a written world language, English has primarily complex syllables. The primary syllabic structure in English is CVC. For single-syllable words (of which English has more than most languages), this structure accounts for 43% of monosyllables (e.g., "cat," "dog," "soap," "look"; see De Cara & Goswami 2002). English also has many CCVC syllables (15% of monosyllables, e.g., "trip," "plan," and "spin"), CVCC syllables (21% of monosyllables, e.g., "fast," "pant," and "jump"), and some CCVCC syllables (6%, e.g., "crust"). Only 5% of monosyllabic words follow the CV pattern ("sea," "go," "do"). Because children find it perceptually challenging to segment a complex syllable such as "pant" into four distinct elements, they often omit sounds such as the penultimate consonant sound when they learn to spell (e.g., writing PAT for "pant," or JUP for "jump"; Treiman 1998). The dominant phonological CVC template in English does not necessarily correspond to a CVC spelling pattern, however – "coat," "book," and all "magic E" words such as "make" and "time" follow a CVC phonological pattern but are spelled with more than three letters.

Sonority profile. There is also variation across languages in the types of sound elements that comprise syllables. This variation is described by the linguistic term "sonority profile." Vowels are the most sonorant sounds that the vocal tract can make, followed in decreasing order by glides (e.g., /w/), liquids (e.g., /l/), nasals (e.g., /n/), and obstruents or plosive sounds (e.g., /p/, /d/, /t/). Linguists have investigated whether there is an optimal sonority profile that is frequently represented across languages because it is easy to produce (e.g., Clements 1990). Theoretically, more sonorant sounds should be nearer to the vowel (we say "tra" but not "rta"). The majority of syllables in English end with plosive or non-sonorant sounds (such as "dog" and "cat" – around 40%). In contrast, the majority of syllables in French either end in liquids or have no consonant coda (almost 50%). To date, the effects of sonority profile have not been investigated systematically across languages with respect to the development of phonological awareness. Nevertheless, it seems likely that sonority profile will affect children's ability to segment syllables into smaller elements of sound.

Phonological neighborhood density. Phonological neighborhood density is an interesting structural factor for an incremental learning approach to child phonology. It was originally proposed by psycholinguists (e.g., Landauer & Streeter 1973; Luce & Pisoni 1998) as a metric for describing similarities and differences between words in terms of shared single sound elements or phonemes (a "phoneme" corresponds to the sounds made by single letters or letter clusters, such as the sound /f/, which corresponds to F and PH). However, phonological neighborhood density analyses for spoken English turned out to highlight the perceptual salience of phonological similarity at the level of rhyme rather than the phoneme (De Cara & Goswami 2002). In these phonological neighborhood density analyses, phonological "neighbors" are defined as words that sound similar to each other. The classical linguistic definition of a phonological neighborhood is the set of words generated by the addition, deletion, or substitution of one *phoneme* to the target (e.g., Landauer & Streeter 1973; Luce & Pisoni 1998). For example, the neighbors of the target *tin* would include *tint, in, tip,* and *tan*. When many words resemble the target, the neighborhood is said to be dense. When few words resemble the target, the neighborhood is said to be sparse. Developmental psycholinguists have also argued that a phonological neighborhood density metric based on the phoneme was unsatisfactory. For example, Dollaghan (1994) reported that the one-phoneme-different criterion led to many intuitively dissatisfying exclusions when she was calculating children's phonological neighborhoods. In particular, the one-phoneme different criterion excluded many rhyme neighbors, such as *clock* and *sock* (you cannot create *clock* by adding or substituting a single phoneme of *sock*).

De Cara and Goswami (2002) provided empirical data that supported Dollaghan's view. They carried out statistical neighborhood analyses for all monosyllabic English words in the CELEX corpus (4086 words; Baayen,

Piepenbrock, & van Rijn 1993), as well as for a number of smaller English lexica controlled for age of acquisition. These statistical analyses demonstrated that most phonological neighbors in English are rhyme neighbors (e.g., *clock/sock*). This means that the phonology of English is rhyme-based, at least at the monosyllabic level. A good example of a dense phonological neighborhood in English is words that rhyme with *fair*. A good example of a sparse phonological neighborhood in English is words that rhyme with *moth*. In later work (Ziegler & Goswami 2005), we carried out similar statistical analyses for German, French, and Dutch. The German and Dutch analyses were based on the monosyllabic words in the CELEX database (Baayen et al. 1993), and the French analyses were based on the monosyllabic words in BRULEX (Content, Mousty, & Radeau 1990). The analyses showed that rhyme neighbors predominate in French, Dutch, and German phonology as well. In all of these languages, the percentage of rhyme neighbors in the monosyllabic lexicon is between 40% and 50%. The phonological neighborhood density structure of different European languages may explain why rhyme awareness is also an early emerging skill.

Changes in Phonological Representation as Literacy Is Learned
Once reading skills are acquired, the way in which the brain represents phonology changes. As Port (2007, p. 143) commented, once we are literate "speech [seems to present] itself to our consciousness in the form of letter-like symbolic units." The ease or difficulty with which the spelling system of a language supports the development of these "letter-like symbolic units" (classically, these units are called *phonemes*) will play a role in literacy acquisition in different languages, and in the transfer of literacy skills between languages. This factor is called *orthographic consistency* or *orthographic transparency*.

We have provided detailed analyses elsewhere to demonstrate that the orthographic consistency of different European languages has dramatic effects on how rapidly children learning those languages develop an awareness of phonemes (Ziegler & Goswami 2005). We have also shown how differences in orthographic consistency are related systematically to how rapidly children learning different languages become efficient at single-word reading (Ziegler & Goswami, 2005, 2006). Our analyses demonstrate that children acquiring reading in languages with high orthographic consistency, that is mainly one-to-one mappings between letters and sounds, learn about phonemes more rapidly. In languages such as Finnish, Greek, German, Spanish, and Italian, a letter corresponds consistently to one phoneme, and children acquire phoneme awareness rapidly. In languages such

Table 5.1. Illustrative Data (% correct) from Studies Comparing Phoneme Counting, Simple Word Reading and Nonword Reading in Different Languages in Kindergarten or Early Grade 1

Language	% phonemes counted correctly	% familiar real words read correctly[8]	% simple nonwords read correctly[8]
Greek	98[1]	98	97
Turkish	94[2]	–	–
Italian	97[3]	95	92
German	81[4]	98	98
Norwegian	83[5]	92	93
French	73[6]	79	88
English	70[7]	34	41

Notes: 1 = Harris & Giannoulis 1999; 2 = Durgunoglu & Oney 1999; 3 = Cossu et al. 1988; 4 = Hoien et al. 1995; 5 = Wimmer et al. 1991; 6 = Demont & Gombert 1996; 7 = Liberman et al. 1974; 8 = Seymour, Aro, & Erskine 2003 (familiar real words = content and function words, nonwords = monosyllabic items only).

as English, French, Portuguese, and Danish, there is a one-to-many mapping between letters and phonemes, and children acquire phoneme awareness more slowly (see Ziegler & Goswami 2005, 2006, for more detailed evidence). English has a particularly high level of orthographic inconsistency. Many letters or letter clusters can be pronounced in more than one way. Examples include *O* in "go" and "do," *EA* in "bead" and "bread," and *G* in "magic" and "bag" (see Berndt, Reggia, & Mitchum 1987; Ziegler, Stone, & Jacobs 1997). Hence children who are learning to read in English show particularly slow acquisition of phoneme awareness.

A table based on studies using the phoneme-counting task, which shows cross-language variation in the development of phoneme awareness, is provided as Table 5.1. Very similar differences between languages are found if children are asked to read aloud simple words and nonwords (i.e., if grapheme-phoneme recoding to sound is the dependent variable). For example, Seymour, Aro, and Erskine (2003) reported large differences in reading achievement during the first year of literacy instruction in 14 European Community languages. This was demonstrated using simple measures of word and nonword reading (and importantly, the word and nonword items used in the study were matched for difficulty across languages). As an example, whereas Finnish children were reading 98% of simple words accurately, English children (in Scotland) were reading only 34% of matched items correctly. Whereas Italian children were reading 95% of items correctly, French children were reading 79% of items correctly. These data are also included in Table 5.1.

According to the theoretical analysis provided here, these cross-language differences in the development of phoneme awareness and simple reading skills are a product of *both* phonological factors and orthographic factors. Children learning to read in languages such as Finnish, Italian, and Spanish are not only learning orthographically consistent languages, they speak languages with predominantly CV syllables. This simplifies the segmentation problem considerably. However, children who are learning to read in languages such as English not only have to acquire an orthographically inconsistent language, they also have a spoken language with predominantly complex syllables. The effects of both phonological and orthographic complexity on learning to be literate are considerable. As shown by the cross-language comparisons in Table 5.1, it takes children longer to learn about phonemes and to become efficient in simple reading skills for languages such as English and French compared to languages such as Finnish, Italian, and Spanish. It should also be noted that another factor that is likely to be important for cross-language differences in phonological development is morphology (Goswami & Ziegler 2006). Morphological or meaning-based changes are frequently signaled by small phonological differences. For example, in Turkish *evim* means "in my house' and *evin* means "in your house." This single phoneme change (/m/ to /n/) is critical for language comprehension. Therefore, it is a priori likely that Turkish morphology affects how rapidly Turkish children become aware of phonemes (Durgunoglu 2006). However, the cross-language database on how morphological differences affect phonological development is currently too small to attempt a systematic analysis.

Educational Difficulties in Learning to Read

So far, we have seen that the child's brain develops phonological "representations" of words in response to spoken language exposure and learning to speak. Extensive cross-language research has shown that the quality of these phonological representations then determines literacy acquisition (see Ziegler & Goswami 2005, for a detailed analysis). When phonological representations are impaired, children will struggle to acquire functional literacy skills across languages. For example, cognitive studies demonstrate that children with developmental dyslexia in all languages so far studied have difficulties with phonological awareness tasks. They find it difficult to count syllables, they find it difficult to recognize rhyme, they find it difficult to decide whether words share phonemes, and they find it difficult to substitute one phoneme for another (e.g., Kim & Davis 2004, *Korean*; Wimmer 1996, *German*; Porpodas, Pantelis, & Hantziou 1990, *Greek*; Share & Levin

1999, *Hebrew*). Numerous studies in English in particular have shown that children with developmental dyslexia remain poor at tasks such as deciding whether words rhyme (Bradley & Bryant 1978). They remain poor at making accurate judgments in counting or same–different judgments (Swan & Goswami 1997), at making oddity judgments about phonemes (Bowey, Cain, & Ryan 1992), and at phoneme swapping tasks (Landerl, Wimmer, & Frith 1997). These difficulties persist into the teenage years (e.g., Bruck 1992).

However, for dyslexic children who are learning to read transparent orthographies, reading has an impact on phonological awareness. Learning consistent letter–sound relationships appears to help children to specify phonological similarities and differences between words. For example, German dyslexic children show age-appropriate phonological skills in some phonological awareness tasks (those that can be solved using letters) by the age of 10 years. A Spoonerism task is an example of a phonological awareness task that can be solved using letter–sound knowledge. In Spoonerism tasks, the child has to swap the beginning sounds in words (like Reverend Spooner, who told students "You have hissed all my mystery lectures"). For example, the child may have to say "Dob Bylan" instead of "Bob Dylan". German dyslexic children eventually became able to do such tasks as well as typically developing control children (Wimmer 1993). However, when German dyslexic children are compared to age-matched English dyslexic children, the Germans perform much better in Spoonerism tasks because of their more transparent spelling system (Landerl et al. 1997).

Despite measurable phonological difficulties in children with developmental dyslexia across languages, for most of the world's languages, differences in the *accuracy* of decoding is only found in the very earliest stages of reading. Studies of young German and Greek children who later turned out to have specific reading difficulties showed that word and nonsense word reading was significantly poorer than that of age-matched controls in the first year of reading instruction, but this difference soon disappeared (Porpodas 1999; Wimmer 1993). Although difficulties with phonology remain for children learning to read transparent orthographies, these difficulties do not impede reading accuracy; rather, they impede reading *speed* and *spelling* accuracy. Developmental dyslexia in most languages other than English is usually diagnosed on the basis of extremely slow and effortful reading, and strikingly poor spelling.

For English children, however, developmental dyslexia is characterized by both inaccurate and effortful reading and by inaccurate spelling. Even dyslexic adults in English remain poor at decoding words accurately (Bruck

1992). Hence the same cognitive phonological deficit can manifest differently in different languages. In fact, English children with developmental dyslexia perform significantly more poorly in tasks such as nonsense word reading compared to German children with developmental dyslexia, even when they are trying to read the same items (e.g., nonsense words such as "grall"; see Landerl et al., 1997). This demonstrates the pervasive effects of learning to read an inconsistent orthography on reading development. The consequences of having a phonological deficit are more profound in developmental terms for literacy in English.

Implications for Education: Phonological Interventions
Current early screening tools for identifying developmental dyslexia are relatively ineffective, generating many false positives. However, we know that effective interventions for developmental dyslexia are based on phonology. The most effective interventions are thus likely to be *generic* interventions that develop excellent phonological skills in *all* children during the early years. Such generic intervention can then be followed by differentiated interventions for those most at risk. For example, teachers can be trained to recognize children who are unresponsive to generic enrichment, thereby identifying those with likely learning difficulties. These children could then receive more specific interventions such as individualized treatments. For phonological difficulties and literacy, early generic intervention with later individualized and differentiated intervention seems likely to offer the highest return on educational investment.

Targeted phonological interventions that include teaching children about letters across languages generally are effective in improving developmental dyslexia (mean effect size 0.67, Bus & van IJzendoorn 1999). Many interventions considered by Bus and van IJzendoorn were for school-aged children, but they reported greater effects for preschool children. The effects can be considerable. For example, a successful generic phonology-based intervention in German with younger pre-reading children (the 20-week program "Hearing, Listening, Learning" developed by Schneider and his colleagues, which is delivered by German kindergarten teachers), reported an effect size of 0.57 for spelling development by Grade 2, with a smaller effect size for reading (0.26; see Schneider, Roth, & Ennemoser 2000). Further studies by Schneider and his colleagues have revealed similar enhancement of reading and spelling following phonological training for migrant children from other language backgrounds, and also for children with spoken language difficulties. Importantly, the phonological training for the migrant children was delivered in the mother tongue (e.g., Turkish migrant children received oral language interventions in Turkish, and this had an impact on learning to read in German). Phonological interventions with older at-risk children in English also show large effect sizes (0.69), which translate into gains of around 7 standardized score points in reading (Hatcher et al. 2006). These studies suggest that phonological interventions that link phonological training to letter–sound relations offer an important tool for early educational intervention.

Parents and the home environment also play a crucial role in literacy development. Connor et al. (2004) estimated that the family environment was the major source of the variability in children's literacy skills at school entry. The learning environment provided by the home influences both phonological development (e.g., via oral language practices in the home such as nursery rhymes and singing) and how much exposure to print the child receives (e.g., the number of books in the home, parental valuation of literacy, etc.). Unsurprisingly, therefore, interventions that are designed to introduce books into the home and to demonstrate optimal "shared reading" practices are also effective in fostering early literacy skills (e.g., Whitehurst et al. 1994). Typical effect sizes are about 0.50, which is medium to large. Interventions that involve shared reading enhance the spoken language that caregivers use with young children as well as providing exposure to print. The spoken language input is important, as overall language skills (vocabulary development and use of complex language) as well as phonological awareness and letter knowledge are extremely strong predictors of later literacy. Effective shared reading program also teach caregivers to use books as a starting point for dialogue. The books thereby increase the complexity of the language used with the child and also make the parent more responsive to the interests of the child ("responsive contingency," Bornstein & Tamis-LeMonda 1989). Responsive contingency is also an important predictor of later independent learning. Hence, interactions around books affect more than the developmental trajectory for later literacy learning: These interactions also affect memory and conceptual development, and the development of social cognition and reasoning skills, as well as the child's ability to manage his or her own behavior.

Chapter Conclusion

The research reviewed here illustrates some of the developmental trajectories that make early language acquisition so critical for later school achievement. Word learning (vocabulary development) is exponential in early childhood. Using the "Child Language Checklist" (now translated into 12 languages), Fenson et al. (1994) showed that median English spoken vocabulary size was 55 words by 16 months of age, 225 words by 23 months, 573 words by 30 months, and 6000 words by age 6. Comprehension vocabulary at age 6 is around 14,000 words (Dollaghan 1994). However, the developmental range can be enormous. For example, at 2 years, the range in word production was from 0 words to more than 500 words (Fenson et al. 1994). New-word learning is extremely rapid, with around 10 new words acquired daily at age 2. Clearly, talking to children and enriching their language experiences via books and other media can play an important role in enhancing later achievement. Most important of all, language is symbolic. This symbolic system enables children to detach themselves from the immediate situation, enabling cognition itself to become the object of thought and reflection. The long-lasting and pervasive effects on memory, reasoning, self-regulation, and theory of mind mean that enhancing early language enhances the child's entire cognitive repertoire.

Acknowledgments

Preparation of this chapter was supported by grants from the National Institute of Health (HD030410 to Waxman) and the Medical Research Council (G0400574 to Goswami). We are indebted to the parents who agreed to have their infants and children participate in the experiments we have described and to the members of our respective labs for their dedication and discoveries. Finally, thanks to Erin Leddon and Jennifer Woodring for editorial assistance.

REFERENCES

Ahn, W. & Luhmann, C. C. (2004). Demystifying theory-based categorization. In L. Gershkoff-Stowe & D. Rakison (Eds.), *Building object categories in developmental time* (pp. 277–300). Mahwah, NJ: Lawrence Erlbaum Associates.

Akhtar, N. & Tomasello, M. (1996). Two-year-olds learn words for absent objects and actions. *British Journal of Developmental Psychology*, **14**, 79–93.

Arunachalam, S. & Waxman, S.R (2010). Meaning from syntax: Evidence from 2-year-olds. *Cognition*, **114**(3), 442–446.

Baayen, R. H., Piepenbrock, R., & van Rijn, H. (1993). *The CELEX lexical database (CD-ROM)*. Philadelphia: Linguistic Data Consortium, University of Pennsylvania.

Baillargeon, R. (2000). How do infants learn about the physical world? In D. Muir & A. Slater (Eds.), *Infant development: The essential readings. Essential readings in development psychology* (pp. 195–212). Malden, MA: Blackwell.

Balaban, M. T. & Waxman, S. R. (1997). Do words facilitate object categorization in 9-month-old infants? *Journal of Experimental Child Psychology*, **64**(1), 3–26.

Baldwin, D. A. & Baird, J. A. (1999). Action analysis: A gateway to intentional inference. In P. Rochat (Ed.), *Early social cognition: Understanding others in the first months of life* (pp. 215–240). Mahwah, NJ: Lawrence Erlbaum Associates.

Baldwin, D. A. & Markman, E. M. (1989). Establishing word-object relations: A first step. *Child Development*, **60**(2), 381–398.

Barsalou, L. W., Santos, A., Simmons, W. K., & Wilson, C. D. (2008). Language and simulation in conceptual processing. In M. De Vega, A. M. Glenberg, & A. C. Graesser (Eds.). *Symbols, embodiment, and meaning* (pp. 245–283). Oxford: Oxford University Press.

Berndt, R. S., Reggia, J. A., & Mitchum, C. C. (1987). Empirically derived probabilities for grapheme-to-phoneme correspondences in English. *Behavior Research Methods, Instruments, & Computers*, **19**, 1–9.

Booth, A. E. & Waxman, S. R. (2009). A horse of a different color: Specifying with precision infants' mappings of novel nouns and adjectives. *Child Development*, **80**(1), 15–22.

Bornstein, M. & Tamis-LeMonda, C. S. (1989). Maternal responsiveness and cognitive development in children. In M. H. Bornstein (Ed.), *Maternal responsiveness, characteristics and consequences*. San Francisco: Jossey-Bass.

Bornstein, M. H., Cote, L. R., Maital, S., Painter, K., Park, S.-Y., & Pascual, L. (2004). Cross-linguistic analysis of vocabulary in young children: Spanish, Dutch, French, Hebrew, Italian, Korean, and American English. *Child Development*, **75**(4), 1115–1139.

Bowey, J. A., Cain, M. T., & Ryan, S. M. (1992). A reading-level design study of phonological skills underlying fourth grade children's word reading difficulties. *Child Development*, **63**, 999–1011.

Bradley, L. & Bryant, P. E. (1978). Difficulties in auditory organization as a possible cause of reading backwardness. *Nature*, **271**, 746–747.

Bruck, M. (1992). Persistence of dyslexics' phonological awareness deficits. *Developmental Psychology*, **28**, 874–886.

Bunger, A. & Lidz, J. (2004). Syntactic bootstrapping and the internal structure of causative events. Proceedings of the 28th Annual Boston University Conference on Language Development. Somerville, MA: Cascadilla Press.

Buresh, J., Wilson-Brune, C., & Woodward, A. L. (2006). Prelinguistic action knowledge and the birth of verbs. In K. Hirsh-Pasek & R. M. Golinkoff (Eds), *Action meets word* (pp. 208–227). Oxford: Oxford University Press.

Bus, A. G. & vanIJzendoorn, M. H. (1999). Phonological awareness and early reading: A meta-analysis of experimental training studies. *Journal of Educational Psychology*, **91**(3), 403–414.

Casasola, M. & Cohen, L. B. (2000). Infants' association of linguistic labels with causal actions. *Developmental Psychology*, **36**(2), 155–168.

Clements, G. N. (1990). The role of the sonority cycle in core syllabification. In J. Kingston & M. E. Beckman (Eds.), *Papers in laboratory phonology 1: Between the grammar and physics of speech* (pp. 283–333). Cambridge: Cambridge University Press.

Connor, C. M., Morrison, F. J., & Katch, L. E. (2004). Beyond the reading wars: Exploring the effect of child-instruction interactions on growth in early reading. *Scientific Studies of Reading*, **8**(4), 305–336.

Content, A., Mousty, P., & Radeau, M. (1990). BRULEX: A computerized lexical data base for the French language/BRULEX. *Une base de donnees lexicales informatisee pour le francais ecrit et parle. Annee Psychologique*, **90**(4), 551–566.

De Cara, B. & Goswami, U. (2002). Statistical analysis of similarity relations among spoken words: Evidence for the special status of rimes in English. *Behavioural Research Methods and Instrumentation*, **34**(3), 416–423.

Dollaghan, C. A. (1994). Children's phonological neighbourhoods: Half empty or half full? *Journal of Child Language*, **21**, 257–271.

Durgunoglu, A. Y. (2006). Learning to read in Turkish. *Developmental Science*, **9**, 437–438.

Durgunoglu, A. Y. & Oney, B. (1999). A cross-linguistic comparison of phonological awareness and word recognition. *Reading & Writing*, **11**, 281–299.

Fennell, C. & Waxman, S. R. (2010). What paradox? Referential cues allow for infant use of phonetic detail in word learning. *Child Development*, **81**(5), 1376–1383.

Fenson, L., Dale, P. S., Reznick, J. S., Bates, E., Thal, D., & Pethick, S. (1994). Variability in early communicative development. *Monographs of the Society for Research in Child Development*, **59**(5), Serial no. 242.

Fernald, A., Taeschner, T., Dunn, J., Papousek, M., Boysson-Bardies, B., & Fukui, I. (1989). A cross-language study of prosodic modifications in mothers' and fathers' speech to preverbal infants. *Journal of Child Language*, **16**, 477–501.

Fernandes, K. J., Marcus, G. F., DiNubila, J. A., & Vouloumanos, A. (2006). From semantics to syntax and back again: Argument structure in the third year of life. *Cognition*, **100**, B10–B20.

Ferry, A. L., Hespos, S. J., & Waxman, S. R. (2010). Categorization in 3- and 4-month-old Infants: An advantage of words over tones. *Child Development*, **81**, 472–479.

Fisher, C. (2002). Structural limits on verb mapping: The role of abstract structure in 2.5-year-olds' interpretations of novel verbs. *Developmental Science*, **5**, 56–65.

Fisher, C., Hall, G., Rakowitz, S., & Gleitman, L. (1994). When it is better to receive than to give: Structural and cognitive factors in acquiring a first vocabulary. *Lingua*, **92**, 333–376.

Gelman, S. A. (2006). Early conceptual development. In K. McCartney & D. Phillips (Eds.), *Blackwell handbook of early childhood development* (pp. 149–166). Malden, MA: Blackwell.

Gelman, S. A. & Kalish, C. W. (2006). Conceptual development. In W. Damon & R. M. Lerner (Series Eds.), & D. Kuhn & R. S. Siegler (Vol. Eds.), *Handbook of child psychology: Vol. 2 cognition, perception, and language* (6th ed., pp. 687–733). Hoboken, NJ: Wiley.

Gentner, D. & Namy, L. (1999). Comparison in the development of categories. *Cognitive Development*, **14**, 487–513.

Gergely, G., Nádasdy, Z., Csibra, G., & Bíró, S. (1995). Taking the intentional stance at 12 months of age. *Cognition*, **56**, 165–193.

Gertner, Y., Fisher, C., & Eisengart, J. (2006). Learning words and rules: Abstract knowledge of word order in early sentence comprehension. *Psychological Science*, **17**, 684–691.

Gleitman, L. (1990). The structural sources of verb meanings. *Language Acquisition: A Journal of Developmental Linguistics*, **1**(1), 3–55.

Gleitman, L. R., Cassidy, K., Nappa, R., Papafragou, A., & Trueswell, J. C. (2005). Hard words. *Language Learning and Development*, **1**(1), 23–64.

Golinkoff, R. M. & Hirsh-Pasek, K. (2006). Introduction: Progress on the verb learning front. In K. Hirsh-Pasek & R. M. Golinkoff (Eds.), *Action meets word: How children learn verbs* (pp. 3–28). NewYork: Oxford University Press.

Gomez, R. (2002). Variability and detection of invariant structure. *Psychological Science*, **13**, 431–436.

Goswami, U. & Ziegler, J. C. (2006). Fluency, phonology and morphology: A response to the commentaries on Becoming Literate in Different Languages. *Developmental Science*, **9**, 451–453.

Harris, M. & Giannouli, V. (1999). Learning how to read and spell in Greek: The importance of letter knowledge and morphological awareness. In M. Harris & G. Hatano (Eds.), *Learning to read and write: A cross-linguistic perspective* (pp. 41–70). Cambridge: Cambridge University Press

Hart, B. H. and Risley, T. R. 1995. *Meaningful differences in the everyday experience of young American children.* Baltimore, MD: Paul H. Brookes.

Hatcher, P. J., Hulme, C., Miles, J. N. V., Carroll, J. M., Hatcher, J., Gibbs, S., Smith, G., Bowyer-Crane, C., & Snowling, M. J. (2006). Efficacy of small-group reading intervention for beginning readers with reading delay: A randomized controlled trial. *Journal of Child Psychology & Psychiatry*, **47**, 820–827.

Hirsh-Pasek, K., Golinkoff, R., & Naigles, L. (1996). Young children's use of syntactic frames to derive meaning. In K. Hirsh-Pasek & R. M. Golinkoff (Eds.), *The origins of grammar.* Cambridge, MA: MIT Press.

Hoien, T., Lundberg, L., Stanovich, K. E., & Bjaalid, I. K. (1995). Components of phonological awareness. *Reading & Writing*, **7**, 171–188.

Huttenlocher, J., Vasilyeva, M., Cymerman, E., & Levine, S. (2002). Language input and child syntax. *Cognitive Psychology*, **45**, 337–374.

Imai, M., Lianjing L., Haryu, E., Okada, H., Hirsh-Pasek, K., Golinkoff, R. M., & Shigematsu, J. (2008). Novel noun and verb learning in Chinese-, English-, and Japanese-speaking children. *Child Development*, **79**, 979–1000.

Jaswal, V. K. (2004). Don't believe everything you hear: Preschoolers' sensitivity to speaker intent in category induction. *Child Development*, **75**, 1871–1885.

Jusczyk, P. & Aslin, R. N. (1995). Infants' detection of the sound patterns of words in fluent speech. *Cognitive Psychology*, **29**(1), 1–23.

Keates, J. & Graham, S. A. (2008). Category labels or attributes: Why do labels guide infants' inductive inferences? *Psychological Science*, **19**, 1287–1293.

Kemler Nelson, D. G., Hirsh-Pasek, K., Jusczyk, P. W., & Cassidy, K. W. (1989). How the prosodic cues in motherese might assist language learning. *Journal of Child Language*, **16**(1), 55–68.

Kersten, A. W. & Smith, L. B. (2002). Attention to novel objects during verb learning. *Child Development*, **73**(1), 93–109.

Kim, J. & Davis, C. (2004). Characteristics of poor readers of Korean Hangul: Auditory, visual and phonological processing. *Reading and Writing*, **17**(1–2), 153–185.

Landau, B. & Gleitman, L. (1985). *Language and experience: Evidence from the blind child.* Cambridge, MA: Harvard University Press.

(1994). Object shape, object name, and object kind: Representation and development. In D. L. Medin (Ed.), *The psychology of learning and motivation: Advances in research and theory* (Vol. 31, pp. 253–304). San Diego, CA: Academic Press.

Landauer, T. K., & Streeter, L. A. (1973). Structural differences between common and rare words: Failure of equivalence assumptions for theories of word recognition. *Journal of Verbal Learning and Verbal Behaviour*, **12**, 119–131.

Landerl, K., Wimmer, H., & Frith, U. (1997) The impact of orthographic consistency on dyslexia: A German-English comparison. *Cognition*, **63**, 315–334.

Landry, S. H. (2005). *Effective early childhood programs: Turning knowledge into Action*. University of Texas Houston Health Science Center, Houston, Texas.

Lehiste, I. (1977) *Suprasegmentals*. Cambridge, MA/London: M.I.T. Press.

Leslie, A. M. & Keeble, S. (1987). Do six-month-old infants perceive causality? *Cognition*, **25**, 265–288.

Liberman, I. Y., Shankweiler, D., Fischer, F. W., & Carter, B. (1974). Explicit syllable and phoneme segmentation in the young child. *Journal of Experimental Child Psychology*, **18**, 201–212.

Luce, P.A., & Pisoni, D. B. (1998). Recognising spoken words: The neighbourhood activation model. *Ear & Hearing*, **19**, 1–36.

Macnamara, J. (1994). Logic and cognition. In J. Macnamara & G. E. Reyes (Eds.), *The logical foundations of cognition. Vancouver studies in cognitive science*, Vol. 4 (pp. 11–34). New York: Oxford University Press.

Markman, E. M. (1989). *Categorization and naming in children: Problems of induction*. Cambridge, MA: MIT Press.

Meyer, M., Leonard, S., Hirsh-Pasek, K., Imai, M., Haryu, E., Pulverman, R., & Addy, D. (2003). *Making a convincing argument: A crosslinguistic comparison of noun and verb learning in Japanese and English*. Paper presented at the 28th Annual Boston Conference on Language Development. Boston University, Boston, MA.

Morgan, J. L. & Demuth, K. (Eds.). (1996). *Signal to syntax: Bootstrapping from speech to grammar in early acquisition*. Mahwah, NJ: Lawrence Erlbaum Associates.

Murphy, G. (2004). *The big book of concepts*. Cambridge, MA: MIT Press.

Naigles, L. (1990). Children use syntax to learn verb meanings. *Journal of Child Language*, **17**, 357–374.

(1996). The use of multiple frames in verb learning via syntactic bootstrapping. *Cognition*, **58**, 221–251.

Naigles, L. & Kako, E. (1993). First contact in verb acquisition: Defining a role for syntax. *Child Development*, **64**, 1665–1687.

Pauen, S. & Träuble, B. (2009). How 7-month-olds interpret ambiguous motion events: Category-based reasoning in infancy. *Cognitive Psychology*, **59**(3), 275–295.

Piccin, T. B. & Waxman, S. R. (2007). Why nouns trump verbs in word learning: New evidence from children and adults in the Human Simulation Paradigm. *Language Learning and Development*, **3**(4), 295–323.

Pierrehumbert, J. (2003). Phonetic diversity, statistical learning and acquisition of phonology. *Language & Speech*, **46**, 115–154.

Porpodas, C. D., Pantelis, S. N., & Hantziou, E. (1990). Phonological and lexical encoding processes in beginning readers: Effects of age and word characteristics. *Reading and Writing*, **2**, 197–208.

Porpodas, C. D. (1999). Patterns of phonological and memory processing in beginning readers and spellers of Greek. *Journal of Learning Disabilities, 32,* 406–416.

Port, R. (2007). How are words stored in memory? Beyond phones and phonemes. *New Ideas in Psychology, 25,* 143–170.

Pruden, S. M., Hirsh-Pasek, K., Maguire, M. J., & Meyer, M. A. (2004). Foundations of verb learning: Infants form categories of path and manner in motion events. In A. Brugos, L. Micciulla & C. E. Smith (Eds.), *Proceedings of 28th annual Boston University Conference on language development* (pp. 461–472). Somerville, MA: Cascadilla Press.

Pulverman, R., Hirsh-Pasek, K., Pruden, S., & Golinkoff, R. M. (2006). Precursors to verb learning: Infant attention to manner and path. In K. Hirsh-Pasek & R. M. Golinkoff (Eds.), *Action meets word: How children learn verbs* (pp. 134–160). New York: Oxford University Press.

Schneider, W., Roth, E., & Ennemoser, M. (2000). Training phonological skills and letter knowledge in children at-risk for dyslexia: A comparison of three kindergarten intervention programs. *Journal of Educational Psychology, 92,* 284– 295.

Seymour, P. H. K., Aro, M., & Erskine, J. M. (2003). Foundation literacy acquisition in European orthographies. *British Journal of Psychology, 94,* 143–174.

Share, D. & Levin, I. (1999). Learning to read and write in Hebrew. In M. Harris & G. Hatano (Eds.), *Learning to read and write: A cross-linguistic perspective* (pp. 89–111). New York: Cambridge University Press.

Shi, R. & Werker, J. F. (2003). The basis of preference for lexical words in 6-month-old infants. *Developmental Science, 6*(5), 484–488.

Sommerville, J. A., Woodward, A. L., & Needham A. (2005). Action experience alters 3-month-old infants' perception of others' actions. *Cognition, 96,* B1–B11.

Spelke, E. S. (2000). Nativism, empiricism, and the origins of knowledge. In D. Muir & A. Slater (Eds.), *Infant development: The essential readings. Essential readings in development psychology* (pp. 36–51). Malden, MA: Blackwell.

Swan, D., & Goswami, U. (1997). Phonological awareness deficits in developmental dyslexia and the phonological representations hypothesis. *Journal of Experimental Child Psychology, 66*(1), 18–41.

Treiman, R. (1998). Beginning to spell in English. In C. Hulme & R. M. Joshi (Eds.), *Reading and spelling: Development and disorders* (pp. 371–393). Mahwah, NJ: Lawrence Erlbaum Associates.

Treiman, R. & Zukowski, A. (1991). Levels of phonological awareness. In S. Brady & D. Shankweiler (Eds.), *Phonological processes in literacy.* Hillsdale, NJ: Erlbaum.

Vihman. M. & Croft, W. (2007). Phonological development: Towards a "radical" templatic phonology. *Linguistics, 45,* 683–725.

Wagner, L. & Carey, S. (2005). 12-month-old infants represent probable endings of motion events. *Infancy, 7*(1), 73–83.

Waxman, S. R. & Booth, A. E. (2001). Seeing pink elephants: Fourteen-month-olds' interpretations of novel nouns and adjectives. *Cognitive Psychology, 43*(3), 217–242.

(2003). The origins and evolution of links between word learning and conceptual organization: New evidence from 11-month-olds. *Developmental Science, 6*(2), 130–137.

Waxman, S. R. & Braun, I. E. (2005). Consistent (but not variable) names as invitations to form object categories: New evidence from 12-month-old infants. *Cognition, 95,* B59–B68.

Waxman, S. R. & Gelman, S. A. (2009). Early word-learning entails reference, not merely associations. *Trends in Cognitive Sciences*, **13**(6), 258–263.

Waxman, S. R. & Lidz, J. (2006). Early word learning. In D. Kuhn & R. Siegler (Eds.), *Handbook of child psychology*, Vol. 2 (6th ed.). Hoboken, NJ: John Wiley & Sons.

Waxman, S. R. & Markow, D. B. (1995). Words as invitations to form categories: Evidence from 12- to 13-month-old infants. *Cognitive Psychology*, **29**(3), 257–302.

(1998). Object properties and object kind: Twenty-one-month-old infants' extension of novel adjectives. *Child Development*, **69**(5), 1313–1329.

Waxman, S. R., Lidz, J. L., Braun, I. E., & Lavin, T. (2009). 24-month-old infants' interpretations of novel verbs and nouns in dynamic scenes. *Cognitive Psychology*, **59**(1), 67–95.

Welder, A. N. & Graham, S. A. (2006). Infants' categorization of novel objects with more or less obvious features. *Cognitive Psychology*, **52**, 57–91.

Werker, J. F., Lloyd, V. L., Pegg, J. E., & Polka, L. (1996). Putting the baby in the bootstraps: Toward a more complete understanding of the role of the input in infant speech processing. In J. L. Morgan & K. Demuth (Eds.), *Signal to syntax: Bootstrapping from speech to grammar in early acquisition* (pp. 427–447). Mahwah, NJ: Lawrence Erlbaum Associates.

Whitehurst, G. J. et al. (1994). A picture book reading intervention in day care and home for children from low-income families. *Developmental Psychology*, **30**, 679–689.

Wimmer, H. (1993). Characteristics of developmental dyslexia in a regular writing system. *Applied Psycholinguistics*, **14**, 1–33.

(1996). The nonword reading deficit in developmental dyslexia: Evidence from children learning to read German. *Journal of Experimental Child Psychology*, **61**, 80–90.

Wimmer, H., Landerl, K., Linortner, R., & Hummer, P. (1991). The relationship of phonemic awareness to reading acquisition: More consequence than precondition but still important. *Cognition*, **40**, 219–249.

Xu, F. & Carey, S. (1996). Infants' metaphysics: The case of numerical identity. *Cognitive Psychology*, **30**(2), 111–153.

Ziegler, J. C. & Goswami, U. (2005). Reading acquisition, developmental dyslexia and skilled reading across languages: A psycholinguistic grain size theory. *Psychological Bulletin*, **131**(1), 3–29.

(2006). Becoming literate in different languages: Similar problems, different solutions. *Developmental Science*, **9**, 429–453.

Ziegler, J. C., Stone, G. O., & Jacobs, A. M. (1997). What's the pronunciation for -OUGH and the spelling for /u/? A database for computing feedforward and feedback inconsistency in English. *Behavior Research Methods, Instruments, & Computers*, **29**, 600–618.

6   Infant Cognitive Functioning and Mental Development

Marc H. Bornstein and John Colombo

... childhood shews the man ...
John Milton (1608–1674), *Paradise Regained (1671), Book 4, line 220.*

This chapter provides an overview of infancy studies that bear on the prediction of future mental development. It does so in the framework of a developmental perspective on information processing. The chapter is organized as follows. First, we review prominent methods and measures of studying cognition in infants. Our focus falls primarily on one measure of infant information processing, visual habituation – the decline in infant attention to stimulation that is increasingly familiar. Measurement studies of the procedural and psychometric characteristics of habituation show robust individual variation and adequate short-term reliability. Arguments for the interpretation of habituation as information processing and as an indicator of infant cognitive functioning are then evaluated. Second, the interpretation of habituation as a measure of cognition is supported with evidence from studies of its concurrent and predictive validity. The predictive ability of habituation in infancy for childhood cognitive performance is reviewed, along with assessments of alternative interpretations in exogenous and endogenous sources. Before we conclude, we raise and address some open questions and some possible fertile future directions in the field.

Methods and Measures of Infant Cognitive Functioning

Although they do not always appear so, even very young infants have an active mental life. They are constantly learning and developing new ideas, and they do so in many different ways. Although not the traditional view, it now appears that the capacities infants demonstrate in learning have consequences for their later development.

Traditional Infant Tests and Their Critics.   Baby biographies of the 19th century constituted the first close published examinations of infants, and the evidence developed from those records had two important implications. First, infants of different ages showed themselves to be competent at a variety of tasks, and, second, baby biographies revealed wide variation among infants of the same age, suggesting that individual infants vary among themselves in motor skills, temperament, and other characteristics. The early 20th century witnessed several attempts in Europe and in the United States to develop standardized tests for infants, and for years these sequences, scales, and schedules (e.g., Bayley, Buhler and Hetzer, Cattell, Gesell, Griffiths, Shirley, and Užgiris and Hunt) proved valuable in defining normative infant development. These traditional infant tests have since evolved as valuable screening tools, useful for diagnostic and clinical purposes. Typically, they represent the infant's developmental status as an aggregate score (the average obtained across different developmental domains).

For the most part, traditional infant tests were modeled after Binet-type assessments originally developed for older children, and they were strongly influenced by the idea of a general or unitary factor of intelligence. In infants, however, there is no obvious external index with which to compare test performance to assess validity. The validity of infant tests has typically been evaluated by documenting the association between infants' performance early in life with their performance years later as children or adults. The presumption in this time-lagged comparison is that, if individuals who perform well on infant tests also do well on standardized intelligence tests later, then the original tests may constitute assessments of "intelligence" in infancy. This general approach relies on the predictive validity of the infant measures.

However, the predictive validities of infant tests have consistently proved poor in normal populations (Bornstein & Sigman 1986; Colombo 1993; Fagan & Singer 1983; Kopp & McCall 1980; but see Siegel 1989). Bayley's (1949) classic longitudinal study exemplifies both the findings and conclusions that characterize the early tradition in infant testing. Bayley followed 27 Berkeley Growth Study children from the first 3 months of life to 18 years of age and then correlated their scores on her California First-Year Mental Scale (later the Bayley Scales of Infant Development (BSID)) with their intelligence test scores in young adulthood. Bayley found essentially no correlation between test performance in the first 3 to 4 years of life and intelligence test performance at 18 years. Only after children reached about 6 to 7 years of age (when they were taking the Stanford-Binet) did the correlation between child scores and eventual adult scores rise to a respectable .68, eventually reaching about ~.85 between 11 and 18 years. Subsequent studies have shown that developmental tests, such as the BSID, administered to children older than 12 months possess somewhat higher predictive power than do tests administered during the first year; predictive relations are generally stronger for high-risk and developmentally challenged infants than for typically developing infants; and infant scores may predict some kinds of nonverbal performance as opposed to intelligence (e.g., Blaga et al. 2009; Humphreys & Davey 1988; Siegel 1989). With a few exceptions, however, scores achieved in the first year of life on traditional infant tests fail to provide meaningful information about later intelligence.

The lack of predictive validity of traditional infant tests led to several significant broad conclusions about a central general question of the development of cognition from infancy. Some theorists opined that this finding reflects the lack of a stable general intelligence factor in mental life. Others argued that, if such a factor exists, it is not fixed or stable across the early part of the life span. Still others contended that mental growth follows a stage-like progression wherein intelligence in infancy differs qualitatively from intelligence in maturity; under this latter model, variation in infancy would therefore not represent stable individual differences, but rather temporary variations in stage progression. These interpretations of human mental development differ from one another, but all are based on the same data showing a lack of cross–age predictability of intelligence from traditional infant tests.

That there is little or no prediction in mental development from infancy based on traditional infant tests has also been challenged on several grounds, however. Many sources of variance could contribute to attenuating a relation between an initial assessment of a person in infancy and a later assessment in childhood or beyond. First, traditional infant tests are themselves not particularly reliable; that is, infant performance on one of these tests at one time does not accurately predict infant performance on the same test just a short time later. Perhaps infancy is a period of rapid "fits and starts" in development; or infants are simply underdeveloped, undermotivated, and underregulated, so that unreliability of performance is inherent to this early phase of life. Statistically speaking, as Spearman noted, unreliability places inexorable limits on predictive validity (Cohen et al. 2003). Second, the kinds of items put to young infants in traditional tests largely tap sensory capacities, the attainment of motor milestones, and responses of questionable cognitive content (e.g., reaching and smiling). Many also rely on imitation of simple actions. Very different items are used in evaluating developing or mature intelligence, such as skills related to language, reasoning, and memory. Thus, the underlying constructs or domains assessed at the two ages bear little or no conceptual relation to one another (Colombo 1993). In essence, children are asked such different "questions" at the different developmental periods that there is little reason to expect individual stability between infant performance on traditional developmental tests and child performance on subsequent intelligence tests. Third, reasons external to individual stability could account for the low age-to-age correlations between infant tests and later intelligence tests; infancy might well represent a stage of extreme susceptibility to environmental influence and experience, so that expressions of infant abilities change rapidly. In essence, it could be that there actually is little or no predictive validity of intelligence from infancy. However, it would be invalid to accept this null hypothesis about human mental development before trying measures that redress the raft of foregoing criticisms.

In lieu of past evaluations, longitudinal assessments of cognitive predictability beginning in infancy might rather assess basic skills such as information processing or mental representation that underlie intelligence and do so in ways that are psychometrically sound; that transcend sensory ability and are relatively free of motor requirements, affective components, and imitation; and that conceptually parallel or serve as foundations for cognitive functions in childhood. In modern systems theory, development is conceived to consist of hierarchically organized characteristics that incorporate earlier emerging ones and increasingly differentiate over time. Moreover, for a developmental process that is both mediated and distal, such as that between information processing in infancy and cognition later in development, tests of indirect paths may be more sensitive, powerful, and theoretically appropriate than tests of simple direct relations (Shrout & Bolger 2002). Intelligence reflects efficiency of a variety of information-processing and mental-representation skills (Cooper & Regan 1986; Dempster 1991; Hunt 1983; see Sternberg 1985). Anderson (1992), among others (Jensen 1992), theorized about the association between measures of information processing and IQ test performance, and diverse measures of reaction time and inspection time (information-processing capacity) correlate with adult IQ in the range of ~ -.30 to ~ -.50 (Deary et al., 2001; Sheppard, 2008). Speed of processing is a pervasive individual-differences factor and component of childhood cognition (Hale 1990; Kail 1991; Nettelbeck 1987; Nettelbeck &

Young 1989, 1990), and processing speed may be "necessary for the appropriate development of intellectual aptitudes" even if not sufficient to determine them (Nettelbeck & Wilson 1994, p. 279). In a developmental study of 7- to 19-year-olds, Fry and Hale (1996) showed that individual differences in speed of information processing exerted a direct effect on working memory, which in turn was a direct determinant of individual differences in fluid intelligence.

Information Processing and Attention

Information processing draws on attention, traditionally viewed as a key factor in the expression of intelligence (Deary 2012; Stankov 1983; Vernon 1987) as well as achievement test scores and grades in school (Alexander, Entwisle, & Dauber 1993; Raver et al. 2005). Using six longitudinal data sets, Duncan et al. (2007) estimated links between three key elements of school readiness – academic, attention, and socioemotional skills – and later school reading and math achievement. Across all studies, attention skills were among the strongest predictors of later achievement. One explanation for this predictive power is that attention skills increase the time children engage and participate in learning activities.

Investigators have long used measures of attention to capture two meaningful indices of information processing in human infants: the rapidity with which attention declines to, or is withdrawn from, an unchanging aspect of the environment (*habituation*), and recovery of attention to some novel aspect of the environment (*novelty responsiveness*). The first of these constructs is indexed by the amount or rate of decay in looking infants give a stimulus that is repeated or is available constantly. Loosely stated, infants who acquire information from the environment more quickly have presumably processed the information more efficiently. Thus, greater decrements, quicker decays, and lower total looking times generally have been considered as indices of more efficient information processing in infants. Recovery of attention is indexed by infants' looking at new information compared with familiar information. Relatively more looking at novel stimuli, and less looking at familiar stimuli, are also generally believed to index efficient information processing on the grounds that infants who have processed the information, and are now familiar with it, ought to recognize that information later and attend to it less, but discriminate new information from the now familiar, attending to it more.

Decrement, look duration, and recovery of attention are believed to encompass the classic components of attention in infants: selection, engagement, disengagement, encoding, and retention of information in

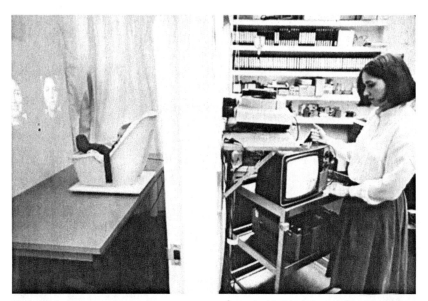

Figure 6.1. The experimental arrangements of a typical habituation study with infants.

the environment. These are all processes that are involved in the construction of some sort of central mental representation of stimulus information and the continuing comparison between incoming information with that mental representation. So, it may be that the sensory, motor, affective, and imitative capacities captured by traditional infant tests do not relate conceptually or empirically to later intelligence, but selection, encoding, and retention processes, presumably measured by attention, could relate to language, reasoning, problem solving, and memory skills that are assessed on tests of intelligence. The balance of this chapter explores their proposition using habituation in typically developing children.

Habituation

Sit a baby in an infant seat, show the baby a stimulus, and observe and record the baby's looking (Figure 6.1). When the stimulus first appears, the baby will normally orient and attend to it. If, however, the same stimulus is made available continuously or is presented repeatedly, the baby's attention to it usually wanes. This decrement in attention in infancy has been likened to the phenomenon of habituation that has been studied widely in the behavioral sciences (Colombo & Mitchell 2009; Rankin et al. 2009).

Formally, researchers have almost universally adopted an infant–control procedure to implement habituation (Bornstein 1985a). Here a single infant look is the unit of analysis, and a stimulus is presented to the infant for the duration that the infant looks at it. The mean of the infant's initial (e.g., first 2 or so) looks is calculated to compute a baseline, and succeeding looks are tracked until a criterion (e.g., 2 or so) successive looks less than or equal to one-half of the baseline is reached. In practice, habituation is typically indexed quantitatively by temporal measures of duration and rate of looking, including the longest or peak look, the cumulative time the infant looks before the habituation criterion is reached, the decrement in looking, the slope, and the number of looks to habituation criterion (Figure 6.2). Of course, it could be that the decrement in infant attention reflects general changes in state, in receptor adaptation, or in effector fatigue, but experimental controls are normally put into place to rule out these alternative interpretations (Bertenthal, Haith, & Campos 1983; Bornstein 1985a).

Habituation has proved to be an important individual-differences variable among infants. In this respect, it has been found to satisfy two prerequisite psychometric criteria reasonably well. Habituation is characterized by adequate individual variation, and it has been shown to be a moderately reliable infant behavior at least over the short term. On the first criterion, from a qualitative view some infants show a linear or exponential decrease in habituation to criterion; other infants first increase then decrease looking; and still other infants show a fluctuating looking pattern (Bornstein & Benasich 1986). This qualitative perspective on habituation is supported by quantitative measures of duration and magnitude. For example, infants who habituate in a linear or exponential fashion require about one-half the accumulated looking time to reach a constant criterion as increase–decrease and fluctuating infants, who require approximately equivalent amounts of time. The range of individual variation for common habituation variables is substantial (Colombo et al. 2004).

A number of studies of the second psychometric criterion of habituation, short-term reliability, have also been conducted. The reliability of habituation has been investigated qualitatively as well as quantitatively. Qualitatively, a nominal scale metric shows significant 10-day test–retest repeatability of habituation pattern (Bornstein & Benasich 1986). More typical are reports of the reliability of quantitative habituation data. Two-day test–retest reliabilities have been reported to exceed .90 (Hood et al. 1996); for longer test–retest durations, reliability naturally attenuates (Colombo & Mitchell 1990; Guttman, 1954; Mayes & Kessen 1989). Variation in reliability of measures of infant habituation can be explained in several ways. For example, estimates can be expected to vary with state of the child, stimulus used, and so forth. Consider, too, that infants at one time in their lives may

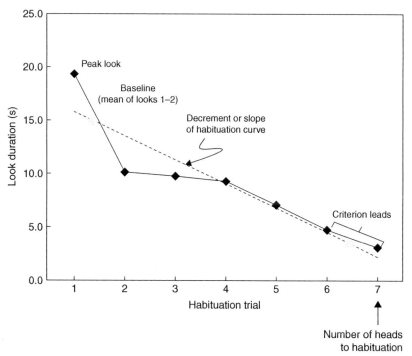

Figure 6.2. Habituation is a process and is characterized multidimensionally by several variables, illustrated in this figure. The average habituation performance of a 5-month-old (from the database for Colombo et al. 2004), who habituated in 7 looks. The figure shows the peak look from the sequence, the criterion looks (which indicate that habituation has occurred), and the decrement or slope of the curve calculated from the baseline (the mean of the first two looks) to criterion (the mean of the last two looks).

process different aspects of the same stimulus than infants do at another time, leading to attenuation of reliability. Furthermore, only one habituation task is normally given to an infant at any one time, and smaller samples are less reliable than larger samples of a behavior. Colombo, Mitchell, and Horowitz (1988) showed that the reliability of infant performance could be improved by combining or aggregating items or tasks.

Habituation *qua* Information Processing
Successful habituation minimally implies neurologic integrity and sensory competence in the infant. Beyond that, habituation represents a form of nonassociative learning (Kandel 2007; Thompson & Spencer 1966; see also Rankin et al. 2009). Habituation is ubiquitous across various levels

of phylogeny (e.g., in *Aplysia*, Kandel 2007; in *C. elegans*, Giles & Rankin 2009), of the nervous system (e.g., in single cells of macaque inferotemporal cortex; Miller, Gochin, & Gross 1991), and of development (e.g., in human fetuses, Hepper & Shahidullah 1992; Leader 1994; Madison, Madison, & Adubato 1986). Aspects of habituation have been interpreted in terms of classical (e.g., Rescorla & Wagner 1972) as well as operant conditioning (e.g., Malcuit, Pomerleau, & Lamarre 1988).

However, the decrement in attention that is habituation is also thought to comprise processes that reflect the infant's passive or active development of some mental representation of stimulus information as well as the infant's ongoing comparison of new information with that representation (Colombo & Mitchell 2009). As a consequence, infant habituation is construed today as (at least) the partial analog in adults of selection, encoding, and retention of information; that is, as information processing. Perhaps habituation in infancy and performance on intelligence tests later in life both reflect efficiency of information processing (Bornstein 1985a, 1989; Colombo 1995). Information processing embraces multiple mental abilities and functions – to detect and discriminate, engage and disengage, encode and store, retrieve and recognize, and compare stimulus information. Thus, infants who habituate efficiently (who require briefer attention deployment to repeated or unchanging stimulation) are infants who scan and pick up information efficiently, detect information easily, encode and store information quickly, and/or retrieve and recognize information from memory faithfully. Children who solve the perceptual, language, reasoning, and memory tasks that are assessed on intelligence tests do likewise (Bjorklund & Schneider 1996; Deary 2012; Detterman 1987; McCall 1994; Nettelbeck 1987; Vernon 1987). That is, IQ presumably reflects efficiency of information processing (Campione, Brown, & Ferrara 1982; Cooper & Regan 1986; Deary 2012) and mental representation skills (Hunt 1983), among other characteristics.

In arriving at this information-processing interpretation, investigators must make intuitions about infant mind, and we therefore require of them considerable evidence. The information-processing interpretation of habituation makes several straightforward predictions in this regard, and there is ample empirical support for each. It is therefore possible to wire a nomological net among age, population, stimulus, mental representation, and validity arguments to support an information-processing interpretation of habituation.

First, on an information-processing interpretation older and more mature babies ought to habituate more efficiently than younger and less mature

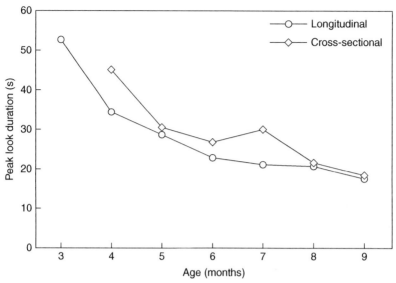

Figure 6.3. Developmental functions for the duration of peak look from the Colombo et al. (2004) database for longitudinal and cross-sectional samples. The two samples do not statistically vary, which indicates that the change across age in the longitudinal sample is a developmental phenomenon, rather than being attributable to repeated measurement or a "practice" effect. (Redrawn with permission from Figure 2 in Colombo et al. 2004)

babies (Colombo et al. 2004; Fantz 1964). Bornstein, Pêcheux, and Lécuyer (1988) recorded total accumulated looking times over weekly habituation sessions in the same infants between 2 and 7 months of age. As they aged across the first year, infants required less and less cumulative exposure to a stimulus to reach a constant habituation criterion. The finding of significant decreases in duration of looking in infants across the initial parts of the first year have been repeated many times (Colombo & Mitchell 2009; Colombo et al. 2004; Courage, Reynolds, & Richards 2006; Shaddy & Colombo 2004; Figure 6.3). There is some ambiguity as to whether looking times continue to decrease beyond the end of the first year (Colombo 2001, 2002; Courage et al. 2006), and this developmental change is a possible consideration in the differential predictive validity of habituation after infancy.

The second prediction of an information-processing interpretation of habituation is related to the first: Normally developing babies ought to habituate more efficiently than babies born at-risk for known cognitive developmental delay. Indeed, preterm infants (Kavšek & Bornstein 2010; Rose, Feldman, & Jankowski 2002; van de Weijer-Bergsma, Wijnroks, &

Jongmans 2008) and children with Down syndrome or brain damage (e.g., micro- or anencephalia) either fail to habituate or habituate relatively inefficiently (Friedman 1975; Hepper & Shahidullah 1992; Lester 1975), as do infants who have been exposed in utero to cocaine (Mayes et al. 1993; Mayes et al. 1995).

The third information-processing prediction is that infants ought to habituate to "simpler" stimuli more efficiently than to more "complex" stimuli. Evidence for this deduction is replete in the literature on perceptual development (Caron & Caron 1969; Colombo, Frick, & Gorman 1997; Maikranz et al. 2001).

Fourth, if habituation involves processing information, infants habituated to one stimulus should later be able to distinguish novel stimulus information in comparison with their mental representation of now-familiar stimulus information. Cognitive or intellectual activity is surely mediated by the brain, and differences in such activity are likely to be reflected in changes in the brain. Slater, Morison, and Rose (1983) habituated newborns to a stimulus, allowing them to use only one eye. On a later test, the babies recovered looking to a new stimulus, compared to the habituation stimulus, when they viewed familiar and novel stimuli through the other eye. This interocular transfer indicates that information about the stimulus acquired via habituation must be processed centrally in the brain.

Validity of Cognition in Infancy

Evidence supporting each of the four foregoing predictions contributes to validating an information-processing interpretation of habituation of attention infants. Further evaluations of habituation as "cognitive" are provided by assessments of its concurrent and predictive validity with respect to other measures of cognition.

As a general rule, developmentalists are interested not only in performance, but also in expressions of stability. As we use the term here, stability describes consistency in the relative ranks of individuals in a group with respect to the expression of some characteristic over time (Bornstein & Bornstein 2008). For example, a stable characteristic would be one that some infants demonstrate at a relatively high level at time 1 and again at a relatively high level at time 2. There are different types of stability. Homotypic stability describes similarity of rank order status on an identical characteristic from time 1 to time 2 (e.g., vocabulary size at 12 months and at 20 months). Heterotypic stability describes similarity of rank order status between two related, but not identical, constructs, related because they presumably share the same underlying process (e.g., vocabulary at 13 months and grammar at 20 months). It could also be that individuals are stable because they maintain their position in a group in terms of their general developmental status, so that at time 1 one child is more developed than a second child, and at time 2 the more-developed child remains ahead of the less-developed child on any given characteristic. Predictive validity is commonly used in the literature to refer to contemporary stability associations as well as to lagged stability associations (such as we have described).

The information-processing interpretation of habituation converges with concurrent individual differences in the normal population. Infants and young children who habituate efficiently explore their environment rapidly, play in relatively more sophisticated ways, solve problems quickly, attain concepts readily, and excel at operant learning, oddity identification, picture matching, and block configuration (for reviews, see Bornstein 1985a; Colombo 1993). Infant attention during habituation relates to visual recognition and discrimination (Frick & Richards 2001; Richards 1997; Shaddy & Colombo 2004).

Moreover, infants with profiles of briefer looking during the first year engage in more extensive stimulus scanning, whereas infants with profiles of longer looking tend to focus for prolonged periods on parts of stimuli (Bronson 1991; see also Jankowski, Rose, & Feldman 2001). Freeseman, Colombo, and Coldren (1993) identified 4-month-olds as short-lookers or long-lookers on the basis of their habituation performance and tested the same children in visual discrimination tasks. Long-looking infants differed from short-looking infants in the speed and nature of their information processing: Short-looking infants required less familiarization with a stimulus to demonstrate a preference for a new stimulus, whereas long-looking infants required more time to process the original stimulus information. Short-looking infants also began by attending to global features and then moved to examine local features as exposure duration increased, a pattern of attention allocation commonly employed by adults. By contrast, long-looking infants focused on local elements during familiarization beyond the time required for discrimination of global features (Colombo et al. 1995). Furthermore, short-looking infants recognized perceptually degraded forms and symmetrical stimuli very quickly, where long-looking infants required more time (Frick & Colombo 1996; Stoecker et al. 1998). Subsequent research showed that the attention of long-looking infants may become fixed ("stuck") on certain visual features (Frick, Colombo, & Saxon 1999).

Most significantly, habituation possesses lagged predictive validity. Since Miller et al. (1976), a substantial body of research has developed that documents that infants who habituate efficiently in the first 6 months of life later, usually between 2 and at least 18 years of age, perform better on assessments of cognitive competence, including standardized psychometric tests of intelligence, measures of representational ability (such as language), and academic achievement. Bornstein et al. (2012) found that habituation at 4 months predicted academic achievement at 14 years, and Sigman, Cohen, and Beckwith (1997) found that (preterm) newborns' fixation duration predicted intelligence and span of apprehension (a speed-of-processing task in which adolescents had to say whether or not a target was present in a tachistoscopically presented array) at 18 years. (Fagan, Holland, and Wheeler, 2007, reported that a measure of memory in infancy predicted academic achievement at 14 years.) A series of meta-analyses of this predictive relation have now been published, including Bornstein and Sigman (1986), Colombo (1993), McCall and Carriger (1993), and most recently Kavšek (2004; and Kavšek & Bornstein 2010, for preterms). Kavšek (2004) included 38 samples from 25 studies. The averaged weighted normalized predictive correlation coefficient (Hedges & Oklin 1985) across studies of habituation in populations of normal infants is about .48; for at-risk samples, it is .36; and for all samples combined, .45. The predictive correlation is not due to extreme scores or random effects, but holds for populations of both normal and at-risk infants across years, samples, ages, laboratories, stimuli, and modalities (including visual and auditory), with different procedures and measures in infancy and childhood. Notably, we know of no correlations that report opposite results. To be fair, of course, we do not know whether (or how many) studies have failed to obtain predictive validity on these infant measures and have fallen into file drawers (Rosenthal 1979). Of course, we also need to interpret effect sizes of these relations taking into consideration both their assumptions and their limitations. For example, there may be subsets of children for whom the relation may be smaller and subsets for whom the relation may be larger. That being said, the available evidence sums to indicate that some infants process information in the habituation paradigm more quickly, needing to look less and reach a habituation criterion more efficiently, and those same children tend to perform better in assessments of cognition, intelligence, and academic achievement.

The degree of prediction between information-processing measures in infancy and cognitive performance in childhood and adolescence reported in these meta-analyses is notably higher than that obtained between traditional infant assessments and later tests of intelligence. This predictive validity could characterize heterotypic stability, if habituation in infancy and later intelligence were related through stability of developmental status or degree of "system integrity" (Deary & Der, 2005), that is if the two did not share any common function(s). More likely, habituation in infancy and cognitive function and intelligence in childhood and adolescence share common characteristics of information processing.

It is important to note that habituation is not an epiphenomenon of laboratory investigation, but is manifest in infants' everyday interactions with people and objects in the world. A study of habituation in naturally occurring, home-based interactions with U.S. American and Japanese infants confirms this (Bornstein & Ludemann 1989). Babies in both cultures habituated, and they were equivalent on measures of habituation. Moreover, quantitative characteristics of habituation at home matched those typically observed in the laboratory. Habituation is thus characteristic of, and similar in, infants growing up in different parts of the world. Furthermore, a case can be made that habituation is broadly adaptive. Not only do infants assimilate environmental information in habituating, but when infants inhibit attending to familiar stimulation, they also liberate attentional and cognitive resources that can then be deployed in new encounters with new stimulation in the environment.

The association between infant habituation performance and childhood cognitive outcome endorses the predictive validity of information processing in early life. Findings of stability from so early in life often in turn entice infancy researchers into believing that endogenous processes may be at work. It would be premature to characterize stability of any infant measure as reflecting shared cognitive processes, however, without considering potential "third variable" roles of other endogenous processes and of exogenous ones rooted in experience and environment. The nature of the longitudinal association is at base correlational, and other endogenous or exogenous variables could theoretically carry or mediate the predictive association.

Exogenous Sources of Stability

Stability in cognitive performance between infancy and maturity might depend, in part or in whole, on stability in the child's social, didactic, or material environments – how significant people interact with the child, how they teach, or what kinds of physical surroundings they provide. Experimental observation shows, however, that, although people and the environment certainly contribute to child cognitive growth, some stability obtains in the child.

Contributions of maternal behavior and the environment to stability assessments have been investigated. In one long-term prospective study extending from 4 months to 4 years, mother-child dyads were seen at three points in children's development (Bornstein 1985b). At 4 months, infant habituation was assessed in the laboratory; at 1 year, infant productive vocabulary was ascertained; and at 4 years, children's intelligence was evaluated using the Wechsler series. At 4 months and at 1 year, didactics in mothers' interactions with children were also recorded during home observations. Didactics included mothers' pointing, labeling, showing, demonstrating, and the like. Path analysis determined direct and unique longitudinal effects of independent variables on dependent variables. Maternal didactic efforts in encouraging infant attention contributed to both 1-year and 4-year child cognitive outcomes. However, infant habituation linked predicatively both to toddler productive vocabulary size at 1 year and to childhood intelligence test performance at 4 years independent of maternal early and late didactic contributions. These findings were replicated and expanded in two shorter-term longitudinal follow-up studies (Tamis-LeMonda & Bornstein 1989, 1993). Similarly, Laucht, Esser, and Schmidt (1994) found that 3-month habituation accounted for a small but significant proportion of variance in 4.5-year IQ after the significant contributions of infants' 3-month Bayley MDI, indexes of biological and psychological risk, and parent education had been partialed out. Finally, Bornstein and colleagues (2006) found, in a large-N study, that parenting as well as maternal education were predictive of children's Denver and Griffith's developmental scores, MacArthur Communicative Developmental Inventories, and Wechsler Full Scale IQ at 6, 18, 24, and 48 months, respectively, but habituation efficiency at 4 months predicted Wechsler IQ at 48 months independent of exogenous factors. In this study, habituation linked to IQ through intervening cognitive measures, and cognitive development was best characterized in terms of a "cascade" initiated by information processing in infancy. This work has since been carried through and replicated to 14-year academic achievement (Bornstein, Hahn, & Wolke 2012). Fry and Hale (1996) likewise placed information processing speed at the start of a cognitive cascade in older children as did Rose et al. (2008) in older infants.

External experiences and family influences, both genetic and experiential, play certain roles in child mental development, but they do not exclusively mediate stability (e.g., Bornstein 1989; Broman, Nichols, & Kennedy 1975; Gottfried 1984; Plomin & DeFries 1985; Scarr, Weinberg, & Waldman 1993). A thread of stability in mental development appears to maintain in the child independent of environmental contributions. Taken together, these findings specifically confirm stability between infant habituation and childhood and adolescent mental development, controlling for diverse experiences, including the physical environment, educational climate, and didactic stimulation, as well as other influences (at least partially) external to the infant, such as maternal IQ. Habituation in infancy appears to predict later cognitive status, and stability in mental performance appears (at least partially) to reside in children.

Endogenous Sources of Stability

Succeeding in infancy at habituation and in childhood on mental assessments requires some noncognitive characteristics including presumably a persistent or vigilant temperament style. Spontaneous exploratory activity in infants does not mediate stability. A comprehensive index of infant activity – derived by tallying infants' looking at objects, touching objects, looking at mother, and nondistress vocalizing – predicts toddler exploratory competence, but infant habituation does so over and above these motor activities (Tamis-LeMonda & Bornstein 1993).

With respect to other noncognitive endogenous characteristics, consider motivation or temperament to be yet another potential mediator of stability in the child. Motivation is often included in constructs of intelligence (e.g., Duckworth et al. 2011). Children's motivation to master the environment often results in longer periods of object exploration (i.e., attention) and therefore increased competence. By contrast, infants who are congenitally distractible are likely to learn more slowly about objects and events because they are unable to attend to or to concentrate on them. Habituation and motivation could share variance in infancy, just as intelligence test performance and motivation share variance in childhood (e.g., Guerin, Gottfried, Oliver, & Thomas 1994; Sigman, Cohen, Beckwith, & Topinka 1987; Zigler, Abelson, & Seitz 1973).

Alternatively, it could be that children who possess an attentive or easy temperament do well at habituation in infancy and later at tests involving an evaluation of intelligence and achievement, independent of their cognitive ability (Slomkowski, Nelson, Dunn, & Plomin 1992; Sternberg, Grigorenko, & Bundy 2001). Pasilin (1986) reported that mothers' ratings of their preschoolers' persistence and attention to tasks related positively to children's achievement.

Thus, besides intelligence, it takes an attentive temperament and perhaps a vigilant or persistent cognitive-style to succeed at testing in infancy and in later life. Attention and temperament could share variance in infancy, just as intelligence test performance and temperament could share variance in maturity. On this account, temperament or motivation could be the stable construct from infancy on, and the predictive association between attention in infancy and intelligence in maturity could be carried by stability in temperament or motivation.

This argument is tempered, however, by two considerations. First, infant performance on traditional infant tests shows little or no predictive validity. That is, there is no reason that infant performance on traditional developmental assessments should not share variance with temperament and/or motivation the way habituation would. Therefore, if temperament or motivation were consistent and carried the longitudinal association to later intelligence and achievement, they should do so for traditional test performance and information processing equivalently. Second, habituation predicts over and above temperament. In their longitudinal study, Bornstein and colleagues (2012), found that habituation efficiency at 4 months was predictive of Wechsler Full Scale IQ at 48 months independent of positive temperament and difficultness, and this relation extended to adolescent academic achievement at 14 years independent of temperament and behavior problems.

In summary, several possible related threads to the fabric of individual stability in child mental development have been woven, and many factors contribute to human mental development. These include efficiency of information processing and personality, as well as supportive experience. Although it is parsimonious to believe that a single mechanism underlies developmental performance, that clearly need not be the case. There is nothing to say that this list of processes is exhaustive, or that these processes themselves are mutually exclusive. Nonetheless, some stability lies in the child, separate from the contribution of the environment and apart from other noncognitive factors in the child. At base, prevailing empirical results substantiate a view of mental development from infancy that incorporates the notion of individual consistency.

Some Open Questions and Future Directions

What Is Habituation?
For all the progress that has been made in this domain of infant assessment over the years, the nature and meaning of habituation per se are far from settled. For example, theoretical understanding of the processes of habituation dates back at least to physiological speculation on the orienting reflex and "comparator model" of Sokolov (1958/1963), which in itself is

not altogether satisfying. Theory as to how habituation occurs is simple or complex, but still theory (see Miller, Galanter, & Pribram 1960). Moreover, whether looking and habituation are active information-processing strategies, or whether the focus should rather fall on the disengagement of looking (Blaga & Colombo 2006; Colombo 1995; Frick, Colombo, & Saxon 1999) or the inhibition of attention (McCall & Mash 1995) are important, but still unanswered questions. Perhaps habituation is *noumenal* in Kant's terminology – an unknown, possibly unknowable, yet logically necessary mental operation.

Individual differences in information processing could reflect individual differences in some aspect of central nervous system functioning, such as speed of neurotransmission, which in infancy might depend on myelinization, extent of dendritic branching, and neurochemical or biophysical parameters (Colombo 1995). In general, mature nervous systems habituate more quickly than do immature nervous systems (Bergström 1969; Graham, Anthony, & Zeigler 1983), and "system integrity" has been identified as a possible common cause (Deary 2012).

Can the Predictive Validity of Habituation Measures Be Improved?
More reliable and valid measures can improve the predictability of infant attention (Colombo et al. 1988, 2004). Correcting for attenuation of reliability (Cohen, Cohen, West, & Aiken 2003) would improve the predictive coefficient of infant measures (the maximum predictive correlation between predictor and criterion is the square root of the product of their reliabilities). Furthermore, studies that employ cardiac measures have demonstrated that infant looking can be parsed into different phases of attentional engagement. Colombo et al. (2001) closely analyzed the several components of a look. Looking during habituation reflects information processing, but there is considerable "noise" in the measure; through the use of heart-rate (HR) defined phases of attention (Richards 2003, 2004) it is possible to assess various components of attention that occur during looking, some of which are more closely associated with true information processing than others (Figures 6.4 and 6.5). As might be expected, longer durations of looking during habituation are associated with more time spent in sustained attention; this finding is consistent with the contention that long looking reflects slower or less-efficient processing. Long looking is also uniformly associated with more time spent in attention termination (Colombo et al. 2001), a phase which reflects the continuation of looking after processing has ended. Thus, along with less efficient processing, the coordination of fixation and processing is less well integrated in cases of prolonged look durations.

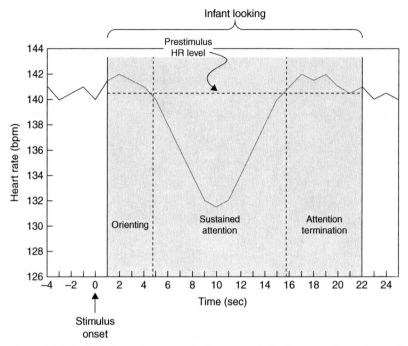

Figure 6.4. Idealized figure demonstrating heart-rate defined phases of attention, as first described by Richards and colleagues. The stimulus onset occurs at time 0, and infant looking to the stimulus is represented by the light shaded area. Infants' marked heart rate deceleration (below a prestimulus HR level) during looking indicates the occurrence of the phase called *sustained attention*, which represents active stimulus processing and encoding. (Redrawn with permission from Figure 3 in Colombo et al. 2004)

Habituation assessments from 2 to 7 months are more predictive than assessments before 2 months or after 7 months. Colombo et al. (2004) studied habituation in infants from 3 to 9 months and the Bayley Scales of Infant Development and the MacArthur CDI in the same children at 12, 18, and 24 months. On the basis of their habituation performance across ages, infants distributed themselves in two main clusters: One group of infants decreased strongly, and another group of infants showed different patterns of change that were not consistent with this normative trend. When assessed later on, the strong habituation group showed increasing levels of predictability from 12 to 24 months. Subsequent analyses of this sample (Colombo et al. 2009) assessed out to 4 years of age have yielded essentially the same conclusions regarding the drop in look duration across ages, especially when accompanied by higher proportions of sustained attention across ages, and later vocabulary and IQ. In addition, outcomes after 6 years

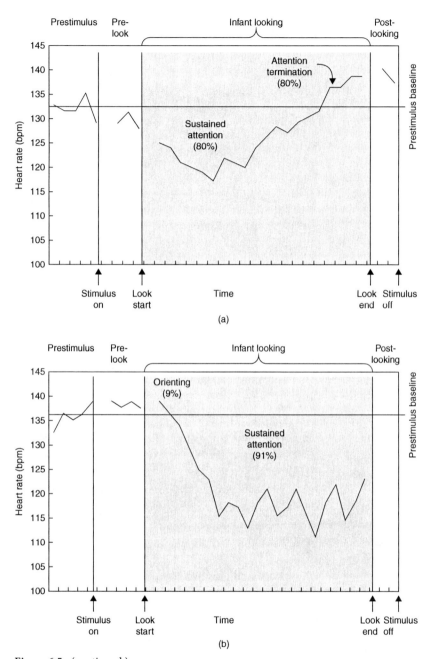

Figure 6.5. (continued.)

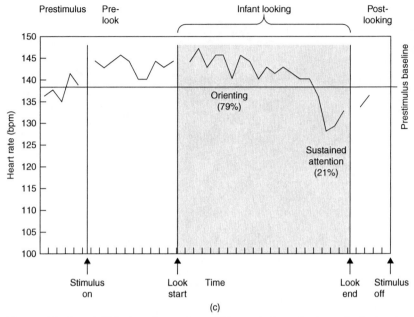

Figure 6.5. Actual HR data from three different infants (a, b, and c) showing approximately the same duration of looking (denoted by light shaded area). Note that the profiles of HR and HR-defined phases differ markedly from one another. Two infants (a, b) show substantial amounts of sustained attention (an indicant of active and engaged information processing), whereas a third (c) shows substantially less.

are stronger than outcomes before 6 years (in apparent contravention of the "simplex structure" of correlation; Guttman 1954). The longest term reported correlation extends from the newborn period to 18 years, $r = -.36$ (Sigman et al. 1997). For mediated, distal developmental processes, such as that between habituation efficiency in infancy and later cognitive function or academic achievement in childhood and adolescence, a test of the indirect path between predictor and criterion may be more sensitive, powerful, and theoretically appropriate than is a test of a simple direct relation between the two (Fry & Hale 1996; Shrout & Bolger 2002).

Chapter Conclusions

A central issue in developmental study is evaluation of forces bound up in ontogenetic advance. Central to understanding developmental advance is recognizing the contributions of interindividual differences, personal experiences, and their transactions. In this chapter, we focused on some ways in which individuals contribute to their development. Notably, infants appear to bring individuality of information processing to their own long-term mental development.

At the same time, experience and environment, often embodied for infants in their parents' characteristics and their experiences, also contribute to cognitive growth. How transactions between the child and parent begin and evolve, the nature of their distribution and sequential structure, what their psychophysiological underpinnings may be, what their consequences are, and how their positive effects may be facilitated in the dyad as a boon to the child, represent critical (and, we add, perennial) research questions in human development. A multivariate and transactional approach promises a more comprehensive characterization of the antecedents in infancy of mature mental competencies.

The predictive validity of mental development from infancy, as we have described it, has several implications. First, it has meaning for developmental science in terms of more fully describing the growth of individuals. Second, it leads to a more complete understanding of the nature and structure of intelligence. Third, it could be that, because there is some thread of prediction in mental performance from infancy, measures of infant cognitive ability might serve as screening and early detection of risk status for delayed development. Likewise, these measures could conceivably, fourth, constitute criteria indicating the effects of enrichment or deprivation. Fifth, insofar as they are true of infants and behaviorally based, these measures may one day serve as culture-free assessments of early cognition. Finally, sixth, "intelligence predicts important things in life," like education, occupation, social mobility, and health (Deary 2012), so knowing more about its origins is valuable.

In relative terms, the adoption of information-processing measures has increased predictability from infancy approximately 15-fold vis-à-vis traditional infant tests; absolutely speaking, however, it is still the case that information-processing measures in infancy share, at best, one-quarter to one-third of variation with measures of later intelligence and academic achievement. That is, infants who are more efficient in processing information tend to score higher on standardized childhood assessments of intelligence and adolescent academic achievement. Although this new perspective on stability in mental ability is telling, it is critical to underscore the fact that it certainly does not mean that intelligence is innate, that the level of a child's intelligence is fixed in early life, or that the infant is alone in the journey of mental development. The stability perspective does, however, substantiate a revised view of mental life from infancy. The data on stability overturn the argument that cognition in infancy is not meaningful in itself and that it is unrelated to later life. Selected cognitive capabilities assessed in the first year relate to selected measures of more mature intelligence and cognitive competence assessed at least through adolescence. We might next return to Alfred Binet's original ideas to ask how this new information can best be used to benefit children. Infancy is a starting point of life. Infancy may also represent a critical setting point in the life of the child.

Acknowledgments

This chapter summarizes selected aspects of our research, and portions of the text have appeared in previous scientific publications cited in the references. The research was supported by the Intramural Research Program of the NIH, NICHD (MHB) and NIH grants HD045430, HD047315, MH084061, P30 DC005803, and P30 HD02528 (JC). Address correspondence to: Marc H. Bornstein, Child and Family Research, National Institute of Child Health and Human Development, National Institutes of Health, Suite 8030, 6705 Rockledge Drive, Bethesda MD 20892–7971, USA (E-mail: Marc_H_Bornstein@nih.gov) or to John Colombo, Schiefelbusch Institute for Life Span Studies, 1052 Dole Human Development Center, University of Kansas, Lawrence, KS 66045–7555, USA (E-mail: colombo@ku.edu).

REFERENCES

Alexander, K. L., Entwisle, D. R., & Dauber, S. L. (1993). First-grade behavior: Its short-and long-term consequences for school performance. *Child Development*, **64**, 801–814.

Anderson, M. (1992). *Intelligence and development: A cognitive theory.* Oxford: Blackwell.

Bayley, N. (1949). Consistency and variability in the growth of intelligence from birth to eighteen years. *Journal of Genetic Psychology*, **75**, 165–196.

Bergström, R. M. (1969). Electrical parameters of the brain during ontogeny. In R. J. Robinson (Ed.), *Brain and early behavior: Development in the fetus and infant* (pp. 15–37). New York: Academic Press.

Bertenthal, B. I., Haith, M. M., & Campos, J. J. (1983). The partial-lag design: A method for controlling spontaneous regression in the infant-control habituation paradigm. *Infant Behavior and Development*, **6**, 331–338.

Bjorklund, D. F., & Schneider, W. (1996). The interaction of knowledge, aptitude, and strategies in children's memory performance. *Advances in Child Development and Behavior*, **26**, 59–89.

Blaga, O. M., Anderson, C. J., Shaddy, D. J., Kannass, K. N., Little, T. D., & Colombo, J. (2009). Structure and continuity of intelligence during early childhood. *Intelligence*, **37**, 106–113.

Blaga, O. M. & Colombo, J. (2006). Visual processing and infant ocular latencies in the overlap paradigm. *Developmental Psychology, 42,* 1069–1076.

Bornstein, M. H. (1985a). Habituation of attention as measure of visual information processing in human infants: Summary, systematization, and synthesis. In G. Gottlieb & N. A. Krashnegor (Eds.), *Measurement of audition and vision in the first year of postnatal life: A methodological overview* (pp. 253–300). Norwood, NJ: Ablex.

   (1985b). How infant and mother jointly contribute to developing cognitive competence in the child. *Proceedings of the National Academy of Sciences USA, 82,* 7470–7473.

   (1989). Sensitive periods in development: Structural characteristics and causal interpretations. *Psychological Bulletin, 105,* 179–197.

Bornstein, M. H. & Benasich, A. A. (1986). Infant habituation: Assessments of short–term reliability and individual differences at five months. *Child Development, 57,* 87–99.

Bornstein, M. H. & Bornstein, L. (2008). Psychological stability. In W. A. Darity, Jr. (Ed.), *International encyclopedia of social sciences* (2nd ed., Vol. 8, pp. 74–75). Detroit, MI: Macmillan Reference.

Bornstein, M. H., Hahn, C.-S., Bell, C., Haynes, O. M., Slater, A., Golding, J., Wolke, D., & ALSPAC Study Team (2006). Stability in cognition from early infancy: A developmental cascade. *Psychological Science, 17,* 151–158.

Bornstein, M. H., Hahn, C.-S., & Wolke, D. (2012). Systems and cascades in cognitive development and academic achievement. *Child Development.*

Bornstein, M. H. & Ludemann, P. L. (1989). Habituation at home. *Infant Behavior and Development, 12,* 525–529.

Bornstein, M. H., Pêcheux, M.-G., & Lécuyer, R. (1988). Visual habituation in human infants: Development and rearing circumstances. *Psychological Research, 50,* 130–133.

Bornstein, M. H. & Sigman, M. D. (1986). Continuity in mental development from infancy. *Child Development, 57,* 251–274.

Broman, S. H., Nichols, P. L., & Kennedy, W. A. (1975). *Preschool IQ: Prenatal and early developmental correlates.* Hillsdale, NJ: Erlbaum.

Bronson, G. (1991). Infant differences in rate of visual encoding. *Child Development, 62,* 44–54.

Campione, J. C., Brown, A. L., & Ferrara, R. A. (1982). Mental retardation and intelligence. In R. J. Sternberg (Ed.), *Handbook of human intelligence* (pp. 392–491). Cambridge: Cambridge University Press.

Caron, A. J. & Caron, R. F. (1969). Degree of stimulus complexity and habituation of visual fixation in infants. *Psychonomic Science, 14,* 78–79.

Cohen, J., Cohen, P., West, S. G., & Aiken, L. S., (2003). *Applied multiple regression/correlation analysis for the behavioural sciences* (3rd ed.). Mahwah, NJ: Erlbaum.

Colombo, J. (1993). *Infant cognition: Predicting later intellectual functioning.* Newbury Park, CA: Sage.

   (1995). On the neural mechanisms underlying developmental and individual differences in visual fixation in infancy: Two hypotheses. *Developmental Review, 15,* 97–135.

   (2001). The development of visual attention in infancy. *Annual Review of Psychology, 52,* 337–367.

(2002). Infant attention grows up: The emergence of a developmental cognitive neuroscience perspective. *Current Directions in Psychological Science*, **11**, 196–199.

Colombo, J., Freeseman, L. J., Coldren, J. T., & Frick, J. E. (1995). Individual differences in infant fixation duration: Dominance of global versus local stimulus properties. *Cognitive Development*, **10**, 271–285.

Colombo, J., Frick, J. E., & Gorman, S.A. (1997). Sensitization during visual habituation sequences: Procedural effects and individual differences. *Journal of Experimental Child Psychology*, **67**, 223–235.

Colombo, J. & Mitchell, D. W. (1990). Individual differences in early visual attention: Fixation time and information processing. In J. Colombo & J. Fagen (Eds.), *Individual differences in infancy: Reliability, stability, prediction* (pp. 193–228). Hillsdale, NJ: Erlbaum.

(2009). Infant visual habituation. *Neurobiology of Learning and Memory*, **92**, 225–234.

Colombo, J., Mitchell, D. W., & Horowitz, F. D. (1988). Infant visual attention in the paired-comparison paradigm: Test-retest and attention-performance relations. *Child Development*, **59**, 1198–1210.

Colombo, J., Richman, W. A., Shaddy, D. J., Greenhoot, A. F., & Maikranz, J. M. (2001). Heart rate-defined phases of attention, look duration, and infant performance in the paired-comparison paradigm. *Child Development*, **72**, 1605–1616.

Colombo, J., Shaddy, D. J., Blaga, O. M., Anderson, C. J., Kannass, K. N., & Richman, W. A. (2009). Attentional predictors of vocabulary from infancy. In J. Colombo, P. McCardle, & L. Freund (Eds.), *Infant pathways to language: Methods, models, and research directions* (pp. 143–168). New York: Psychology Press.

Colombo, J., Shaddy, D. J., Richman, W. A., Maikranz, J. M., & Blaga, O. M. (2004). The developmental course of habituation in infancy and preschool outcome. *Infancy*, **5**, 1–38.

Cooper, L. A., & Regan, D. T. (1986). Attention, perception, and intelligence. In R. J. Sternberg (Ed.), *Handbook of human intelligence* (pp. 123–169). Cambridge: Cambridge University Press.

Courage, M. L., Reynolds, G. D., & Richards, J. E. (2006). Infants' attention to patterned stimuli: Developmental change from 3 to 12 months of age. *Child Development*, **77**, 680–695.

Deary, I. J. (2012). Intelligence. *Annual Review of Psychology*, **63**, 453–482.

Deary, I.J., & Der, G, (2005). Reaction time explains IQ's association with death. *Psychological Science*, **16**, 64–69.

Deary, I.J., Der, G., & Ford, G. (2001). Reaction times and intelligence differences: a population-based cohort study. *Intelligence*, **29**, 389–399.

Dempster, F. N. (1991). Inhibitory processes: A neglected dimension of intelligence. *Intelligence*, **15**, 157–173.

Detterman, D. K. (1987). Theoretical notions of intelligence and mental retardation. *American Journal of Mental Deficiency*, **92**, 2–11.

Duckworth A.L., Quinn, P.D., Lynam, D.R., Loeber, R., & Stouthamer-Loeber, M. (2011). Role of test motivation in intelligence testing. *Proceedings of the National Academy of Sciences USA*, **108**, 7716–7720.

Duncan, G. J., Dowsett, C. J., Claessens, A., Magnuson, K., Huston, A. C., Klebanov, P., & Japel, C. (2007). School readiness and later achievement. *Developmental Psychology*, **43**, 1428–1446.

Fagan, J. F., Holland, C. R., & Wheeler, K. (2007). The prediction, from infancy, of adult IQ and achievement. *Intelligence*, **35**, 225–231.

Fagan, J. F. & Singer, L. T. (1983). Infant recognition memory as a measure of intelligence. In L. P. Lipsitt (Ed.), *Advances in infancy research* (Vol. 2, pp. 31–79). Norwood, NJ: Ablex.

Fantz, R. L. (1964). Visual experience in infants: Decreased attention to familiar patterns relative to novel ones. *Science*, **146**, 668–670.

Freeseman, L. J., Colombo, J., & Coldren, J. T. (1993). Individual differences in infant visual attention: Four-month-olds' discrimination and generalization of global and local stimulus properties. *Child Development*, **64**, 1191–1203.

Frick, J. E. & Colombo, J. (1996). Individual differences in infant visual attention: Recognition of degraded visual forms by four-month-olds. *Child Development*, **67**, 188–204.

Frick, J. E., Colombo, J., & Saxon, T. F. (1999). Individual and developmental differences in disengagement of fixation in early infancy. *Child Development*, **70**, 537–548.

Frick, J. E. & Richards, J. E. (2001). Individual differences in infants' recognition of briefly presented visual stimuli. *Infancy*, **2**, 331–352.

Friedman, S. (1975). Infant habituation: Process, problems, and possibilities. In N. Ellis (Ed.), *Aberrant development in infancy: Human and animal studies* (pp. 217–239). New York: Halstead Press.

Fry, A. F. & Hale, S. (1996). Processing speed, working memory, and fluid intelligence: Evidence for a developmental cascade. *Psychological Science*, **7**, 237–241.

Giles, A. C. & Rankin, C. H. (2009). Behavioral and genetic characterization of habituation using *Caenorhabditis elegans*. *Neurobiology of Learning and Memory*, **92**, 139–147.

Gottfried, A. W. (1984). Issues concerning the relationship between home environment and early cognitive development. In A. W. Gottfried (Ed.), *Home environment and early cognitive development* (pp. 1–4). New York: Academic Press.

Graham, F. K., Anthony, B. J., & Zeigler, B. L. (1983). The orienting response and developmental processes. In D. Siddle (Ed.), *Perspectives in human research* (pp. 371–430). New York: Wiley.

Guerin, D. W., Gottfried, A. W., Oliver, P. H., & Thomas, C. W. (1994). Temperament and school functioning during early adolescence. *Journal of Early Adolescence*, **14**, 200–225.

Guttman, L. (1954). A new approach to factor analysis: The radex. In P. F. Lazarfeld (Ed.), *Mathematical thinking in the social sciences* (pp. 258–349). Glencoe, IL: Free Press.

Hale, S. (1990). A global developmental trend in cognitive processing speed. *Child Development*, **61**, 653–663.

Hedges, L. L. & Oklin, I. (1985). *Statistical methods for meta-analysis*. Orlando, FL: Academic Press.

Hepper, P. G. & Shahidullah, S. (1992). Habituation in normal and Down's Syndrome fetuses. *The Quarterly Journal of Experimental Psychology*, **44**, 305–317.

Hood, B. M., Murray, L., King, F., Hooper, R., Atkinson, J., & Braddick, O. (1996). Habituation changes in early infancy: Longitudinal measures from birth to 6 months. *Journal of Reproductive and Infant Psychology*, **14**, 177–185.

Humphreys, L. G. & Davey, T. C. (1988). Continuity in intellectual growth from 12 months to 9 years. *Intelligence*, **12**, 183–197.

Hunt, E. B. (1983). On the nature of intelligence. *Science*, **219**, 141–146.

Jankowski, J. J., Rose, S. A., & Feldman, J. F. (2001). Modifying the distribution of attention in infants. *Child Development*, **72**, 339–351.

Jensen, A. R. (1992). The importance of intraindividual variation in reaction time. *Personality and Individual Differences*, **13**, 869–881.

Kail, R. (1991). Developmental change in speed of processing during childhood and adolescence. *Psychological Bulletin*, **109**, 490–501.

Kandel, E. C. (2007). *In search of memory: The emergence of a new science of mind*. New York: W. W. Norton.

Kavšek, M. (2004). Predicting later IQ from infant visual habituation and dishabituation: A meta-analysis. *Journal of Applied Developmental Psychology*, **25**, 369–393.

Kavšek, M. & Bornstein, M. H. (2010). Visual habituation and dishabituation in preterm infants: A review and meta-analysis. *Research in Developmental Disabilities*, **31**, 951–975.

Kopp, C. B. & McCall, R. B. (1980). Stability and instability in mental test performance among normal, at–risk, and handicapped infants and children. In P. B. Baltes & O. G. Brim, Jr. (Eds.), *Life-span development and behavior* (Vol. 4, pp. 33–61). New York: Academic Press.

Laucht, M., Esser, G., & Schmidt, M. (1994). Contrasting infant predictors of later cognitive functioning. *Journal of Child Psychology and Psychiatry*, **35**, 649–662.

Leader, L. R. (1994). Fetal habituation in growth retardation and hypoxia. In H. C. Lou, G. Greisen, & J. F. Larsen (Eds.), *Brain lesions in the newborn* (pp. 326–329). Munksgaard, Copenhagen: Alfred Benzon Symposium 31.

Lester, B. M. (1975). Cardiac habituation of the orienting response to an auditory signal in infants of varying nutritional status. *Developmental Psychology*, **11**, 432–442.

Madison, L. S., Madison, J. K., & Adubato, S. A. (1986). Infant behavior and development in relation to fetal movement and habituation. *Child Development*, **57**, 1475–1482.

Maikranz, J. M., Colombo, J., Richman, W. A., & Frick, J. E. (2001). Autonomic indicators of sensitization and look duration in infancy. *Infant Behavior and Development*, **23**, 137–151.

Malcuit, G., Pomerleau, A., & Lamarre, G. (1988). Habituation, visual fixation and cognitive activity in infants: A critical analysis and an attempt at a new formulation. *Cahiers de Psychologie Cognitive*, **8**, 415–440.

Mayes, L. C., Bornstein, M. H., Chawarska, K., & Granger, R. H. (1995). Information processing and developmental assessments in three-month-old infants exposed prenatally to cocaine. *Pediatrics*, **95**, 539–545.

Mayes, L. C., Granger, R. H., Frank, M. A., Schottenfeld, R., & Bornstein, M. (1993). Neurobehavioral profiles of infants exposed to cocaine prenatally. *Pediatrics*, **91**, 778–783.

Mayes, L. C. & Kessen, W. (1989). Maturational changes in measures of habituation. *Infant Behavior and Development*, **12**, 437–450.

McCall, R. B. (1994). What process mediates prediction of childhood IQ from infant habituation and recognition memory? Speculations on the roles of inhibition and rate of information processing. *Intelligence*, **18**, 107–125.

McCall, R. B. & Carriger, M. S. (1993). A meta-analysis of infant habituation and recognition memory performance as predictors of later IQ. *Child Development*, **64**, 57–79.

McCall, R. G. & Mash, C. W. (1995). Infant cognition and its relation to mature intelligence. *Annals of Child Development*, **10**, 27–56.

Miller, E. K., Gochin, P. M., & Gross, C. G. (1991). Habituation-like decrease in the response of neurons in inferior temporal cortex of the macaque. *Visual Neuroscience*, **7**, 357–362.

Miller, G. A., Galanter, E., & Pribram, K. H. (1960). *Plans and the structure of behavior*. New York: Holt, Rinehart and Winston.

Miller, D. J., Sinnott, J. P., Short, E. J., & Hains, A. A. (1976). Individual differences in habituation rates and object concept performance. *Child Development*, **47**, 528–531.

Nettelbeck, T. (1987). Inspection time and intelligence. In P. A. Vernon (Ed.), *Speed of information processing and intelligence* (pp. 295–346). Norwood, NJ: Ablex.

Nettelbeck, T. & Wilson, C. (1994). Childhood changes in speed of information processing and mental age: A brief report. *British Journal of Developmental Psychology*, **12**, 277–280.

Nettelbeck, T. & Young, R. (1989). Inspection time and intelligence in 6-year-old children. *Personality and Individual Differences*, **10**, 605–614.

  (1990). Inspection time and intelligence in 7-year-old children. *Personality and Individual Differences*, **11**, 1283–1289.

Pasilin, H. (1986). Preschool temperament and performance on achievement tests. *Developmental Psychology*, **22**, 766–770.

Plomin, R. & DeFries, J. C. (1985). *Origins of individual differences in infancy: The Colorado Adoption Project*. New York: Academic Press.

Rankin, C., Abrams, T., Barry, R., Bhatnagar, S., Cerruti, D., Fang, C.-W., & Thompson, R. (2009). Habituation: An evaluation and revision of Thompson and Spencer (1966). *Neurobiology of Learning and Memory*, **92**, 135–138.

Raver, C. C., Smith-Donald, R., Hayes, T., & Jones, S. M. (2005, April). *Self-regulation across differing risk and sociocultural contexts: Preliminary findings from the Chicago School Readiness Project*. Paper presented at the biennial meeting of the Society for Research in Child Development, Atlanta, GA.

Rescorla, R. A. & Wagner, A. R. (1972). A theory of Pavlovian conditioning: Variations in the effectiveness of reinforcement and nonreinforcement. In A. H. Black & W. F. Prokasy (Eds.), *Classical conditioning II: Current research and theory* (pp. 64–99). New York: Appleton-Century-Crofts.

Richards, J. E. (1997). Effects of attention on infants' preference for briefly exposed visual stimuli in the paired-comparison recognition-memory paradigm. *Developmental Psychology*, **33**, 22–31.

  (2003). The development of visual attention and the brain. In M. de Haan & M. H. Johnson (Eds.), *The cognitive neuroscience of development* (pp. 73–98). Hove: Psychology Press.

(2004). The development of sustained attention in infants. In M. I. Posner (Ed.), *Cognitive neuroscience of attention* (pp. 342–356). New York: Guilford Press.

Rose, S. A., Feldman, J. F., & Jankowski, J. J. (2002). Processing speed in the 1st year of life: A longitudinal study of preterm and full-term infants. *Developmental Psychology*, **38**, 895–902.

Rose, S. A., Feldman, J. F., Jankowski, J. J., & VanRossem, R. (2008). A cognitive cascade in infancy: Pathways from prematurity to later mental development. *Intelligence*, **36**, 367–378.

Rosenthal, R. (1979). The file drawer problem and tolerance for null results. *Psychological Bulletin*, **86**, 638–641.

Scarr, S., Weinberg, R. A., & Waldman, I. D. (1993). IQ correlations in transracial adoptive families. *Intelligence*, **17**, 541–555.

Shaddy, D. J. & Colombo, J. (2004). Developmental changes in infant attention to dynamic and static stimuli. *Infancy*, **5**, 355–365.

Sheppard, L. D. (2008). Intelligence and information processing: A review of 50 years of research. *Personality and Individual Differences*, **44**, 533–549.

Shrout, P. E. & Bolger, N. (2002). Mediation in experimental and nonexperimental studies: New procedures and recommendations. *Psychological Methods*, 7(4), 422–445.

Siegel, L. S. (1989). A reconceptualisation of prediction from infant test scores. In M. H. Bornstein & N. A. Krashnegor (Eds.), *Stability and continuity in mental development: Behavioral and biological perspectives* (pp. 89–103). Hillsdale, NJ: Erlbaum.

Sigman, M., Cohen, S. E., & Beckwith, L. (1997). Why does infant attention predict adolescent intelligence? *Infant Behavior and Development*, **20**, 133–140.

Sigman, M., Cohen, S. E., Beckwith, L., & Topinka, C. (1987). Task persistence in 2-year-old preterm infants in relation to subsequent attentiveness and intelligence. *Infant Behavior and Development*, **10**, 295–305.

Slater, A. M., Morison, V., & Rose, D. (1983). Locus of habituation in the human newborn. *Perception*, **12**, 593–598.

Slomkowski, C. L., Nelson, K., Dunn, J., & Plomin, R. (1992). Temperament and language: Relations from toddlerhood to middle childhood. *Developmental Psychology*, 28(6), 1090–1095.

Sokolov, Y. N. (1958/1963). *Perception and the conditioned reflex* (S. W. Waydenfeld, Trans.). New York: Macmillan.

Stankov, L. (1983). Attention and intelligence. *Journal of Educational Psychology*, **75**, 471–490.

Sternberg, R. J. (1985). *Beyond IQ: A triarchic theory of intelligence*. Cambridge: Cambridge University Press.

Sternberg, R. J., Grigorenko, E. L., & Bundy, D. A. (2001). The predictive value of IQ. *Merrill-Palmer Quarterly*, **47**, 1–41.

Stoecker, J. J., Colombo, J., & Frick, J. E., & Ryther, J. S. (1998). Long- and short-looking infants' recognition of symmetrical and asymmetrical visual forms. *Journal of Experimental Child Psychology*, **71**, 63–78.

Tamis-LeMonda, C. S. & Bornstein, M. H. (1989). Habituation and maternal encouragement of attention in infancy as predictors of toddler language, play, and representational competence. *Child Development*, **60**, 738–751.

(1993). Antecedents of exploratory competence at one year. *Infant Behavior and Development*, **16**, 423–439.

Thompson, R. F. & Spencer, W. A. (1966). Habituation: A model phenomenon for the study of neuronal substrates of behavior. *Psychological Review*, **73**, 16–43.

van deWeijer-Bergsma, E., Wijnroks, L., & Jongmans, M. J. (2008). Attention development in infants and preschool children born preterm: A review. *Infant Behavior & Development*, **31**, 333–351.

Vernon, P. E. (Ed.). (1987). *Speed of information-processing and intelligence*. Norwood, NJ: Ablex.

Zigler, E., Abelson, W. D., & Seitz, V. (1973). Motivational factors in the performance of economically disadvantaged children on the Peabody Picture Vocabulary Test. *Child Development*, **44**, 294–303.

7 Early Hazards to Brain Development: The Effects of Early Institutionalization on Brain and Behavioral Development

Charles A. Nelson III, Nathan A. Fox, and Charles H. Zeanah

Developmental psychologists have, for many years, argued that early experience can have a profound effect upon the course of human development. Studies of human infants demonstrate that learning takes place from a very early age and sets the course for trajectories of either adaptive or maladaptive behavior. And, recent evidence would suggest that there are certain periods during early development when experiences have a more significant effect than others. These periods, called sensitive or critical periods, are thought of as windows of opportunity during which certain types of experience have a foundational effect upon the development of skills or competencies. Thinking about the effects of early experience on development has been solidified with advances in neuroscience that describe the pattern of brain development during the early months and years of life and the role that experience has in shaping development. Huttenlocher (Huttenlocher & Dabholkar 1997) and Rakic (Granger et al. 1995) illustrated changes in synaptic density, increases in neural connections, and the subsequent pruning or decreases in synaptic number that occurred during the postnatal period. This blooming and pruning occurred in different brain areas at different times, particularly during postnatal development. Sensory and perceptual regions displayed these changes early in life whereas these changes occurred later in areas of the brain involved in higher cognition. In related work Hubel and Wiesel (1970) described in specific detail how certain types of sensory/perceptual experience were necessary, at particular early periods of postnatal development, for the mature functioning of visual cortex. The animal had to engage actively in the perceptual world to stimulate the development of neural structures that underlay typical depth perception and other perceptual abilities. Together this work underscored the argument that the quality and timing of early experience was critical for typical brain and behavioral development. Much of the work on the effects of early experience and sensitive periods on later development has been with rodents or nonhuman primates. Data in human infants have been primarily in visual perceptual development (e.g., the work of Maurer and colleagues (1999)) or auditory perceptual development and language (e.g., the work of Kuhl (Kuhl et al. 1992) and Neville (Neville & Bevellier 1998)). Examination of the effects of more general psychosocial deprivation and neglect in human infants has until recently been missing from the research field.

Studies of infants who have been abandoned at birth and placed into institutions where they have received minimum basic care but have been deprived of typical psychosocial stimulation have filled the gap in our knowledge about the effects of these experiences on later cognitive and social development. These studies have been in the literature for some time (e.g., Tizard & Rees 1974) but only recently has there been a systematic attempt to examine issues of timing and sensitive periods across a wide array of domains of cognitive and socio-emotional behavior (e.g., Rutter, O'Connor et al. 2004). The work we describe in this chapter derives from a longitudinal project begun in 2000, concerned with the effects of early institutionalization on brain-behavioral development (see Zeanah et al. 2003). It is the first randomized clinical trial (RCT) of foster care as an intervention for early institutionalization.

We begin by placing our work in a broader cultural context: Specifically, what led a country of 22 million people to institutionalize over 150,000 children? In 1966, Nicolai Ceausescu, then the leader of Romania, decided that he could increase his power over the country if he could raise production. He believed the way to increase productivity was to increase the population. He accomplished these goals by outlawing all contraception, forbidding abortion, and taxing families who produced fewer than 5 children. As a result, the birthrate skyrocketed and poverty became even more widespread. Because many families could not afford to keep their children, Ceausescu supported a network of institutions into which many families placed infants for whom they could not afford to care. Rather than stigmatizing such families, abandonment was implicitly encouraged under communism because the state raising productive children was preferable to having them live in poverty. As a result, a cultural shift occurred, which essentially led to increasingly large numbers of children being placed very early in their lives into these institutions. It is important to be aware that the majority of these children were not orphaned in the conventional sense;

rather, they were abandoned. Moreover, many parents did not give up their legal rights to the child and some even visited their children in the institution at periodic intervals.

In 1989 there was a revolution, and Ceausescu was overthrown and later executed. The Western media then gained access to the country and revealed the horrific conditions under which many children were being raised. Life in an institution was characterized by deprivation and regimentation. Young children spent their time languishing in cribs, and as a rule, were not stimulated in any conventional sense of the word. There was little access to caregivers (the ratio of caregivers to children might be 1:15), and the quality of caregiving was poor in most cases (e.g., most caregivers were poorly educated and had no training in child development). Because of the unfavorable caregiver-child ratio, there was a high level of regimentation (e.g., children went to the bathroom at the same time, went to bed at the same time, were dressed similarly, and were fed on schedule in an impersonal manner).

As has been documented by many authors dating back well into the early part of the 20th century (Dennis & Najarian 1957; Doolittle 1995; Spitz 1945; Tizard & Rees 1979) children do not thrive in such conditions. Not surprisingly, as families in the West learned of the plight of these children and began to adopt them in large numbers, they became quickly overwhelmed with the special needs of these children. Many were very small for their age, had significant cognitive and language delays, behavior problems (particularly hyperactivity), and perhaps most noticeable, problems in forming and maintaining relationships with significant others.

Despite the consensus that institutional rearing can, in many cases, lead to poor developmental outcomes, there remains some uncertainty as to *why* this is the case. On the one hand, there is abundant work from animals (particularly monkeys) that underscores the role of deprivation in poor developmental outcomes. For example, the landmark studies by Harry Harlow demonstrated that infant monkeys reared without their mothers suffered significant emotional damage (Harlow 1959). On the other, one must ask whether it is institutional rearing per se versus *why* a child winds up in an institution that is to blame. In other words, perhaps children who are abandoned to institutions may somehow be different from those who are not abandoned. For example, perhaps children abandoned to institutions have biological mothers who experienced more prenatal complications; perhaps these children were born with genetic defects (Down Syndrome) or they suffered perinatal complications (cerebral palsy). Undoubtedly, the families of institutionalized children were from low socio-economic strata. Thus, poor developmental outcomes may not be due to the children's rearing as much as what landed them in an institution to begin with.

There is an additional issue of whether prior studies of post-institutionalized children have actually *underestimated* the long-term effects of institutionalization on brain and behavioral development. Specifically, in studies of children adopted out of institutions, there is the potential for sample bias. That is, might there be something different about children who are adopted from institutions versus those who stay behind that lead to a mischaracterization of the effects of institutionalization? For example, it may be the case that only the healthiest, most responsive, or better-looking children get adopted. If this is true, then adoption studies examining the effects of institutionalization might actually be under-reporting problems.

The Bucharest Early Intervention Project

In the late 1990s the first author of this chapter was asked by the John D. and Catherine T. MacArthur Foundation to launch a research network on *early experience and brain development*.[1] The work of this group was focused on how the structure of experience weaves its way into the structure of the brain. The Bucharest Early Intervention Project (BEIP) was one of several ambitious projects this group conducted. The BEIP is a randomized controlled trial (RCT) of foster care as an intervention for children abandoned and then placed in an institution (see Zeanah et al. 2003). The project recruited participants from all six of the institutions for young children in Bucharest, Romania. The study began with comprehensive baseline assessments of 136 institutionalized children and their caregiving environments prior to randomization. These children were selected from a larger group of children (>180) and had been found to be relatively healthy, with no obvious chromosomal or major handicapping condition (e.g., cerebral palsy or fetal alcohol syndrome).

Once the baseline assessment had been completed, half the children in the study were randomly assigned either to foster care created specifically for the study (Smyke et al. 2009) or to care as usual, meaning continued institutional care. The average age at foster care placement was 22 months (range = 6–31 months). Following randomization, all children were seen for follow-up assessments at 30, 42, and 54 months, and the development of children in foster care was compared to the development of children in institutions and to a group of typically developing Romanian children, recruited from pediatric clinics (they had never been institutionalized; N = 72). We assessed the children comprehensively, including measures of physical growth, cognitive function, social-emotional development, attachment, problem behaviors and psychiatric symptomatology, language development, caregiving environment, genetics, and brain functioning. We are currently completing an extensive assessment of these children at age 8, which also includes structural MRI imaging.

Since the study began, we have been reporting our results in the scientific literature (Ghera et al. 2009; Jeon et al. in press; Marshall et al. 2004, 2008; Moulson et al. 2009; Moulson, Westerlund, & Nelson 2009; Nelson et al. 2006, 2007; Parker et al. 2005; Pollak et al. in press; Smyke et al. 2007, 2009, in press; Windsor et al. 2007; Zeanah, et al. 2003, 2005, 2006a, 2006b, 2009;); in addition, we and others have extensively discussed some of the ethical issues involved in this project (Nelson et al. 2007; Zeanah et al. 2006a, 2006b, 2009). We refer the reader to these papers for more detail. In this chapter we will review findings from four areas of study: cognitive development (IQ), brain development (EEG), face processing (ERP), and socio-emotional development (attachment). In two of these areas (IQ and EEG) we are able to review data through assessment of the children in our study when they were 8 years old. For ERP and attachment our findings focus on data up through 42 months of age. In all instances, we examine both the effects of early experience (intervention effects) and sensitive periods (timing of intervention).

Findings

Précis to the Discussion of Findings

The BEIP was designed as a randomized clinical trial so as to maximize our ability to identify effects that were a result of the intervention and not a result of a child's previous history or circumstance prior to randomization. Presumably, these early experiential differences and even prenatal differences among the institutionalized children were randomly distributed amongst the 136 children, and thus children in both the intervention group and the group that was assigned to remain in the institution had similar histories and backgrounds. Indeed, examination of child characteristics such as birth-weight found no differences between the two randomized groups. However, one important aspect of this study was our agreement with the authorities in Romania that we would not interfere with the "natural" history of any child either within the institution or in our foster care homes. Practically this meant that if a child assigned to one of these two groups was returned to his/her biological family or adopted, we would not interfere. A second occurrence complicated the design even further. Early on in our study, when we presented our initial findings to the Romanian authorities, they set up government-sponsored foster care homes for institutionalized children. Thus, some of the children originally randomized to remain in the institution were during our study moved out of the institution into government-sponsored foster homes.

As we present the findings from our work below it is important to remember that the data were analyzed using an intent-to-treat approach. This means that even though a child may have left his or her initial group assignment for any of the reasons described, we continued to consider that child as if he/she were still in the original group. For example, if a child originally assigned to remain in the institution was placed in government foster care, or if a child originally assigned to our intervention/foster care group was reunited with his/her biological family we still considered each of these children as members of his or her original group. Examining the group differences this way actually biases the effects away from our hypotheses.

Brain Functioning

The BEIP is the first study of its kind to measure brain activity in infants and young children at the onset of the study and over the course of the longitudinal investigation. We accomplished this goal by recording the electroencephalogram (EEG), and its subset, the event-related potential (ERP). To measure brain activity, children were fitted with a lycra stretch cap (much like a swimmer's cap) that contains small sensors that permit us to record brain electrical activity. Two measures were generated from the brain activity that was recorded: *power,* which reflects the amount of voltage or energy the brain generates at different scalp locations (presumably from different areas of the brain) and *coherence,* which reflects the degree to which two EEG signals of identical frequency are oscillating at the same phase. Coherence has been interpreted as reflecting connectivity in the brain between regions.

EEG Power and Coherence

The EEG was recorded from 15 electrodes during an activity designed to elicit quiet attention in infants and young children. Power in three frequency bands (3–5 Hz as theta, 6–9 Hz as alpha, 10–18 Hz as beta) was computed at each electrode site using both the absolute and relative power metrics. Findings from the baseline assessment (see Marshall et al. 2004) indicated that children in the institutionalized group showed a higher level of relative theta power and a reduction in alpha and beta power compared to the

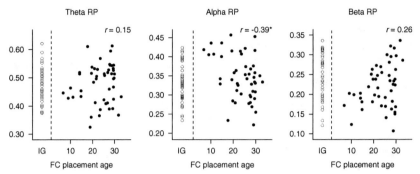

Figure 7.1. Baseline assessment of relative power (RP) in three different frequency bands (middle: 6–9 Hz as alpha; right: 10–18 Hz as beta, left: 3–5 Hz as theta) of an institutionalized group (IG) and a non-institutionalized group (NIG) of children as measured on different electrodes (F3, C3, P3, O1, T7) for the left hemisphere (left) and the right hemisphere (right); data from Marshall et al. (2004)

group of age-matched children living in the community (see Figure 7.1). This pattern of findings suggests a delay in brain development among the institutionalized children.

We next examined the efficacy of foster care by looking at the 42-month EEG power data (Marshall et al. 2008). To our surprise, we found few differences between the foster care and institutionalized groups. Both showed similar levels of EEG power across all bands. However, within the foster care group there were hints that our intervention was having an effect. Age of foster care placement (the age the child was randomized to foster care) was significantly correlated with both alpha power and EEG coherence (see Figure 7.2).

The younger a child was at time of placement into foster care, the higher the child's EEG power in the alpha band and coherence was at age 42 months. Higher EEG power reflects typical maturation of brain activity, and increased EEG coherence reflects greater brain connectivity. Thus, at 42 months there were hints that the intervention was affecting brain activity in children with a history of institutionalization.

Our next follow-up assessment occurred when children were 8 years of age. Again, we examined their EEG power while they sat quietly wearing the EEG caps that had the sensors embedded in them. Surprisingly, we found effects of early experience some seven years on into the study. Children who were originally placed into foster care displayed higher alpha power (6–9 Hz) compared to those originally randomized to care as usual in the institution (Vanderwert et al. 2010). As well, there was a timing effect: Children removed from the institution and placed into our foster care intervention before they were 24 months of age were indistinguishable from community controls at age 8 in their alpha power (see Figure 7.3).

Children removed and placed in our foster care intervention who were older than 24 months of age looked no different on this measure than the children who remained in the institution. In addition, the care-as-usual

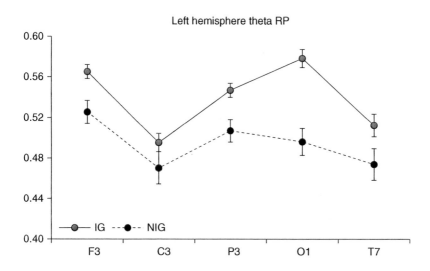

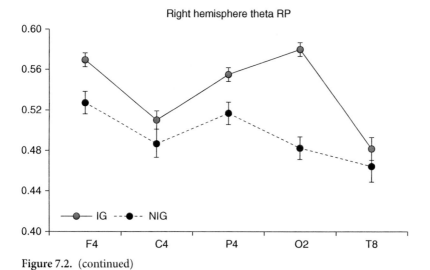

Figure 7.2. (continued)

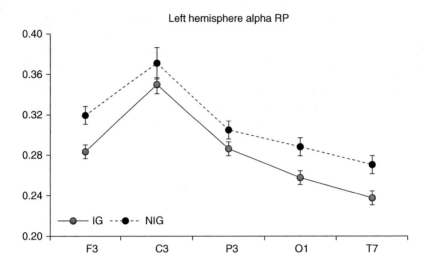

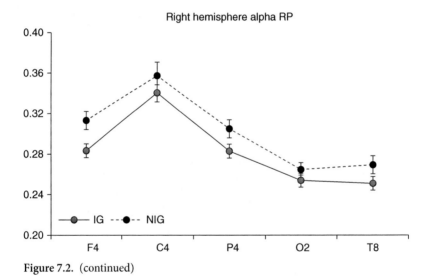

Figure 7.2. (continued)

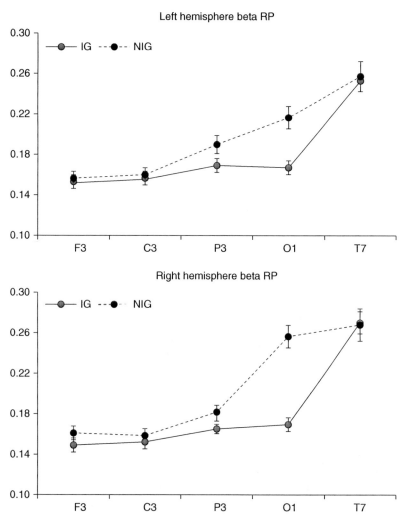

Figure 7.2. Data from an institutionalized group (IG). Correlation between age of foster care (FC) placement (in months) and baseline EEG coherence for three different frequency bands (left: 3–5 Hz as theta; middle; 6–9 Hz as alpha; right: 10–18 Hz as beta); see also Marshall et al. (2008).

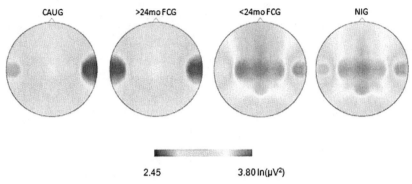

Figure 7.3. Baseline EEG power of school-aged children in a Care As Usual Group (CAUG)," children placed into foster care after 24 months of age (>24mo FOG) and before that time (<24mo FOG), as well as children of a Non-Institutionalized Group (NIG); see also Vanderwert et al. (2010).

group displayed higher theta (slow wave) activity (over the left hemisphere in the temporal region) compared to the intervention group. The normalization of alpha power in the foster care group who were removed from institutions before they were 24 months of age suggests that intervention, if it occurs early in life, does have significant positive effects on brain activity. As well, the continued low alpha power and higher slow wave power in the institutionalized group indicates that early psychosocial deprivation if not ameliorated early continues to exert a detrimental influence on brain functioning during childhood.

Processing of Facial Expressions of Emotion
Faces are an important visual stimulus that primates use for social communication. They provide information about conspecifics including identity, sex, age, and emotional state. Most adults are experts at processing faces, and infants quickly become expert as well over the first year of life (e.g., Pascalis et al. 1995). There is some debate within the face processing and neuroscience literatures about the degree and timing of experience with faces that is necessary for primates to utilize these important functions. Nelson (2001) argued that the development of face perception is an experience-expectant, activity-dependent process in which infants' experiences with faces early in life shape the neural systems that underlie expertise in face processing. There is support for this position from studies of the other race effect (e.g., Bar-Haim et al. 2006) as well as from studies of infants' abilities to recognize faces of nonhuman primates (e.g., Pascalis, de Haan, & Nelson 2002). Early

adverse environments could affect the development of face processing. For example, Pollak and colleagues (2000) reported that children raised in abusive environments showed altered face processing of emotion (they overidentified angry vs. other emotions on the face). Institutionalization may be another example of an adverse early environment that may affect face perception. For that reason we investigated this competency in the children in the BEIP sample.

The event-related potential (ERP) represents the brain's response to the presentation of a distinct event. ERPs have been extensively used in the study of a variety of perceptual and cognitive abilities in infants and children; Nelson & Monk 2001; DeBoer, Scott, & Nelson 2004). We performed two ERP studies at all ages: The first involved presenting children with pictures of facial emotion (fear, angry, happy, and sad) (see Parker et al. 2005a); the second involved presenting children with alternating images of their caregiver's face and the face of a stranger (see Parker et al. 2005b). In both cases we examined both the peak amplitude and latency of various ERP components whose functional significance has been well documented in the research literature. We noted several differences among children living in institutions and children living in families. First, amplitudes were smaller for several ERP components in the institutionalized compared to the community children. This pattern continued through 42 months (Moulson et al. 2009; Moulson, Westerlund, & Nelson 2009). Second, latencies for these components were longer in the institutionalized group compared to the community group, indicating slower processing in children with a history of institutionalization. Finally, children in the never-institutionalized group demonstrated right-hemispheric specialization for faces (the expected response), whereas children in the institutionalized group did not.

In terms of specific findings, two emerged that we found surprising. First, children in the institutionalized group and the never-institutionalized group both showed typical (i.e., normal) differentiation of facial emotion (e.g., larger ERP response to fear than the other emotions). Second, both groups showed appropriate differentiation of caregiver face versus stranger face. In hindsight we have interpreted these normal patterns of response as reflective of how little experience is required to perceptually distinguish one face from another or one facial expression from another (cf., Sugita 2008). That is, the perceptual apparatus involved in telling apart one facial emotion from another may require little experiential input. On the other hand, *recognizing* or labeling an emotion, or deriving meaning from facial expressions, may be compromised in children who experienced early psychosocial deprivation (indeed, these abilities are currently being targeted in our 8-year follow-up).

Cognitive Development-IQ
Because of language and cultural differences, we were challenged to ascertain the effects of early institutionalization on cognitive development. We eventually settled on using the Bayley Scales of Infant Development at baseline, 30 and 42 month, and the Wechsler Preschool Primary Scales of Intelligence (WPPSI-R) at 54 months. We observed that children reared in institutions showed greatly reduced intellectual performance compared to children raised with their biological families; for example, at baseline the mean Bayley Mental Developmental Index (MDI) scores were 66 for children in the institutionalized group and 103 for children in the community group (Smyke et al. 2007).

Having established that early institutionalization has a very detrimental effect on cognitive development, we next turned our attention to intervention effects (Nelson et al. 2007). Here we asked two questions: Was our intervention effective, and was there an effect of age at placement? In terms of the first question, as predicted, children in the foster care group experienced significant gains in cognitive function compared to children in the institutional group. For example, at 42 months, the mean Developmental Quotient (DQ) was 86 for children in the Foster Care Group (FCG) compared to 77 for children in the Institutionalized Group (IG) and 103 for children in the Never Institutionalized Group (NIG). At 54 months, mean Intelligence Quotient (IQ) was 81 for children in the FCG compared to 73 for children in the IG and 109 for children in the NIG.

In terms of the second question, the answer appears to be affirmative. For example, at 42 and 54 months, respectively, the DQ/IQ of children placed in foster care before 18 months was 94/85; those placed between 18 and 24 months: 89/87; those placed between 24 and 30 months: 80/78; and those placed after 30 months of age: 80/72[2] (for discussion, see Nelson et al. 2007).

The next assessment point was when children were eight years of age (Fox et al. in press). At that time we administered the Wechsler Intelligence Scale for Children (WISC-IV; Wechsler 2003). We computed sub-domain scores in verbal comprehension, perceptual reasoning, working memory, and processing speed and from these computed a full-scale IQ score. It should be noted that there was a great deal of mobility in the subject populations of both the CAUG and the FCG children over the period of time between the last assessment at age 54 months and the one when children were 96 months of age. Only 15 children of the original 68 remained institutionalized when they were 8 years old, and only 31 of the original 68 children assigned to our foster care intervention remained in these homes when they were 8. Nevertheless, we analyzed the IQ data with an intent-to-treat approach and found that the children originally assigned to our foster care intervention had higher scores on the verbal subscale compared to children originally assigned to the CAUG. There was also a marginally significant effect (p = .07) for full-scale IQ, with the FCG group scoring higher than the CAUG. As for timing effects, these two were marginally significant. FCG children placed earlier than 26 months of age had higher processing speed scores than FCG children placed into the intervention at a later age. There were no other timing effects for other subscales or full-scale IQ. Interestingly, there were effects of continuity of placement on IQ. Specifically, children who remained in the BEIP foster care homes over the 7- to 8-year period scored higher on full-scale IQ, verbal comprehension, and processing speed compared to children who left those homes (e.g., were reunited with their biological parents) or any of the CAUG.

The data suggest that even using a conservative intent-to-treat analysis, children assigned to the BEIP intervention exhibited better IQ scores compared to those assigned to CAUG. And, it also appears that the context of the intervention maintained these scores over time. Indeed, the timing effects were best sustained with consistent high-quality environmental experiences.

Attachment.   There is a large literature on the effects of institutionalization on children's socio-emotional behavior, with all of these studies having been completed on children who have been adopted or placed into families after a history of early deprivation. The most stable and persistent finding in children who have experienced early institutionalization is their display of social disinhibition, also termed indiscriminate sociability, indiscriminate friendliness, and disinhibited attachment disorder. This pattern of behavior has been characterized by an undiscriminating social approach to others, lack of awareness of social boundaries, and difficulty in identifying or responding to social cues about what is socially appropriate when engaging with other people (O'Connor et al. 2003; O'Connor, Rutter, & English and Romanian Adoptees Study Team 2000).

The caregiving environment in institutions is one of routine but also one of instability of unique specific caregivers. Caregivers rotated shifts often and had little-to-no education in child development, nor was there any motivation to form attachment relationships with individual children.

Thus, problems with attachment and indiscriminate behavior are not unexpected in this less-than-typical caregiving environment.

We assessed the quality of the child's relationship with his or her caregivers using the Ainsworth Strange Situation Procedure (SSP) (Ainsworth et al. 1978). This moderately stressful procedure assesses the child's balance between exploratory behavior and seeking closeness and comfort from the parent/caregiver rather than the stranger. Based upon the child's behavior directed towards the stranger and the familiar attachment figure, trained coders classify the child's attachment as secure, or one of various forms of insecure. Prior to randomization all children who were either 11 months or older (both in chronological age and mental age) were tested. Results revealed that the majority of infants did not display behaviors that could be described as reflecting an attachment relationship with the caregiver. Indeed, many displayed bizarre and unusual responses in this testing context. Over 65% of the institutionalized children had a disorganized attachment with their favorite caregiver, and another 13% had so little attachment behavior that they could not even be classified. In contrast, only 22% of the children living with their families had disorganized attachments to their mothers. More importantly, 100% of the attachments of the community children were rated as being fully developed, but only 3% of the institutionalized children were rated as having fully formed attachments.

What were the effects of the intervention? At 42 months, the preschool version of the Strange Situation Procedure was administered and episodes were coded using a preschool coding scheme. All children were seen with their primary caregivers – mothers, foster mothers or institutional caregivers.

In brief, the foster care intervention favorably impacted attachment relationships. At 42 months, nearly 50% of children placed in foster care demonstrated secure attachments as compared to only 18% of children in the institutionalized group. As a point of comparison, children living with their parents in the community, approximately 65% were securely attached.

Chapter Conclusions

In virtually every domain we have examined, children living in institutions suffer from delays or disorders. Importantly, because by age 96 months only 15 children are still living in an institution, and because we have adopted a strict intent-to-treat approach to our data analyses, our findings may actually underestimate the toll early institutionalization takes on the course of child and brain development.

As discouraging as the news is regarding the effects of early institutionalization, our foster care program appears to be very efficacious in ameliorating many of the disorders and delays that result from early institutionalization. Thus, we find improvements in virtually every domain examined. However, we must qualify this statement in two important ways. First, in many domains there is a relation between how old the child was when placed in foster care and the degree of recovery; as a rule, the earlier the better, and after approximately 24 months of age, recovery may be limited. Second, in virtually *no* domain do we see our foster care children obtaining the same level of performance on our battery of tasks as our never-institutionalized children. Thus, for example, although 54-month-old children assigned to foster care before 18 months have IQs that are 25+ points higher than those assigned to the institutionalized group, and 96-month-old children assigned to foster care have higher full-scale IQ scores than those who were taken out later, these children still test below children who never spent time in an institution.

Overall, our findings emphasize the need to raise children in families. For those placed early in life in institutions, it is imperative to get them out of the institution and into a family as soon as possible. The implications of these findings are discussed next.

Let us now turn to the implications of our work. What are the problems with being raised in institutions? First and foremost, infants and young children are deprived of typical, expected environments in which they receive loving, contingent, and responsive caregiving. Second, children are not provided with the range of stimulation important for the development of language and cognitive abilities. And third, life in the institution is routinized. Children all eat at the same time, toilet at the same time, and go to sleep at the same time. Yet we know that there are important individual differences in children's physiology and temperament that necessitate more nuanced, individualized approaches to their caregiving. The BEIP has attempted to address these issues by instituting a foster care program in Bucharest. And the project may already have had an impact in Romania, which, after our preliminary findings were available, passed a law forbidding the institutionalization of children under 2 years of age unless the child is severely handicapped. Second, our project has implications for the nearly 100,000,000 orphaned or abandoned children around the world. A common societal response to such children is to place them in institutions. Our study calls into question this practice and also speaks to the importance of removing children from institutions as early in life as possible. Third, there are thousands of children in the child protection system in the United States (and likely thousands more in other countries), and our work has implications for these children, as well. Specifically, adverse early experiences need not have lifelong effects if children can be placed in quality stable foster care while their parents attempt remediation. If young children remain in neglectful or abusive homes for too long, the risk of long-term harm is great. Finally, our work has implications for our understanding of sensitive periods in human brain development. This, in turn, may lead to a better understanding of how the structure of experience weaves its way into the structure of the brain, which in turn may lead to renewed efforts on behalf of policy makers to do all they can to ensure that our children get off to a good start in life.

Acknowledgments

The authors gratefully acknowledge the support of the John D. and Catherine T. MacArthur Foundation, who supported the work reported in this chapter. For information about this chapter, contact the first author at the Laboratories of Cognitive Neuroscience, Children's Hospital Boston/ Harvard Medical School, 1 Autumn Street, 6th Floor, Boston, MA 02215; charles.nelson@childrens.harvard.edu.

NOTES

1 The network's members consisted of David Amaral, Judy Cameron, B. J. Casey, Nathan Fox, Eric Knudsen, Pat Levitt, Susan McConnell, Jack Shonkoff, Marian Sigman, Charles Zeanah, and Charles A. Nelson (chair).
2 Because the two different test instruments were used at 42 and 54 months (Bayley vs. WIPSI), the scores at 54 months tend to be lower than at 42 months, simply because the instrument provides a more conservative assessment of IQ.

REFERENCES

Ainsworth, M. D. S., Blehar, M. C., Waters, E., & Wall, S. (1978). *Patterns of attachment.* Hillsdale, NJ: Erlbaum.
Bar-Haim, Y., Ziv, T., Lamy, D., & Hodes, R.M. (2006). Nature and nurture in own-race face processing. *Psychological Science, 17,* 159–163.
DeBoer, T., Scott, L., & Nelson, C.A. (2004). Event-related potentials in developmental populations. In T. Handy (Ed.), *Event-related potentials: A methods handbook* (pp. 263–297). Cambridge, MA: MIT Press.
Dennis, W. & Najarian, P. (1957). Infant development under environmental handicap. *Psychological Monographs: General and Applied, 71,* 1–13.

Doolittle, T. (1995). The long term effects of institutionalization on the behavior of children from Eastern Europe and the former Soviet Union: Research, diagnoses, and therapy options. Parent Network for Post-Institutionalized Children. Retrieved July 17, 2004 from http://www.mariaschildren.org/english/ babyhouse/ effects.html.

Fox, N. A., Almas, A. N., Degnan, K. A., Nelson, C. A., & Zeanah, C. H. (in press). The effects of severe psychosocial deprivation and foster care intervention on cognitive development at 8 years of age: Findings from the Bucharest Early Intervention Project. *Journal of Child Psychology and Psychiatry*.

Ghera, M., Marshall, P., Fox, N., Zeanah, C., Nelson, C. A., & Smyke, A. (2009). The effects of foster care intervention on socially deprived institutionalized children's attention and positive affect: Results from the BEIP study. *Journal of Child Psychology and Psychiatry*, **50**, 246–253.

Granger, B., Tekaia, F., LeSourd, A. M., Rakic, P., & Bourgeois, J. P. (1995). Tempo of neurogenesis and synaptogenesis in the primate cingulate mesocortex: Comparison with the neocortex. *The Journal of Comparative Neurology*, **360**, 363–376.

Harlow, H. F. (1959). Love in infant monkeys. *Scientific American*, **200**(6), 68–74.

Hubel, D. H. & Wiesel, T. N. (1970). The period of susceptibility to the physiological effects of unilateral eye closure in kittens. *Journal of Physiology* (London), **206**, 419–436.

Huttenlocher, P. R., & Dabholkar, A. S. (1997). Regional differences in synaptogenesis in human cerebral cortex. *Journal of Comparative Neurology*, **387**, 167–178.

Jeon, H., Nelson, C.A., & Moulson, M. (in press). The effects of early experience on emotion recognition: A study of institutionalized children in Romania. *Infancy*.

Harry, H. F. (1958). The nature of love. *American Psychologist*, **3**, 673–685.

Kuhl, P. K., Williams, K. A., Lacerda, F., Stevens, K. N., & Lindblom, B. (1992). Linguistic experience alters phonetic perception in infants by 6 months of age. *Science*, **255**, 606–608

Marshall, P. J., Fox, N. A., & Bucharest Early Intervention Project Core Group (2004). A comparison of the electroencephalogram between institutionalized and community children in Romania. *Journal of Cognitive Neuroscience*, **16**, 1327–1338.

Marshall, P., Reeb, B.C., Fox, N.A., & BEIP Core Group (2008). Effects of early intervention on EEG power and coherence in previously institutionalized children in Romania. *Development and Psychopathology*, **20**, 845–859.

Maurer, D., Lewis, T. L., Brent, H. P., & Levin, A. V. (1999). Rapid improvement in the acuity of infants after visual input. *Science*, **286**, 108–110.

Moulson, M. C., Fox, N. A., Zeanah, C. H., & Nelson, C. A. (2009). Early adverse experiences and the neurobiology of facial emotion processing. *Developmental Psychology*, **45**(1), 17–30.

Moulson M. C., Westerlund A., & Nelson C. A. (2009). The effects of early experience on face recognition: An event-related potential study of institutionalized children in Romania. *Child Development*, **80**(4), 1039–1056.

Nelson, C. A. (2001). The development and neural bases of face recognition. *Infant and Child Development*, **10**(1–2), 3–18.

Nelson, C. A., & Monk, C. (2001). The use of event-related potentials in the study of cognitive development. In C. A. Nelson & M. Luciana (Eds.), *Handbook of developmental cognitive neuroscience* (pp. 125–136). Cambridge, MA: MIT Press.

Nelson, C. A., Parker, S. W., Guthrie, D., & BEIP Core Group (2006). The discrimination of facial expressions by typically developing infants and toddlers and those experiencing early institutional care. *Infant Behavior and Development*, **29**, 210–219.

Nelson, C. A., Zeanah, C. H., Fox, N. A., Marshall, P. J., Smyke, A., & Guthrie, D. (2007). Cognitive recovery in socially deprived young children: The Bucharest Early Intervention Project. *Science*, **318**, 1937–1940.

Neville, H. & Bavellier, D. (1998). Neural organization and plasticity for language. *Current Opinions in Neurobiology*, **8**(2), 254–258.

O'Connor, T. G., Marvin, R. S., Rutter, M., Olrick, J. T., Britner, P. A., & English and Romanian Adoptees Study Team. (2003). Child-parent attachment following early institutional deprivation. *Development and Psychopathology*, **15**(1), 19–38.

O'Connor, T. G., Rutter, M., & English and Romanian Adoptees Study Team. (2000). Attachment disorder behavior following early severe deprivation: Extension and longitudinal follow-up. *Journal of the American Academy of Child and Adolescent Psychiatry*, **39**(6), 703–712.

Parker, S. W., Nelson, C. A., et al. (2005a). The impact of early institutional rearing on the ability to discriminate facial expressions of emotion: an event-related potential study. *Child Development*, **76**, 54–72.

Parker, S. W., Nelson C.A., & BEIP core group (2005b). An event-related potential study of the impact of institutional rearing on face recognition. *Development and Psychopathology*, **17**, 621–639.

Pascalis, O., deHaan, M., & Nelson, C. A. (2002). Is face processing species-specific during the first year of life? *Science*, **296**(5571), 1321–1323.

Pascalis, O., deSchonen, S., Morton, J., Derulle, C., & Fabre-Grenet, M. (1995). Mother's face recognition in neonates: A replication and an extension. *Infant Behavior and Development*, **18**, 79–85.

Pascalis, O., Scott, L. S., Kelly, D. J., Shannon, R. W., Nicholson, E., Coleman, M., et al. (2005). Plasticity of face processing in infancy. *Proceedings of the National Academy of Sciences USA*, **102**, 5297–5300.

Pollak, S. D., Cicchetti, D., Hornung, K., & Reed, A. (2000). Recognizing emotion in faces: Developmental effects of child abuse and neglect. *Developmental Psychology*, **36**, 679–688.

Pollak, S. D., Nelson, C. A., Schlaak, M., Roeber, B., Wewerka, S., Wiik, K., Loman, M., & Gunnar, M. R. (in press). Neurodevelopmental effects of early deprivation in post-institutionalized children. *Child Development*.

Reeb, B. C., Fox, N. A., Nelson, C. A., & Zeanah, C. H. (2009). The effects of early institutionalization on social behavior and underlying neural correlates. In M. de Haan & M. Gunnar (Eds.), *Handbook of social developmental neuroscience* (pp. 477–496). London: Guilford Press.

Rutter, M., O'Connor, T. G., & and ERA (2004). Are there biological programming effects for psychological development: Findings from a study of Romanian Adoptees. *Developmental Psychology*, **40**, 81–94.

Smyke, A. T., Koga, S. F., Johnson, D. E., Fox, N. A., Marshall, P. J., Nelson, C. A., Zeanah, C. Z., & BEIP Core Group (2007). The caregiving context in institution reared and family reared infants and toddlers in Romania. *Journal of Child Psychology and Psychiatry*, **48**, 210–218.

Smyke, A. T., Zeanah, C. H., Fox, N. A., Nelson, C. A., & Guthrie, D. (in press). Placement in foster care enhances quality of attachment among very young institutionalized children. *Child Development.*

Smyke, A. T., Zeahah, C. H., Fox, N. A., & Nelson, C. A. (2009). A new model of foster care for young children: The Bucharest Early Intervention Project. *Child and Adolescent Psychiatry Clinics of North America,* 18(3), 721–734.

Spitz, R. (1945). Hospitalism: An inquiry into the genesis of psychiatric conditions in early childhood. *Psychoanalytic Study of the Child,* 1, 53–74.

Sugita, Y. (2008). Face perception in monkeys reared with no exposure to faces. *Proceedings of the National Academy of Sciences USA,* 105, 394–398.

Tizard, B. & Rees, J. (1974). A comparison of the effects of adoption, restoration to the natural mother, and continued institutionalization on the cognitive development of four-year-children. *Child Development,* 45, 92–99.

Vanderwert, R. E., Marshall, P. J., Nelson, C. A., Zeanah, C. H., & Fox, N. A. (2010). Timing of intervention affects brain electrical activity in children exposed to severe psychosocial neglect. *PLosONE.* 5 (7), 1–5. PMCID: PMC2895657.

Windsor, J., Glaze, L. E., Koga, S. F., & BEIP Core Group (2007). Language acquisition with limited input: Romanian institution and foster care. *Journal of Speech, Language, and Hearing Research,* 50, 1365–1381.

Zeanah, C. H., Nelson, C. A., Fox, N. A., Smyke, A. T., Marshall, P., Parker, S. W. et al. (2003). Designing research to study the effects of institutionalization on brain and behavioral development: The Bucharest Early Intervention Project. *Development and Psychopathology,* 15, 885–907.

Zeanah, C. Z., Smyke, A. T., Koga, S. F., Carlson, E., & BEIP Core Group (2005). Attachment in institutionalized and community children in Romania. *Child Development,* 76, 1015–1028.

Zeanah, C. H., Koga, S. F., Simion, B., Stanescu, A., Tabacaru, C. L., Fox, N. A., Nelson, C. A., & BEIP Core Group (2006a). Ethical considerations in international research collaboration: The Bucharest Early Intervention Project. *Infant Mental Health Journal,* 27, 559–576.

Zeanah, C. H., Koga, S. F., Simion, B., Stanescu, A., Tabacaru, C. L., Fox, N. A., Nelson, C. A., & BEIP Core Group (2006b). Response to summary: Ethical considerations in international research collaboration: The Bucharest Early Intervention Project. *Infant Mental Health Journal,* 27, 581–583.

Zeanah, C. H., Egger, H. L., Smyke, A. T., Nelson, C. A., Fox, N. A., Marshall, P. J., & Guthrie, D. (2009) Altering early experiences reduces psychiatric disorders among institutionalized Romanian preschool children. *American Journal of Psychiatry,* 166, 777–785.

8 Non-Parental Care and Emotional Development

Michael E. Lamb

My goal in this chapter is to consider the importance of early relationships with adults other than parents. This is a multifaceted topic and I want to limit my focus to four issues. First, I address the popular misconception that humans have, as a species, come to have significant relationships with non-parental care-providers only in comparatively recent times. Next, I briefly and selectively review some recent work on the effects of non-parental care on children before discussing the available evidence on the formation and significance of relationships with non-parental carers. Finally, I say a little about the policy implications of what we have learned. I have explored these and related issues in much greater depth elsewhere, and refer those who are interested in a fuller picture to these other publications, all cited in recent reviews (Hewlett & Lamb 2005; Lamb & Ahnert 2006; Lamb & Lewis 2010). The present chapter contains a comprehensive summary of my work on this issue.

The History of Non-Parental Child-Care

Non-parental child-care has been the focus of heated ideological debate for more than 30 years, at least in part because social commentators and social scientists tend to have a very myopic view of human history, and thus consider recent practices to be species-typical universals. Non-parental care in early childhood has aroused great concern, for example, even though non-parental care has deep historical roots. As briefly summarized below, decisions and arrangements about children's care and supervision are amongst the oldest problems faced by human society. The fact that they were not discussed frequently in the past may reflect the failure of the men with political and intellectual power to discuss a "women's issue" as well as the fact that maternal care at home was the dominant mode of early child-care in the cultures and eras most familiar to contemporary social and political scientists.

Our species is one in which decisions about child-care arrangements and the division of time and energy among child-care, provisioning, and other survival-relevant activities have always been necessary (Lamb & Ahnert 2006; Lancaster et al. 1987). Humans are born at a much earlier stage of development than are the young of any other mammalian species and a larger proportion of development takes place outside of the womb in humans than in any other mammal (Altmann 1987). The period of dependency, and thus the process of socialization, is extremely prolonged among humans, with offspring dependent on conspecifics into adulthood whereas the young of most mammals become nutritionally independent at the time of weaning. As a result, parental investment in each human child is extremely high and recent scholarship makes clear that non-parents typically make invaluable contributions as well (Hrdy 1999, 2005a, 2005b, 2009). Humans have long been forced to develop complex and extended alliances and arrangements with others in order to ensure the survival of both themselves and their offspring; studies in many contemporary cultures underscore the survival value of these contributions (Hewlett & Lamb 2005; Hrdy 1999, 2005a, 2005b, 2009). Pair-bonding represents one adaptation to the basic needs of human parents to cooperate in the provisioning, defence, and rearing of their offspring (Lancaster & Lancaster 1987) and in many environments, multifamily units developed to maximize individual survival in circumstances where, for example, hunting or gathering required cooperative strategies. Hrdy (1999, 2005a, 2005b, 2009) has argued persuasively, furthermore, that humans evolved as cooperative breeders and thus that human child-rearing has always been characterized by extensive involvement by multiple relatives and conspecifics. Non-parental care is thus a universal practise with a long history, not a dangerous innovation representing a major deviation from species-typical and species-appropriate patterns of child-care (Hrdy 2009; Lamb & Sternberg 1992). In addition, research over the last 30 years has demonstrated conclusively that most infants form attachments to their fathers as well as their mothers, challenging beliefs that infants form relationships to their parents serially rather than at about the same time (Lamb & Lewis 2010).

Studies of modern hunter-gatherers (such as those described in Hewlett and Lamb's recent anthology) provide insight into the social organizations that might have developed in circumstances such as those in which humans are believed to have emerged as a species. In many such societies, within-family divisions of responsibility between men and women are paralleled by cooperative hunting and gathering strategies sometimes involving both men and women. Depending on the task, the season, the children's ages, the availability of alternatives, and the women's condition, children accompany one or other parent at work or are left under the supervision of "alloparents," often older children or adults. Prior to weaning, mothers assume the heaviest portion of child-care responsibilities in most societies, although fathers are frequently present and alloparents are typically active long before weaning (Fouts, Hewlett, & Lamb 2005, 2012). Although the strategies of provisioning, protection, and child-care are different in industrialized countries and in those societies where pastoral or agricultural traditions have replaced nomadic foraging, similar choices have always and must always be made. Exclusive maternal care throughout the period of dependency was never an option in what Bowlby (1969) called "the environment of evolutionary adaptedness" and was seldom an option in any phase of human society even through early childhood; it emerged as a possibility for a small elite segment of humanity during one small recent portion of human history. Nor is it normative cross-culturally: In 40% of the cultures sampled by Weisner and Gallimore (1977), infants were cared for more than half the time by people other than their mothers, and rates are surely higher where toddlers, preschoolers, and young children are concerned. It is thus testimony to the power of recent mythology and ignorance of the dominant human condition throughout history that exclusive maternal care came to be labelled as the "traditional" or "natural" form of human child care, with all deviations from this portrayed as unnatural and potentially dangerous. Only the need for parents in industrialized countries to leave their children in the care of paid care-providers, rather than neighbours or kin, *is* novel, and the implications of this change warrant consideration.

Does Non-Parental Care Psychologically Harm Young Children?

Whether or not non-parental child-care is a long-standing tradition, social commentators, policy makers, and researchers around the world have expressed concern about the adverse effects of extensive non-parental care on children's behaviour and adjustment. Perhaps the most important and persuasive evidence came from the NICHD Early Child Care Research Network which reported in 2003 that a history of extensive out-of-home care predicted externalizing behaviour problems in early childhood. Although it is easy to draw the simplistic conclusion that non-parental care has direct adverse effects on early development, the finding is best interpreted in the context of the complex, multifaceted, psychobiological and behavioural changes that take place when infants and toddlers begin to receive regular non-parental care, particularly in group contexts.

It is helpful to consider the differences and similarities between the daily life experiences of families who do and do not make use of out-of-home care arrangements. In one study, we observed a group of middle-class German children throughout the day both at home and, when relevant, in their child-care centres (Ahnert, Rickert, & Lamb 2000). Our observations confirmed that patterns of parental care changed significantly when families made use of child-care centres. Most importantly, mothers of children in out-of-home care compensated for the time they spent away from their children by interacting at increased intensity when they were with their children in the early morning and evening hours. As a result, the total amount of attention the children received from adults was the same, whether or not they were enrolled in out-of-home care. These parents also remained central figures in their children's lives, providing the types and amounts of care, stimulation, and intimate interaction that the children might have missed while at the centres. Even though the parents counted on the centres to provide stimulation and communication, furthermore, they spent significant amounts of time engaged in those activities as well. In addition, morning hours before child-care were used primarily for communication and basic care, whereas evenings were preferred for stimulation and soothing. Bedtime routines were characterised by particularly high levels of intimate emotional exchange. This careful equilibration of responses to the children's needs at home and in the out-of-home care settings was less apparent when we observed the toddlers' patterns of behavioural distress, however. Whereas home-reared toddlers were periodically and minimally distressed throughout the day, the toddlers in child-care showed heightened levels of distress around the time that they were picked up from their child-care centres.

Many other studies have confirmed that regular, full-day placement in child-care is emotionally and physiologically stressful for many if not most infants and toddlers (Ahnert et al. 2004; Watamura et al. 2003) and, other things being equal, the seriousness of the challenge increases as the length of time spent in care increases. Ahnert et al. (2004) used cortisol measures to track the adaptation to child-care and reported that adjustment was in part dependent on the quality of prior child–mother attachment relationships. Although child–mother attachment security was unrelated to cortisol levels at home, securely attached toddlers had markedly lower cortisol levels in the centres than insecurely attached toddlers as long as the mothers were also present, suggesting that secure child–mother relationships buffered the stressfulness of entry into child-care. When daily mother–child separations began, however, cortisol levels were similarly elevated in securely and insecurely attached toddlers. The importance of parental support in managing the toddlers' stress levels was also evident in the fact that child–mother attachments remained secure or shifted from insecure to secure when mothers spent more days adapting their children to child-care.

Why are care-providers often unable to reduce levels of stress effectively, particularly as most children develop meaningful relationships with their care-providers? Early studies emphasised that enrolment in child-care allowed children to form significant relationships with providers but did not lead care-providers to displace mothers as primary attachment figures (Lamb & Ahnert 2006). In more recent studies, focus has switched from whether or not children form attachments to the quality or security of the relationships formed. In a meta-analysis of studies assessing nearly 3000 toddlers, Ahnert, Pinquart, and Lamb (2006) found that secure relationships to care-providers were less common than secure relationships to mothers or fathers. Nevertheless, the security of children's attachments to their mothers, fathers, and care-providers were modestly but significantly intercorrelated, suggesting that children indeed construct intertwined internal working models of significant relationships with adults, as many attachment theorists (including Bowlby) had suggested. For the most part, however, the characteristics of interaction with particular individuals shape the quality of specific relationships and, as a result, the security of child-care-provider attachment is not simply determined by the security of child–parent attachment.

As with parents, instead, the security of infant–care-provider attachment is associated with the sensitivity, involvement, and quality of the care given by care-providers. Highly trained care-providers can appear even more sensitive than mothers in one-on-one free play situations (Goosens & van IJzendoorn 1990), but dyadic sensitivity necessarily decreases in group settings because care-providers have to divide their attention among multiple children (Goosens & Melhuish 1996). In our meta-analysis, Ahnert et al. (2006) showed that children's relationships with care-providers, especially in centres, were predominantly shaped by behaviour toward the group as a whole. Only in small groups was the security of relationships with care-providers predicted by measures of dyadic responsiveness similar to those that predict the security of children's attachments to their parents (De Wolff & van IJzendoorn 1997). Sensitive care-providers clearly need to monitor children's emotional needs, and in small groups (or those with low child–adult ratios) they may be able to respond to almost every social bid. They cannot do so in large groups, however, so the association between dyadic responsiveness and attachment security is attenuated, just as it is in large family units (Ahnert, Meischner, & Schmidt 2000).

Interestingly, secure relationships with care-providers are also more common in home-based than in centre-based facilities (Ahnert et al. 2006). Does this mean that home-based settings facilitate the development of emotionally supportive relationships with care-providers, whereas child-care centres have difficulty providing the types of care that promote secure child–adult relationships? Because groups in home-based settings are very small and the providers are typically not professionals, children's relationships with providers in home-based settings (like attachments to mothers) are almost exclusively associated with dyadic sensitivity. In contrast, care-providers in centre-based settings have to deal sensitively with larger and more diverse groups of children and, as a result, the factors shaping the quality of child–care-provider relationships in these contexts differ from those known to shape child–mother and child–father attachments, with the group-oriented sensitivity of care-providers, rather than the sensitivity of their responses to individual children, affecting the quality of their relationships. Not surprisingly, time post entry is also positively associated with secure attachment to care-providers whereas older children who have had discontinuous histories of child-care are less likely to form secure attachments to their care-providers (Ahnert et al. 2006). This underscores the importance of stable care experiences during the time that children are forming attachments with their care-providers.

Clearly, then, there is substantial evidence both that toddlers and young children indeed form relationships to care-providers and that these relationships differ in important respects from the types of relationships these children form to their parents. Relationships with care-providers do affect children's development, furthermore. For example, the security of both infant–mother and infant–care-provider attachment are correlated with the level of social competence evident when playing with both adults and peers (Howes & Hamilton 1993; Howes, Matheson, & Hamilton 1994). More impressively, Israeli infants who were securely attached to their early care-providers ("metaplot") were less ego controlled (i.e., less mature) and more empathic, dominant, purposive, achievement-oriented, and independent four years later than those whose relationships with metaplot were insecure-resistant, regardless of the quality of infant-parent attachments (Oppenheim, Sagi, & Lamb 1988). School children's perceptions of their relationships with teachers are also predicted by the quality of their first attachments to care-providers, underscoring the long-lasting impact of these early relationships (Howes, Hamilton, & Philipsen 1998).

Modulating Stress

In the context of these findings, it is somewhat sobering that care-providers often appear unable to modulate the increased levels of stressful arousal that infants and toddlers experience when in child-care facilities. They not only fail to respond effectively to toddlers' patterns of distress on many occasions, but (perhaps as a result) are seldom sought out in that regard once children have adjusted to child-care (Ahnert & Lamb 2000). Perhaps this is because child–parent and child–care-provider attachments are functionally and ontogenetically different. Adopting a pedagogical perspective, care-providers focus on cognitive-stimulation and on minimizing misbehaviour in order to promote group harmony. By contrast, parents are better attuned to their children's emotions and can thus anticipate and perceive their children's reactions to child-care and take steps to minimize the associated distress. Children in child-care thus typically need nurturant parental intervention to help them cope with the levels of distress that accumulate over the course of the long days spent in child-care settings.

Unfortunately, our observations revealed that the German mothers of children in child-care tended to respond less promptly to their toddlers' signals of distress than home-making mothers did (Ahnert et al. 2000). Their failures to respond promptly to distress may reflect (among other possibilities) the consequences of stress at work, competing demands of other chores, or misinterpretations of the distress signals. Interestingly, the NICHD Early Child Care Network (1999) also reported that American mothers behaved less sensitively when their children spent many hours in child-care, suggesting that our findings were not unique to our sample of German mothers. I suspect we would have found similar patterns in the UK as well.

To reiterate, toddlers often need sensitive support from their parents in order to re-equilibrate emotionally, particularly at the end of extended periods in non-parental care settings. When parents do not deal effectively with manifestations of distress and requests for soothing and comforting, those toddlers may return to child-care the next day inadequately reassured and characterized by elevated levels of cortisol even before their day in child-care commences (Watamura et al. 2003). Repeated daily experiences of this sort may constrain the development and elaboration of coping capacities as well as other socially competent behaviours. Not surprisingly, therefore, angry-aggressive children (mostly boys) have higher levels of cortisol than children who engage in more appropriate social interactions and are well-liked by their peers (Tout et al. 1998). In addition, there is growing evidence that diurnal neuroendocrine rhythms are altered by child-care experiences such that abnormally high cortisol levels are evident in the afternoons when children spend long hours in child-care settings (Dettling, Gunnar, & Donzella 1999; Tout et al. 1998; Watamura et al. 2003). The maladaptive externalizing behaviour that reportedly characterizes some young children in child-care settings may thus reflect the inability of parents to buffer the enhanced levels of stress experienced by their infants and toddlers.

Clearly, children need to spend sufficient amounts of time with parents who can interact sensitively and respond appropriately to their emotional needs because, on the whole, care-providers tend not to do so adequately. Parents who use child-care must recognize the need to address their children's negative emotions in order to foster their confidence and security, especially when the children are developmentally vulnerable (e.g., preterm infants) or highly irritable. Home remains the centre of children's lives even when children spend considerable amounts of time in child-care, and poor-quality relationships at home magnify the adverse effects of the high stress levels associated with child-care. It is desirable, therefore, both to limit the amount of time spent in child-care and to ensure that children spend as much time as possible with supportive, sensitive parents.

The quality of care also makes an important contribution. In the same issue of *Child Development* in which the report from the NICHD Early Child Care Research Network (2003) appeared, there was another article (Love et al. 2003) indicating that similar associations between early non-parental care and behaviour problems were *not* evident in three other large multi-site studies. Love et al. attributed the differences to the fact that the NICHD researchers studied centres that tended to provide care of mediocre quality, whereas the centres he and his co-authors studied provided care of higher quality. Quality of care also proved to be important in a fourth multi-site study involving children from low-income families in three cities. Specifically, Votruba-Drzal, Coley, and Chase-Lansdale (2004) reported that 2- to 4-year-old children had fewer behaviour problems the higher the quality of out-of-home care experienced, and for these children, increases in the amount of time spent in non-parental care facilities had a salutary effect, rather than the adverse effect reported by the NICHD Early

Child Care Research Network (2003)! Boys, in particular, benefited from more care of higher quality.

In sum, whether or not it is mediated through the quality of attachments to care-providers, the quality of non-parental child-care appears to modulate its effects on many aspects of child behaviour and adjustment, although family experiences also have an important impact. Thus, although children who have experienced non-parental care from infancy sometimes appear to be more aggressive, more assertive, and less compliant with adults than peers who have not had these experiences, the associations are weaker, if not non-existent, when the quality of care is better. As mentioned earlier, furthermore, the behaviour problems seem to be consequences of inadequate buffering of the children's levels of arousal by the adults responsible for their care, not the inevitable consequences of non-parental care.

Chapter Conclusions

The onset of regular non-parental care for infants and toddlers has complex psychobiological and behavioural effects on their functioning both at home and in child-care centres. As a result, maladaptive behaviour on the part of children who spend many hours in child-care may reflect, if and when it occurs, not the direct effects of non-parental care, but the inability of parents to buffer the enhanced levels of stress occasioned by the time spent in child-care. Secure child–parent relationships do not appear to help children cope with these stresses as much as attachment theorists originally believed, and thus familiarization programs and supportive child–care-provider relationships are needed to help children adjust to the onset of child-care. Successful adaptation demands careful equilibration of the contrasting limitations and benefits of the two environments, with parental sensitivity remaining a key determinant of children's adjustment even after the onset of child-care. The life changes that accompany the onset of child-care often affect the quality of parental behaviour, and families need to find ways to compensate for the time they spend apart. Supportive and secure child–care-provider relationships can also play an important role in promoting children's well-being. In addition, child-care facilities can help modulate the amount of stress that children experience by minimizing group sizes, noise levels, and staff changes, and by ensuring that children have adequate opportunities to rest and retreat from high levels of stimulation and arousal.

Child-care experiences need not have harmful effects on children's development and on their family relationships, although they can do so. Most children's relationships with their parents do not differ systematically depending on whether or not they receive regular non-parental care, and most children in out-of-home facilities remain securely attached to their parents. Meaningful relationships are often established with peers and care-providers, however, and these can affect children's later social behaviour and personality maturity. In addition, exposure to peers may offer some children (e.g., those who are singletons or have shy temperaments) opportunities they could not experience at home, thereby launching them on different developmental trajectories.

Children in high-quality facilities who enjoy good relationships with both parents and stable providers are not reliably more aggressive than peers who have experienced care only from their parents, but early exposure to non-parental care of poor quality can foster excessive assertiveness, aggression, and behaviour problems. Insecure parent–child attachments do not modulate these effects, as once believed, but poor relationships with care-providers do appear to mediate the effects of non-parental care on children's aggressiveness.

Non-parental child-care is characteristic, not only of our species, but also of many others. Most human children around the world continue to experience non-parental care in a variety of incarnations, and there is no evidence that such forms of care necessarily harm children's well-being. Urbanisation, industrialisation, and social mobility have altered the ecology of childhood dramatically, however, raising new challenges as we strive to ensure that children's emotional and psychological needs are met throughout their long years of dependency and need. Extrapolating from contemporary trends, it seems likely that child-care in the future will involve continued increase in both paternal care and non-parental care in facilities such as centres. Ensuring that this care is of high quality must become a major societal commitment.

REFERENCES

Ahnert, L., Gunnar, M., Lamb, M. E., & Barthel, M. (2004). Transition to child care: Associations of infant-mother attachment, infant negative emotion and cortisol elevations. *Child Development, 75*, 639–650.

Ahnert, L. & Lamb, M. E. (2000). Infant-careprovider attachments in contrasting German child care settings II: Individual-oriented care after German reunification. *Infant Behavior and Development, 23*, 211–222.

Ahnert, L., Meissner, T., & Schmidt, A. (2003). Maternal sensitivity and attachment in East German and Russian family networks. In P. M. Crittenden & A. H. Claussen (Eds.), *The organization of attachment relationships: Maturation, culture and context* (pp. 61–74). Cambridge: Cambridge University Press.

Ahnert. L., Pinquart, M., & Lamb, M. E. (2006). Security of children's relationships with non-parental care providers: A meta-analysis. *Child Development, 74*, 664–679.

Ahnert, L., Rickert, H., & Lamb, M. E. (2000). Shared caregiving: Comparisons between home and child care settings. *Developmental Psychology, 36*, 339–351.

Altmann, J. (1987). Life span aspects of reproduction and parental care in anthropoid primates. In J. B. Lancaster, J. Altmann, A. S. Rossi, & L. R. Sherrod (Eds.), *Parenting across the life span: Biosocial perspectives* (pp. 15–29). Hawthorne, NY: Aldine de Gruyter.

Bowlby, J. (1969). *Attachment and loss* (Vol. 1): *Attachment*. New York: Basic Books.

Dettling, A. C., Gunnar, M. R., & Donzella, B. (1999). Cortisol levels of young children in full-day childcare centers: Relations with age and temperament. *Psychoneuroendocrinology, 24*, 519–536.

De Wolff, M. S. & vanIJzendoorn, M. H. (1997). Sensitivity and attachment: A meta-analysis on parental antecedents of infant attachment. *Child Development, 68*, 571–591.

Fouts, H. N., Hewlett, B. S., & Lamb, M. E. (2005). Parent-offspring conflicts among the Bofi farmers and foragers of Central Africa. *Current Anthropology, 46*, 29–50.

(2012). A bio-cultural approach to breastfeeding interactions in Central Africa. *American Anthropologist, 114*, 123–136.

Goossens, F. A. & Melhuish, E. C. (1996). On the ecological validity of measuring the sensitivity of professional caregivers: The laboratory versus the nursery. *European Journal of Psychology of Education, 11*, 169–176.

Goossens, F. A. & vanIJzendoorn, M. H. (1990). Quality of infants' attachments to professional caregivers: Relation to infant-parent attachment and day-care characteristics. *Child Development, 61*, 832–837.

Hewlett, B. S. & Lamb, M. E. (Eds.) (2005). *Hunter-gatherer childhoods: Evolutionary, developmental, and cultural perspectives*. New Brunswick, NJ: Aldine/ Transaction.

Howes, C. & Hamilton, C. E. (1993). The changing experience of child care: Changes in teachers and in teacher-child relationships and children's social competence with peers. *Early Childhood Research Quarterly, 8*, 15–32.

Howes, C., Hamilton, C. E., & Philipsen, L. C. (1998). Stability and continuity of child-caregiver and child-peer relationships. *Child Development, 69*, 418–426.

Howes, C., Matheson, C. C., & Hamilton, C. (1994). Maternal, teacher, and child care history correlates of children's relationship with peers. *Child Development, 65*, 264–273.

Hrdy, S. B. (1999). *Mother nature*. New York: Pantheon.

(2005a). Comes the child before man: How cooperative breeding and prolonged postweaning dependence shaped human potential. In B. S. Hewlett & M. E. Lamb (Eds.), *Hunter-gatherer childhoods: Evolutionary, developmental, and cultural perspectives* (pp. 65–91). New Brunswick NJ: Transaction/Aldine.

(2005b). Evolutionary context of human development: The cooperative breeding model. In C. S. Carter et al. (Eds.), *Attachment and bonding: A new synthesis* (pp. 9–32). Cambridge, MA: MIT Press.

(2009). *Mothers and others*. Boston: Belknap/Harvard University Press.

Lamb, M. E. & Lewis, C. (2010). The development and significance of father-child relationships in two-parent families. In M. E. Lamb (Ed.), *The role of the father in child development* (5th ed., pp. 94–153). New York: Wiley.

Lamb, M. E. & Ahnert, L. (2006). Nonparental child care: Context, concepts, correlates, and consequences. In W. Damon, R. M. Lerner, K. A. Renninger, & I. E. Sigel
(Eds.), *Handbook of child psychology* (Vol. 4) *Child psychology in practice* (6th ed.,
pp. 950–1016). Hoboken, NJ & Chichester: Wiley.

Lamb, M. E. & Sternberg, K. J. (1992). Sociocultural perspectives on nonparental child
care. In M. E. Lamb, K. J. Sternberg, A. Broberg, & C. P. Hwang (Eds.), *Child care in
context: Cross-cultural perspectives* (pp. 1–23). Hillsdale, NJ,: Erlbaum.

Lancaster, J. B. & Lancaster, C. S. (1987). The watershed: Change in parental investment
and family formation strategies in the course of human evolution. In J. S. Lancaster,
J. Altmann, A. Rossi, & L. R. Sherrod (Eds.), *Parenting across the life span: Biosocial
perspectives* (pp. 187–205). Hawthorne, NY: Aldine de Gruyter.

Lancaster, J. B., Rossi, A., Altmann, J., & Sherrod, L. R. (Eds.). (1987). *Parenting across
the life span: Biosocial perspectives*. Hawthorne, NY: Aldine de Gruyter.

Love, J. M., Harrison, L., Sagi-Schwartz, A., vanIJzendoorn, M. A., Ross, C., Ungerer, J.
et al. (2003). Child-care quality matters: How conclusions may vary with context.
Child Development, **74**, 1021–1033.

NICHD Early Child Care Research Network (1999). Child care and mother-child interaction in the first 3 years of life. *Developmental Psychology*, **35**, 1399–1413.

   (2003). Does amount of time spent in child care predict socioemotional adjustment
during the transition to kindergarten? *Child Development*, **74**, 976–1005.

Oppenheim, D., Sagi, A., & Lamb, M. E. (1988). Infant-adult attachments on the kibbutz
and their relation to socioemotional development four years later. *Developmental
Psychology*, **24**, 427–433.

Tout, K., deHaan, M., Campbell, E. K., & Gunnar, M. R. (1998). Social behavior correlates of cortisol activity in child care: Gender differences and time-of-day effects.
Child Development, **69**, 1247–1262.

Votruba-Drzal, E., Coley, R. L., & Chase-Lansdale, P. L. (2004). Child care and low-income
children's development: Direct and moderated effects. *Child Development*, **75**,
296–312.

Watamura, S., Donzella, B., Alwin, J., & Gunnar, M. (2003). Morning to afternoon
increases in cortisol concentrations for infants and toddlers at child care: Age differences and behavioral correlates. *Child Development*, **74**, 1006–1020.

Weisner, T. S., & Gallimore, R. (1977). My brother's keeper: Child and sibling caretaking.
Current Anthropology, **18**, 971–975.

Index

THE JACOBS FOUNDATION SERIES ON ADOLESCENCE
(*continued from page iii*)